Intersections of Crime and Terror

During the last ten years an increasing number of government and media reports, scholarly books and journal articles, and other publications, have focused our attention on the expanded range of interactions between international organized crime and terrorist networks. A majority of these interactions have been in the form of temporary organizational alliances (or customer-supplier relationships) surrounding a specific type of transaction or resource exchange, like document fraud or smuggling humans, drugs or weapons across a particular border. The environment in which terrorists and criminals operate is also a central theme of this literature.

These research trends suggest the salience of this book which addresses how organized criminal and terrorist networks collaborate, share knowledge and learn from each other in ways that expand their operational capabilities. The book contains broad conceptual pieces, historical analyses, and case studies that highlight different facets of the intersection between crime and terrorism. These chapters collectively help us to identify and appreciate a variety of dynamics at the individual, organizational, and contextual levels. These dynamics, in turn, inform a deeper understanding of the security threat posed by terrorists and criminal networks and how to respond more effectively.

This book was published as a special issue of *Terrorism and Political Violence*.

James J. F. Forest is associate professor at the University of Massachusetts Lowell and senior fellow at Joint Special Operations University. He is the former director of terrorism studies at the U.S. Military Academy, West Point, and has published dozens of books, articles and commentary about terrorism and counterterrorism.

Intersections of Crime and Terror

Edited by
James J. F. Forest

Routledge
Taylor & Francis Group

LONDON AND NEW YORK

First published 2013
by Routledge
2 Park Square, Milton Park, Abingdon, Oxfordshire OX14 4RN

Simultaneously published in the USA and Canada
by Routledge
711 Third Avenue, New York, NY 10017

First issued in paperback 2015

Routledge is an imprint of the Taylor & Francis Group, an informa business

British Library Cataloguing in Publication Data
A catalogue record for this book is available from the British Library

ISBN 13: 978-1-138-94575-3 (pbk)
ISBN 13: 978-0-415-63961-3 (hbk)

Typeset in Times New Roman
By Taylor & Francis Books

Publisher's Note
The publisher would like to make readers aware that the chapters in this book may be referred to as articles as they are identical to the articles published in the special issue. The publisher accepts responsibility for any inconsistencies that may have arisen in the course of preparing this volume for print.

Contents

Citation Information

The chapters in this book were originally published in *Terrorism and Political Violence*, volume 24, issue 2 (2012). When citing this material, please use the original page numbering for each article, as follows:

Chapter 1
Criminals and Terrorists: An Introduction
James J. F. Forest
Terrorism and Political Violence, volume 24, issue 2 (2012) pp. 171-179

Chapter 2
Osama bin Corleone? Vito the Jackal? Framing Threat Convergence through an Examination of Transnational Organized Crime and International Terrorism
John T. Picarelli
Terrorism and Political Violence, volume 24, issue 2 (2012) pp. 180-198

Chapter 3
When Politicians Sell Drugs: Examining Why Middle East Ethnopolitical Organizations are Involved in the Drug Trade
Victor Asal, Kathleen Deloughery, and Brian J. Phillips
Terrorism and Political Violence, volume 24, issue 2 (2012) pp. 199-212

Chapter 4
The Opium Trade and Patterns of Terrorism in the Provinces of Afghanistan: An Empirical Analysis
James A. Piazza
Terrorism and Political Violence, volume 24, issue 2 (2012) pp. 213-234

Chapter 5
Surreptitious Lifelines: A Structural Analysis of the FARC and the PKK
Vera Eccarius-Kelly
Terrorism and Political Violence, volume 24, issue 2 (2012) pp. 235-258

Chapter 6
The Terrorism Debate Over Mexican Drug Trafficking Violence
Phil Williams
Terrorism and Political Violence, volume 24, issue 2 (2012) pp. 259-278

Criminals and Terrorists: An Introduction

On January 24, 1878, a Russian revolutionary named Vera Zasulich became a populist hero after shooting and seriously wounding Colonel Fyodor Trepov, the oppressive and widely reviled governor of St. Petersburg who had recently abused a political prisoner. At her trial, when asked why she threw down her gun after the attack, she responded, "I am a terrorist not a murderer."[1] Vera's belief in the legitimacy of her actions—to her, the shooting was an act of political justice, not criminality—reflects a common theme throughout the world of terrorism, a world full of ideological attempts to justify violence. Criminals are motivated by a broad spectrum of reasons like personal enrichment, revenge, hatred of others, passion, psychological angst, and so forth, while terrorists believe that their actions—even the most violent or criminal—are justified by a higher cause. And yet, it remains difficult sometimes to separate terrorist and criminal activity. For example, terrorists maim, kill, and destroy, and it would be difficult to find a court of law anywhere in the civilized world that does not view these as crimes, regardless of motives or ultimate goals. Terrorists have also routinely engaged in money laundering, theft, fraud, extortion, smuggling (including drugs, weapons, and humans), bank robbery, and many other kinds of criminal activity.

In truth, as Alex Schmid notes, criminal and terrorist organizations have much in common: both are rational actors, they produce victims, they use similar tactics such as kidnapping and assassination, they operate secretly, and both are criminalized by the ruling regime and stand in opposition to the state.[2] However, by portraying their criminality with a cloak of ideological justification, politically violent actors demonstrate how purpose matters. As David Rapoport recently observed, the act of robbing a bank or engaging in drug trafficking can be to enrich oneself as a person, or to get money for an organization that sees itself as creating a better society.[3] Further, as Schmid notes, terrorism and crime are distinguished not only by different purposes (e.g., political motivation versus a greater share of illicit markets), but also by their violence (e.g., terrorists tend to be less discriminate than criminals), and by their communication strategies (e.g., terrorists claim responsibility for violent acts and use the media to propagate their cause, whereas criminals usually avoid the media).[4]

It is also important to note that terrorists generally loathe being labeled as ordinary criminals. However, the story of Vera above represents one of relatively few examples in which the term "terrorist" was embraced by the perpetrators of the violence. Groups and individuals engaging in terrorism have much preferred to use labels like "freedom fighters," or in the case of some religious groups, "holy warriors." For example, Menachem Begin, the leader of an Israeli terrorist group known as Irgun, insisted that he led a group of "freedom fighters" and that the *British* were terrorists.[5] In his September 13, 1982 court statement, Weather Underground member David Gilbert declared, "We are neither terrorists nor criminals. It is precisely because of our love of life, because we revel in the human spirit, that we became freedom fighters against this racist and deadly imperialist system."[6] More recently, Osama bin Laden often referred to al Qaida and other militant Islamists as "freedom fighters."[7]

According to David Rapoport's essential "Four Waves of Terrorism," this intense desire for terrorists to portray their actions using different terms has changed in curious ways over the last century. In his analysis, modern non-state terror began in the 1870s and produced four successive overlapping waves. The "Anarchist" wave was basically completed by the 1920s; the "Anti-Colonial" wave succeeded it and lasted until the 1960s. The "New Left" wave then began and was virtually over by 2000, and the "Religious" Wave (which he describes as the contemporary era) began in 1979. Each completed wave lasted approximately forty years or a generation.[8] First wave participants were particularly obsessed with distinguishing themselves from criminals. Early modern groups proudly identified themselves as terrorists, a description their opponents were pleased to use too.[9] European anarchists decided to throw the bomb, which was particularly dangerous, because criminals would never use bombs that way.[10] They refused to take hostages, even for the purpose of getting prisoners released, because hostage taking was associated with criminal activity and piracy. Groups in the second wave did take hostages, but only to get prisoners released. It was only in the third wave that hostages were taken for other reasons (like monetary ransoms), and criminal activity became widespread, especially in Latin America where the taking of hostages first became common.[11] This is also when we saw a skyrocketing number of airplane hijackings, particularly in the Middle East, during which demands were made for political concessions like the release of imprisoned colleagues.

According to Rapoport, it was only during the first wave that individuals like Vera called themselves terrorists, while in the second wave, terrorist group leaders like Begin preferred to emphasize the purpose of their violence, rather than the methods used. During this and subsequent waves of terrorism, virtually all politically violent groups have refuted the term "terrorist" to describe themselves. Meanwhile, governments have often preferred to use the term to describe a broad range of rebel or non-state groups that used violence. Rapoport observes that by the late 1960s, the mass media "confused or corrupted the language further by obscuring the distinction between ends and means altogether, using terms freedom fighter and terrorist as virtually interchangeable."[12]

Overall, terrorist groups over the past 120 years have shown a keen interest in shaping perceptions about their activities—a concern not usually found among ordinary criminals. This historical perspective informs our understanding of contemporary terrorism and the nature of its relationship with criminal networks. But as John Picarelli notes in his contribution to this special issue of *Terrorism and Political Violence*, there are many ways in which scholars and scientists can contribute further to this understanding. He offers several framing questions and ideas for engaging the academic community in identifying and analyzing new kinds of research on the intersections of crime and terrorism. Particularly useful areas for study address the desire for definitional clarity, and often focus on specific attributes of organizations and their operating environments. These are the general themes addressed by the research articles in this Special Issue.

Definitional Challenges

Studies of crime and terror often grapple with the central debate over definitions: What separates a terrorist group from a criminal organization, a liberation movement or some other entity? From the U.S. Department of State's view, the term "terrorism" means "premeditated, politically motivated violence perpetrated against non-combatant targets by sub-national groups or clandestine agents, usually intended to influence an audience."[13] According to Rapoport:

> Terror is violence with distinctive properties used for political purposes both by private parties and states. That violence is unregulated by publicly accepted norms to contain violence, the rules of war and the rules of punishment. Private groups using terror most often disregard the rules of war, while state terror generally disregards rules of punishment, i.e., those enabling us to distinguish guilt from innocence. But both states and non-state groups can ignore either set of rules.[14]

Similarly, Bruce Hoffman defines terrorism as "the deliberate creation and exploitation of fear through violence or the threat of violence in the pursuit of political change...[it is] designed to have far-reaching psychological effects beyond the immediate victim(s) or object of the terrorist attack...[and] to create power where there is none or to consolidate power where there is very little."[15]

In these and other definitions of terrorism, a common theme is that motives matter. Phil Williams also distinguishes terrorist and criminal organizations by their motives: at the heart of terrorist organizations is the desire to bring about political change, while criminal organizations focus on profit generation and maximization.[16] Further, he notes, terrorist attacks should be seen as a sum total of activities that include fundraising, recruitment, training, development of special skills, and preparation for an attack which can stretch over several months or even years. Criminal organizations focus much of their energies on protecting themselves from peer competitors or government and law enforcement agencies, and pursue strategies to manage, avoid, control, or mitigate risk—but of course, many terrorist groups do this as well.[17] Loretta Napoleoni draws clear distinctions between terrorists and criminals in how they view money. Criminal organizations run their operations like private corporations, with the accumulation of profit as the ultimate goal. In contrast, terrorist organizations are more interested in money disbursements than money laundering; instead of accumulation, money is to be distributed within the network of cells to support operations.[18]

Thus, the scholarly literature is rich with thoughtful arguments for how terrorists should be viewed as different from ordinary criminals. However, a growing number of authors have begun to suggest that the distinctions between the two may be fading. For example, Walter Laqueur has argued that fifty years ago a clear dividing line existed between terrorism and organized crime, but that "more recently this line has become blurred, and in some cases a symbiosis between terrorism and organized crime has occurred that did not exist before."[19] Other scholars such as Tamara Makarenko, Thomas Sanderson, Chris Dishman, R. T. Naylor, Rachel Ehrenfeld, Louise Shelley, and John Picarelli have described the phenomenon as a nexus, a confluence, a continuum, or some other kind of paradigm involving fluid, constantly changing relationships among members of terrorist and criminal networks.[20]

According to Makarenko, the end of the Cold War and subsequent decline of state sponsorship for terrorism forced groups to seek new revenue sources, and most often this led them to engage in various kinds of organized crime activities.[21] Some groups—like the FARC in Colombia and the Abu Sayyaf Group in the

Philippines—have slowly moved away from their original commitment to political violence and more toward increasing levels of purely criminal activity. In the case of the FARC, these Marxist guerillas in Colombia began taxing and protecting the drug trade, and are now seen by many as more of a peer competitor with Colombian drug cartels than as an ideologically-motivated group seeking political change. For the Abu Sayyaf Group, there are indications that profit derived from criminal activity has supplanted socio-political ideology as the organization's *raison d'être.* Loretta Napoleoni refers to these developments as a "new economy of terror" in which sources of revenue include remittance from diaspora members, charities, profits diverted from legal and illegal businesses, kidnapping, piracy, and many other kinds of criminal activity.[22]

These definitional issues are explored by several contributors to this special issue of *Terrorism and Political Violence.* For example, Phil Williams argues that although traffickers routinely torture, kill, and decapitate rivals (as well as police chiefs and local politicians), Mexico is not a victim of growing terrorism. He then offers a three-layered framework (rational strategic competition, factionalism and outsourcing, and anomic violence) to describe how the violence in Mexico is a rather different phenomenon from terrorism and one that cannot be captured under the rubric of political violence nor characterized as narco-terrorism or a criminal insurgency. Shawn Teresa Flanigan compares Mexican drug cartels to more "traditional" terrorist organizations like Hamas and Hizballah, noting commonalities in their provision of public goods, motivations for using violence, organizational structure, and other dimensions. She then explores how shifts in tactics and behavior may determine whether an organized crime group should be considered a terrorist organization.

In her comparison of the Kurdish ethno-nationalist group, the PKK, and the Colombian leftist group FARC, Vera Eccarius-Kelly describes how fluid interactions between terrorist groups and criminal networks and the sharing of knowledge about smuggling operations, money laundering systems, communications technologies, document forgery, and so forth can advance the interests and skills of both types of organizations. In some cases, terrorists and criminals are seen to cooperate within the same territory, share intelligence information, rely on the same corrupt government officials, and even conduct joint operations. These mutually beneficial relationships diminish the precision with which definitional categories can be applied to a specific organization. McKenzie O'Brien describes how the Abu Sayyaf Group in the Philippines has fluctuated between an emphasis on terrorism and on criminal activity. And Jennifer Varriale Carson, Gary LaFree, and Laura Dugan observe that while most scholars of terrorism (as well as policymakers and practitioners) have characterized domestic radical environmental and animal rights groups as terrorists, thus far their attacks have been overwhelmingly a specific type of criminal activity—causing property damage—rather than injuring or killing humans, which is more commonly associated with terrorism.

To sum up, many kinds of analytical frameworks have been used to define and differentiate terrorism from other kinds of activity, but a common approach has proved elusive. Contributors to this special issue add to the conceptual diversity, and offer new perspectives on how crime and terrorism may be overlapping or converging. The cornerstone of research on these criminal-terrorist intersections is the organizational level of analysis. For some terrorist organizations, continued existence has become contingent upon aligning themselves with criminal organizations and engaging in criminal activity. Further, as many scholars have noted, terrorist groups and organized crime networks are learning from one another's successes and failures.[23] Thus a significant number of articles in this Special Issue are case studies that examine specific organizational and environmental dimensions of these crime-terror intersections.

Organizational and Environmental Attributes

Organizations are comprised of individuals, most of whom have a keen survival instinct that influences organizational decision-making. Naturally, the field of terrorism studies is filled with scholars who explore the characteristics of organizations and individuals, including those attributes that enable various kinds of crime-terror collaboration. Some studies have illustrated how both kinds of organizations are driven by strategic concerns, and when those concerns intersect, collaboration is more likely. For example, terrorists and criminals share a desire for the preservation and growth of illicit economies like weapons and drug trafficking. In some cases, a terrorist group's involvement in—or protection of—illicit economies like the drug trade can help them attain local legitimacy. In zones of competing governance, where violent non-state actors compete against central governments for influence and control, these illicit economies are often a central or primary means of commerce and livelihood for local populations.[24] This struggle for influence is critical, and there are many different ways that a terrorist group's involvement in illicit economic activities can help it acquire and wield political capital as well as new operational capabilities.

Another important area of research examines how individual relationships facilitate temporary organizational alliances. Often, ties between terrorist and criminal organizations are basic customer-supplier relationships established to facilitate a specific type of transaction or resource exchange, like document fraud or smuggling humans, drugs, or weapons across a particular border. But not just anyone can forge such relationships. For clandestine networks engaged in illicit activities, collaboration at the individual level is usually dependent upon "trusted handshakes"— personal bonds established through shared ethnic, tribal, religious, or community affiliation, or by mutual background experiences, like prison or years of suffering imposed by a brutally oppressive regime.[25] Individuals who share common bonds and trust are the lynchpins for establishing mutually beneficial collaboration between divergent organizations.

Without some fundamental basis of trust, collaboration between criminal and terrorist networks would be virtually impossible. As Mark Galeotti recently observed, "on the whole organized crime groups have not shown any particular enthusiasm to work with terrorists, whom they regard as not only unreliable and amateurish but also dangerous, in that any evidence of such a connection is likely to trigger a much more immediate and heavy-handed law enforcement response in the post-11 September era."[26] It is thus important to analyze and understand environmental factors that may facilitate this collaboration. For example, researchers can gather and analyze data that helps them identify patterns among environments in which we see high levels of criminal and terrorist network activities. Research questions include: Are there particular environmental enablers—like economic globalization, corruption, weak political institutions, etc.—that contribute to collaboration between criminals and terrorists? If studies reveal identifiable patterns among these factors, do they provide meaningful insights about places in the world that could emerge as enabling environments for a convergence of terrorism and crime in the future?

Common factors that influence a terrorist or criminal organization's activities include access to weapons, illicit economies, and safe haven—these are often referred to as "enablers." Studies of these enablers are often driven by the desire to understand where and when criminal or terrorist activities (including collaboration) are most likely, and why. According to this area of research, there are specific locations throughout the world within which greater criminality, terrorism, and crime-terror collaboration have been facilitated in the past or are likely in the future. For example, the presence of organized crime may attract terrorists into a particular location, where they offer themselves as protectors of the population against the deficiencies of the states and the predatory behavior of criminal groups, and in return they expect support for their ideological agenda.[27] Scholars have drawn links between terrorism, crime, and local conditions like government oppression or corruption, foreign occupation, poverty, discrimination (ethnic, racial, religious), injustice (real or perceived), and a lack of political or socio-economic opportunities. Numerous books, journal articles, and reports—including The Fund for Peace's annual Failed State Index[28]— highlight the importance of a central government's weakness as a potential enabler for criminal and terrorist activity. In-depth case studies of the crime-terror nexus have also been published on the Black Sea region, Chechnya and the Northern Caucasus, the Afghanistan-Pakistan border region, the Horn of Africa, the Tri-Border area of Latin America (where the borders of Argentina, Brazil, and Paraguay intersect), and many other regions.[29]

Trends in globalization have also contributed to the capabilities of—and opportunities for—terrorist and criminal networks to operate and collaborate. According to Yuri Fedotov, the Executive Director of the United Nations Office of Drugs and Crime, "Thanks to advances in technology, communication, finance and transport, loose networks of terrorists and organized criminal groups that operate internationally can easily link with each other. By pooling their resources and expertise, they can significantly increase their capacity to do harm."[30] It is also quite likely that successful counterterrorism strategies can lead to greater levels of collaboration between terrorists and criminals; a constrained operating environment may compel an organization to pursue any and all options to achieve their objectives, or in some cases just to ensure their survival.

Essentially, there are many examples in the scholarly literature that describe how organizational and environmental attributes can enable (or constrain) terrorist and criminal activities. After all, terrorism and crime are—as many have observed—largely contextual phenomena. A majority of the contributions to this special issue of *Terrorism and Political Violence* address these issues of organizational and environmental attributes, in several instances highlighting the intersection of terrorism and drug trafficking. For example, Victor Asal, Kathleen Deloughery, and Brian J. Phillips examine how and why ethnopolitical organizations in the Middle East are involved in the drug trade; James A. Piazza examines longitudinal trends of opiate production, trafficking, and sales in different regions of Afghanistan to explain patterns of terrorist activity undertaken by Afghan-based extremist groups; and Vera Eccarius-Kelly describes how the FARC and the PKK have adapted to changing environmental conditions in ways that include varying levels of involvement in drug trafficking. Phil Williams also examines the intersection of drugs and violence in his analysis of Mexican drug cartels, as does Shawn Flanigan in her comparison of Mexican drug cartels with Hamas and Hizballah.

Other types of criminal activity highlighted in this special issue include McKenzie O'Brien's study of the Abu Sayyaf Group's involvement in kidnapping; Thomas J.

Holt's article on how modern computer hacking tools and malware can be used by cyber criminals and terrorists to exploit online vulnerabilities of their targets; and the analysis by Jennifer Varriale Carson, Gary LaFree, and Laura Dugan, focusing on property damage by radical environmental and animal rights groups in the United States. As the articles in this special issue demonstrate, there is a wide spectrum of research on organizations and enabling environments that can contribute to our understanding of crime-terror intersections—and more importantly, what to do about them.

Conclusion

Much of the literature in the fields of criminology and terrorism studies is intended to help policymakers and practitioners develop more effective ways to disrupt and defeat criminal and terrorist networks. Underlying questions of concern include: How have governments historically responded to criminal and terrorist groups, and what have been the major shortcomings of those responses? How *should* governments respond, and why? Do modern government responses to terrorism and organized crime reflect a sophisticated understanding of diverse group characteristics and environmental enablers? At the end of the day, a government's legal system plays a central role in responding to terrorists; are the laws used for prosecution and imprisonment of criminals equally relevant for combating terrorist networks?

Certainly, there are similarities in how governments view the threats of terrorism and transnational organized crime. Effective strategies for combating both kinds of organizations require a comprehensive integration of a nation's key elements of power (diplomatic, intelligence, military, economic, financial, informational, and legal). This integrated perspective is emphasized in recent U.S. strategies released by the Obama administration, particularly the *National Strategy for Counterterrorism* and the *National Strategy to Combat Transnational Organized Crime*.[31] Further, it is noteworthy that contemporary training programs for security, intelligence, and law enforcement professionals often address the same topics and skills for combating both organized crime and terror. In recent years, several programs—informed by scholarly analysis—have incorporated new approaches to understanding the financial aspects of clandestine networks, the necessity of international and interagency cooperation, and the role of "street perception" in the success or failure of a terrorist or criminal organization.[32]

To conclude, research on crime-terror intersections has important practical implications. The variety of topics and questions discussed here suggest there is a great deal of interesting and useful research being produced by scholars of terrorism and counterterrorism. Further, research that results in a better understanding of the intersections between crime and terrorism will surely contribute to new strategies for disrupting and defeating these kinds of organizations. Making such a contribution to this important security challenge of the 21st century is a central goal of this special issue of *Terrorism and Political Violence*. Sincere gratitude is extended to all the contributors for their hard work and commitment to this effort, and for inspiring others to pursue further study in these areas.

James J. F. Forest
University of Massachusetts Lowell; and Joint Special Operations University

Notes

1. Richard Pipes, "The Trial of Vera Z," *Russian History* 37, no. 1 (2010): 5–82. See also Ana Siljak, *Angel of Vengeance: The "Girl Assassin," The Governor of St. Petersburg, and Russia's Revolutionary World* (London: St. Martin's Press, 2008).

2. Alex P. Schmid, "The Links between Transnational Organized Crime and Terrorist Crimes," *Transnational Organized Crime* 2, no. 2 (Winter 1996): 66–67.

3. Personal correspondence with David Rapoport, Sept. 6, 2011.

4. Schmid (see note 2 above), 67–68.

5. See David C. Rapoport, "Before the Bombs There Were the Mobs: American Experiences with Terror," *Terrorism and Political Violence* 20, no. 2 (2008): footnote 11; and David Rapoport, "The Politics of Atrocity," in *Terrorism: Interdisciplinary Perspectives,* ed. Yonah Alexander and Seymore M. Finger (New York: John Jay Press, 1977), 46–63.

6. David Gilbert, *Students for a Democratic Society and the Weather Underground Organization* (Toronto: Arm the Spirit, 2001).

7. Bin Laden said the rebels in Saudi Arabia were freedom fighters, not terrorists in an interview with CNN, as noted in Gilles Kepel and Jean-Pierre Milelli, *Al Qaeda in its Own Words* (Cambridge, MA: Harvard University Press, 2009), 52.

8. David C. Rapoport, "The Four Waves of Terrorism," in *Attacking Terrorism: Elements of a Grand Strategy*, ed. Audrey Kurth Cronin and James M. Ludes (Washington, DC: Georgetown University Press, 2004); and David Rapoport (see note 5 above, 2008), 167–194.

9. David Rapoport (see note 5 above, 2008), footnote 11.

10. Personal correspondence with David Rapoport.

11. Ibid.

12. David Rapoport (see note 5 above, 2008), footnote 11; and David Rapoport (see note 5 above, 1977), 46–63.

13. 22 United States Code, Section 2656 (d) - cit. *United States Department Patterns of Global Terrorism, 1999* (Washington, DC: Department of State Publications, April 2000), p. viii.

14. David Rapoport (see note 5 above, 2008), footnote 12.

15. Bruce Hoffman, *Inside Terrorism*, Rev. ed. (New York: Columbia University Press, 2006), 40–41.

16. Phil Williams, "Strategy for a New World: Combating Terrorism and Transnational Organized Crime," in *Strategy in the Contemporary World,* ed. John Baylis et al. (Oxford University Press, 2007), 195–196.

17. Phil Williams (see note 16 above), p. 196.

18. Loretta Napoleoni, "The New Economy of Terror: How Terrorism is Financed," *Forum on Crime and Society* 4, nos. 1 and 2 (December 2004): 31–33.

19. Walter Laqueur, *The New Terrorism* (Oxford University Press, 1999), 211.

20. Tamara Makarenko, "The Ties the Bind: Uncovering the Relationship between Organized Crime and Terrorism," in *Global Organized Crime: Trends and Developments,* ed. Dina Siegel, Henk Van De Bunt, and Damian Zaitch (Dordrecht: Kluwer, 2003), 159–170; R. T. Naylor, *Wages of Crime: Black Markets, Illegal Finance and the Underworld of Economy* (Ithaca, NY: Cornell University Press, 2002), 44–87; Chris Dishman, "Terrorism, Crime and Transformation," *Studies of Conflict and Terrorism* 24, no. 1 (2001): 43–58; Thomas M. Sanderson, "Transnational Terror and Organized Crime: Blurring the Lines," *SAIS Review* 24, no. 1 (Winter-Spring 2004): 49–61; John T. Picarelli, "Turbulent Nexus of Transnational Organised Crime and Terrorism: A Theory of Malevolent International Relations," *Global Crimes* 7, no. 1 (2006): 1–24; Rachel Ehrenfeld, *Funding Evil: How Terrorism is Financed, and How to Stop it* (Chicago: Bonus Books, 2003); Louise Shelley and John Picarelli, "The Diversity of the Crime-Terror Interaction," *International Annals of Criminology* 43 (2005): 51–81; and Louise Shelley and John Picarelli, "Organized Crime and Terrorism," in *Terrorism Financing and State Responses: A Comparative Perspective,* ed. Jeanne Giraldo and Harold Trinkunas (Stanford, CA: Stanford University Press, 2007), 39–55.

21. Tamara Makarenko, "The Crime-Terror Continuum: Tracing the Interplay between Transnational Organized Crime and Terrorism," *Global Crime* 6, no. 1 (February 2004): 129.

22. Loretta Napoleoni (see note 18 above), 31–33.

23. Makarenko (see note 21 above), 135; James J. F. Forest, ed., *Teaching Terror: Strategic and Tactical Learning in the Terrorist World* (Lanham, MD: Rowman & Littlefield, 2006).

24. See James J. F. Forest, "Engaging Non-State Actors in Zones of Competing Governance," *Journal of Threat Convergence* 1, no. 1 (Fall 2010): 10–21.

25. James J. F. Forest, "Collaboration between International Organized Crime and Terrorist Networks," Annual Joint Conference of the International Security and Arms Control Section of the American Political Science Association and the International Security Studies Section of the International Studies Association, Providence, RI, 2010.

26. Mark Galeotti, "Hard Times – Organized Crime and the Financial Crisis," *Jane's Intelligence Review* (July 24, 2009).

27. Vanda Felbab-Brown and James Forest, "Political Violence and the Illicit Economies of West Africa," *Terrorism and Political Violence* (Summer 2012, forthcoming).

28. The Failed State Index compiles a variety of social, economic, and political indicators and is produced annually by The Fund for Peace and published in *Foreign Policy* magazine. For more information, please see http://www.fundforpeace.org.

29. For example, see Louise Shelley, John Picarelli, et al., "Methods and Motives: Exploring Links between Transnational Organized Crime and International Terrorism" (June 23, 2005: Final report of research sponsored by the National Institute of Justice, Grant No. 2003-IJ-CS-1019), 59–75; and case studies published by The Center for the Study of Threat Convergence at The Fund for Peace, available online at: http://www.fundforpeace.org/tc

30. "Growing Links Between Crime and Terrorism the Focus of UN Forum," *UN Press Service,* 16 March 2011, http://www.un.org/apps/news/story.asp?NewsID-37780&cr=terrorism&cr1

31. The White House, National Strategy for Counterterrorism (June 2012), http://www.whitehouse.gov/sites/default/files/counterterrorism_strategy.pdf; and The White House, National Strategy to Combat Transnational Organized Crime (July 2012), http://www.whitehouse.gov/sites/default/files/Strategy_to_Combat_Transnational_Organized_Crime_July_2011.pdf

32. For studies of the latter, see James. J. F. Forest, ed., *Influence Warfare: How Terrorists and Governments Fight to Shape Perceptions in a War of Ideas* (Westport, CT: Praeger Security International, 2009); James J. F. Forest, "Exploiting the Fears of Al-Qaida's Leadership," *The Sentinel* 2, no. 2 (2009): 8–10; James J. F. Forest, "Influence Warfare and Modern Terrorism," *Georgetown Journal of International Affairs* 10, no. 1 (2009): 81–90; and James J. F. Forest, "Exploiting al-Qaida's Inconvenient Truths," *Perspectives on Terrorism* (Winter 2012, forthcoming).

Osama bin Corleone? Vito the Jackal? Framing Threat Convergence Through an Examination of Transnational Organized Crime and International Terrorism

JOHN T. PICARELLI

National Institute of Justice, U.S. Department of Justice, Washington, DC, USA

Nation-states and security planners continue to place a high emphasis on threat convergence, such as that which emanates from the links between transnational organized crime and international terrorism. The social and behavioral sciences are not silent on this topic. This article frames the existing literature on crime-terror interaction to demonstrate that threat convergence is more complex than policy-makers and practitioners often realize. With terror and crime groups evolving to resemble one another, convergence is undermining the conventional wisdom that limited crime-terror interaction to short-term relationships due to divergent motives. The contemporary threat environment is promoting longer-term cooperation between organized crime and terrorism, in some cases resulting in hybrid organizations that merge elements of both. This article concludes by giving suggestions for future multidisciplinary research in this field as well as supporting the formation of new strategies to combat threat convergence.

The dangers we face are unprecedented in their complexity. Ethnic conflict and outlaw states threaten regional stability. Terrorism, drugs, organized crime, and proliferation of weapons of mass destruction are global concerns that transcend national boundaries and undermine economic stability and political stability in many countries.

—President Bill Clinton, 1997[1]

This article not subject to U.S. copyright law.

John T. Picarelli is a social science analyst at the National Institute of Justice, the research, development and evaluation branch of the U.S. Department of Justice. There, he oversees research programs on transnational threats such as trafficking in human beings and transnational organized crime.

The views expressed in this article do not necessarily represent the views of the Department of Justice of the United States.

Criminal networks are not only expanding their operations, but they are also diversifying their activities, resulting in a convergence of trans-national threats that has evolved to become more complex, volatile, and destabilizing.

—President Barack Obama, 2011[2]

The group was led by two men, one a hashish dealer from Morocco and the other an economics doctoral candidate from Tunisia. Together, they operated a transnational criminal enterprise of a half-dozen perpetrators that imported hashish from Morocco into Europe. The group had money, weapons, safe houses, disposable mobile phones, and the other infrastructure required of a drug trafficking organization (DTO). In late February, this simple case took an unanticipated turn—the DTO bartered 66 pounds of hashish for 440 pounds of explosives stolen earlier that month from a mine. The next month, Spain learned that this was not just a DTO when backpack bombs shattered the calm and hundreds of lives on board Madrid commuter trains.

The inquiry into the March 11, 2004, bombings in Madrid reinforced a central tenet of contemporary transnational threats—it is more difficult today to categorize malevolent non-state actors using declarative labels like terrorist or organized crime. Terror organizations seeking to replace the state sources of funding they lost after the Cold War have turned to organized crime. Transnational organized crime groups seeking security for their illicit enterprises has deployed political violence against governments. And both criminal and terrorist organizations have leveraged the infrastructures of globalization to advance their causes, often using common facilitators in the process. These developments and others have led to increased opportunities for these groups to collaborate with one another and have led to a collapse of the clear, bright lines that once separated them.

Researchers have been examining the crime-terror nexus for some time. Experts from a variety of academic disciplines have explored the nature and scope of the interactions between transnational organized crime and terrorism. In their works, they have provided case studies of collaboration, identified the reasons supporting and deterring cooperation, detailed the degree to which each group has appropriated the activity of the other, and suggested ways to mitigate or eliminate these hybrid threats. The literature is a starting point for any policy or program that will tackle crime-terror interaction, and it is also the foundation for a host of questions that remain about the nature of collaboration between these two malevolent non-state actors.

Threat convergence is undermining the conventional wisdom on crime-terror interaction. For some time, the conventional wisdom has held that criminal and terrorist organizations employ similar methods and thus will cooperate in the short term, but the divergence of their motives will preclude long-term collaboration. Yet for a host of reasons, the contemporary threat environment provides transnational organized crime and international terrorist organizations the means and reasons to collaborate and, in some rare cases, merge. In order to evaluate if the conventional wisdom still holds true or if we are witnessing a shift in the threat landscape, science needs to provide more information and analysis of contemporary crime-terror interaction that government agencies can use to develop new policies and programs.

The literature on crime-terror interaction is therefore a crucial first step to improving our understanding of how transnational organized crime and international terrorism overlap. The article is broken into three sections. The first section explores the definitions of organized crime and terrorism to demonstrate one source of confusion in the current narrative of the crime-terror nexus. The terms "organized crime" and "terrorism" are applicable to describe not just activities but also the organizations that perpetrate these activities. Moreover, the scope of activities can vary across definitions of organized crime and terrorism, leading to significant issues when comparing parallel studies of threat convergence. This section lays the foundations for the second section, which explores the two predominant analytical foci for understanding threat convergence—organizational linkages and activity appropriation—and locates them in those spaces most conducive to threat convergence. The international political economy approach is an example of how analysts can capture the who, the how, and the where of threat convergence to form a more comprehensive picture of the phenomenon.

The article concludes with a discussion of how scientific research and data collection can improve this picture of threat convergence. While most of the research on threat convergence is limited in its scope and thus difficult to generalize, some recent examples of empirically-based analyses of crime-terror interaction demonstrate that science is on a trajectory to deliver explanations of the etiology and methodology of crime-terror interaction. These examples lead into a discussion of the most useful research and data sets that social science can deliver. The guiding principle of this activity should be empirical in method but practical in analysis, aiming to generate insights that practitioners can use to implement new strategies designed to fight threat convergence.

Definitions Matter: Not Who or How

The discussion of definitions is a required starting point for any analysis of threat convergence. Identifying the definitions of transnational organized crime and terrorism serves three purposes. The first is to clarify when an analysis is considering crime-terror interaction as rooted in organizational linkages, operational overlaps, or both. Definitions therefore must focus on organized crime and terrorism as forms of organization, as a type of activity, or both. Angela Veng Mei Leong builds on these sentiments when she notes that "one of the major difficulties preventing effective interdiction is that the phenomena of organised crime and terrorism are fundamentally difficult to define and often overlap."[3] Her article correctly identifies neither organized crime nor terrorism as a homogenous term. Rather, organized crime and terrorism are both an organization and an activity. Organized crime and terrorism are labels that apply to forms of social activity and to the organizations that conduct those activities. Hence, one can speak of smuggling or fraud as organized crime just as one can speak of a DTO or a mafia family as organized crime.

Bringing in this definitional clarification leads to what is the most frequently cited form of crime-terror interaction: activity appropriation. Crime-terror interaction is not limited to organizational linkages. A criminal organization can engage in terrorism and a terrorist organization can engage in organized crime. Examples of activity appropriation abound in the literature.[4] For example, Longmire and Longmire detail dozens of examples when Mexican DTOs have engaged in terrorist campaigns of violence.[5] Their analysis concludes that these campaigns allow for governments to list DTOs as terrorist organizations:

> Violent acts committed by DTOs and their enforcers are currently viewed as criminal acts. Yet, most of those acts are identical in nature to acts committed by traditional terrorist groups like al-Qaeda, the FARC, and the Provisional Irish Republican Army (IRA), and with similar intentions.... Most importantly, the intention of all these groups is the same—to intimidate the populace and change the behavior of a government.[6]

Reasonable experts will disagree as to whether Mexican DTOs are terrorists or not. Indeed, Longmire and Longmire admit that the ideological motives of terrorism are absent in their analysis of Mexican DTOs and this would normally preclude them for consideration as terrorism organizations. But equally important is to recognize that these organized crime groups are engaging in campaigns of violence that far exceed the normal levels found in drug markets.

Definitions also set the scope of what is considered in analyses of crime-terror interaction. Definitions set the boundaries for what organizations and activities fall into categories like "transnational organized crime" or "terrorism," a fact that in turn can prejudice the findings of a given study. On the one hand, using narrow definitions of these terms will lead to a situation where crime-terror interactions almost never occur. On the other hand, broad definitions lead to a situation where most any illicit activity is the result of criminals and terrorists collaborating.

Moreover, organized crime and terrorism are terms that obfuscate the wide range of groups that engage in these activities. The terrorism literature contains numerous examples of how to categorize different terror groups, such as through their political aims (e.g., ethno-nationalist, religious, ideological, etc.) or the scope of their activities. Some have made the case that careful categorization of terrorist groups can improve our understanding of crime-terror interaction. Hutchinson and O'Malley, for example, note that some groups tend to engage in acts of terrorism according to an "ephemeral-sporadic" basis, and that these groups are far less likely to collaborate with organized crime groups than more "organized-enduring" groups.[7]

Unlike the scholarship on terrorism, few experts ever consider a diversity of transnational organized crime groups. This leads to analyses that lump groups with clear organizational, operational, and even ideological divisions into the same category.[8] Yet as Picarelli and Shelley have argued, a diversity does exist. They argue that there are two or more forms of transnational organized crime; each has its own unique approach to working with terrorist organizations.[9] On the one hand, traditional criminal groups are rooted in a nationalist pride that often precludes them from collaborating with terror organizations for fear of harm to their fellow countrymen. On the other hand, globalized crime groups have an active hostility to the state and thus are more prone to collaborate with terror groups.

Last, being clear and transparent about the definitions used in an analysis of crime-terror interaction is important for avoiding "threat creep." By using clear definitions of organized crime and terrorism, analysts can avoid meaningless conflations with other threats. For example, the term narcoterrorism was coined in 1983 to describe DTOs who used excessive violence against law enforcement and other government agencies. The analyses that employed this term largely ignored if it indeed represented a new form of terrorism. More reasoned arguments that start with definitions of organized crime, drug trafficking, insurgency, and terrorism have resulted in analyses that detail exactly how DTOs and other organized crime groups overlap with terrorism and insurgency.[10] For example, Björnehed applies Makarenko's analytical model to terrorism and drug trafficking to pinpoint the intersections between the two phenomena and concludes with an evaluation of best practices employed against narcotics trafficking tied to terrorism.[11]

Such precision of terminology is not limited to the academic sphere. Practitioners have recently started to adopt the term "threat convergence" to capture the challenges arising from collaboration between drug trafficking, organized crime, terrorism, and proliferation. David Luna has developed this line of thinking, noting how the overlaps between organized crime, terrorism, and corruption yield challenges to national and international security that require interagency and international responses.[12] He notes that "interlinked illicit threats not only undermine the integrity of vital governmental institutions meant to protect peace and security, but cost economies tax revenue and jobs, and promote a culture of impunity..." and concludes that "prosecuting the battle against converging threat networks is not an easy endeavor—we must take the fight directly to these threats, dismantle transnational threat networks, and unravel the illicit financial nodes that sustain a web of criminality and corruption. It will require a constant evaluation of the types of illicit threats that will confront us all in the years to come."[13] It is therefore no surprise that the 2011 *U.S. Strategy to Combat Transnational Organized Crime* is subtitled "Addressing Converging Threats to National Security."

The Past as Prologue: Actors, Activities, and the Conventional Wisdom

What is clear from the discussion of definitions is that one can view crime-terror interaction from an organizational or operational perspective. An organizational analysis will focus on how transnational criminal and terrorist groups use the other's institutional structures for mutual advantage. For example, Aftab Ansari's Indian organized crime group collaborated with and provided funding to Pakistani terrorist cells of Syed Omar Sheikh, a terrorist who was later convicted for the Daniel Pearl murder. When viewing the crime-terror interaction as one that exists between organizations, the analytical focus lies on identifying the linkages between two or more groups and demonstrating how those linkages help each organization further progress towards its goals. An organizational analysis is often expressed through a typology that catalogues the depth of collaboration. For example, Williams' analysis of crime-terror interaction focuses on three organizational models: full integration into a single hybrid organization, a more arms-length tie between terrorist and criminal groups, and an even more distant relationship wherein one group influences the activities of the other.[14]

An operational analysis of crime-terror interaction focuses not on the organizational linkages but on the activities of organized crime and terrorist groups. The analytical focus is the documentation of the criminal activities that terror groups conduct or the terrorist attacks that criminal organizations perpetrate. The emphasis here is first to document the scope of activity appropriated from the other type of group and second to determine the degree to which this helps the group accomplish its goals. For example, Lowe explores a crime-terror interaction by detailing the ways in which terrorists use counterfeiting to fund their operations and concludes that terror groups will become more reliant on illicit sources of funding in the future.[15]

A threat convergence analysis should employ a merger of these two approaches and consider both organizational and operational facets of interaction. Rollins and Wyler, for example, have ten separate analytical categories of crime-terror interaction that each incorporates some elements of the organizational and operational approaches.[16] Similar is a study comparing the Provisional Irish Republican Army to D-Company in India that uses both organizational and operational evidence of crime-terror interaction in its analysis.[17]

Where both of these analytical frameworks generally agree, however, is on a general assessment about the longevity of crime-terror interactions that is often referred to using the shorthand "methods, not motives."[18] This conventional wisdom holds that transnational organized crime and international terrorism will frequently collaborate or appropriate the activity of the other in the short term due to shared interests (i.e., methods). However, over the long term, the criminal's interest in economic gains will clash with the terrorist's interest in political change and this will drive the two apart (i.e., motives). In his analysis of the links between organized crime, terrorism, and insurgency, Naylor makes this succinct conclusion:

> A world of difference exists between the motives of insurgent versus criminal groups. Criminals commit economic crimes to make money. The buck, so to speak, stops there. But to an insurgent group, money is merely a tool—one that is necessary but not sufficient to achieve the group's goals.[19]

The conventional wisdom in this field is that criminal organizations and terrorist groups come together for short-term gain and occasionally dabble in the other's area of expertise, but rarely if ever form long-term bonds.

Yet some are starting to question the utility of this conventional wisdom, suggesting that it oversimplifies a far more complex reality. While still rare and thus difficult to generalize from, it is nevertheless true that some organized crime and terror groups have merged or transformed into new hybrid organizations that no longer fit neatly into either category. As organized crime and terror groups appropriate the other's activity, they themselves can transform and lose their original modus operandi in favor of the goals of the appropriated activity (e.g., a terrorist group can transform into a DTO). Add to this a number of catalysts that create spaces conducive to crime-terror interaction, and it is easy to see why some analysts have raised the caution flag on assuming that long-term cooperation will not occur. Indeed, this three-part analytical framework is one that analysts can apply to most any form of threat convergence, as the following sections suggest.

Converging: The Formation of Hybrid Organizations

In 1997, the Defense Science Board authored a study that foretold of the situation nation-states face today. The two-volume *Summer Study Task Force on DOD Responses to Transnational Threats* outlined a prescient analysis of the threat from threat convergence.[20] The study listed five forms of transnational threat—terrorism, cyberwarfare, narcotics trafficking, the proliferation of weapons of mass destruction, and organized crime. The report was far-reaching not just for its recognition of the potential for mass casualty terrorism in the U.S. or for its call for a coordinated U.S. government effort to defend the homeland, but for its recognition that threats as varied as drug traffickers and terrorists represented the *same potential threat* to the U.S. The Defense Science Board urged the Department of Defense to focus on these threats as an emerging security threat and to pay particular attention to threat convergence arising from collectives of two or more of these threats—such as crime-terror hybrids.

Researchers examining the relationship between transnational organized crime and international terrorism have confirmed this early analysis of the Defense Science Board by focusing on the convergence of groups.[21] Convergence relies more on the organizational analytical tradition, looking within groups for hints as to why they cooperate. For example, Mullins explores the demographic profile and social self-identification of both criminals and terrorists, concluding that the similarities are significant enough to suggest a predilection towards collaboration between the two.[22] Another study uses a similar approach but focuses on gender, employing a pathway analysis to examine the similar life courses of women who engaged in crime and terrorism.[23] Last, Björnehed notes significant similarities in terms of structure and tangible and intangible resources as reasons supporting collaboration between organized crime and terrorist groups.[24]

Networked forms of organization are giving criminals and terrorists greater opportunity, and motive, for collaborating with one another. A number of studies have noted that advancements in information technology and globalized business practices have allowed crime and terror groups to adopt flatter organizational structures with distributed decisionmaking powers. Members of these networks tend to have an entrepreneurial spirit and have more opportunities to exploit it than members of hierarchical organizations.[25] When applied to terrorist and organized crime groups, it is clear that their ability to adapt quickly to changed circumstances is rooted in a sense of entrepreneurship that also undergirds a growing predilection to collaborate with one another.[26] For example, Dishman notes that as organized crime and terrorist groups have adopted networked forms of organization, it has given increased latitude for individuals to make decisions throughout the network.[27] Dishman thus argues that those individuals at the edges of organized crime and terrorist groups have more freedom to engage in collaborative arrangements.

Some have taken this approach to task, most often focusing on the misapplication of network theory or the lack of rigor in the analysis. Challenging the analogy of business firms that many scholars use when analyzing organized crime and terror groups, Eilstrup-Sangiovanni and Jones point to reasons why organized crime and terrorist networks are not as adaptable or resilient as once thought.[28] The authors cite issues related to community, trust, distance, coordination, and security as posing serious organizational difficulties for illicit networks. Similarly, Stohl conducts a review of the literature on networks and concludes that networked forms of organizations cannot alone explain collaboration between criminals and terrorists. Rather, analysis should focus on the flows of information within and between these networked organizations. Stohl also provides a useful reminder of the diversity of interests in terror organizations, noting that "a terrorist network is at the nexus of multiple groups and constituencies who are linked in significant but non hierarchical ways and can only be understood in context."[29] Thus, an entire terrorist organization might not collaborate with organized crime but rather only some individuals or cells in a network might work with criminals.

Another way to demonstrate convergence is more indirect and focuses on third parties that act as common nodes between criminal and terrorist organizations. Investigators and other practitioners have started to call such third parties "facilitators" since they most often play a role in promoting organized crime, terrorism, or other forms of transnational threats. An excellent example of this in practice is the use of money launderers to move funds around the globe. Numerous analyses have demonstrated that both organized crime and terrorists use money launderers, and sometimes organized crime will provide this service to terrorists for a fee. Rudner provides a detailed analysis of Hezbollah's financial apparatus and notes that terrorist organizations tend to launder their funds through the formal and informal banking structures of countries with high levels of criminal profits.[30] Likewise, Horgan and Taylor examine the money laundering strategies of the Provisional Irish Republican Army and note its connections with organized crime.[31]

Facilitators are not limited to money laundering. Another area of overlap between organized crime and terrorist groups arises from their need for forged documents. Members of organized crime and terrorist organizations need to travel internationally, and therefore the demand for false or stolen documents to hide their travel is an operational requirement. Recent research has demonstrated that both criminal and terrorist organizations covet the passports of certain European countries and of the U.S. for the familiarity they provide to border inspectors around the globe.[32] The same analysis notes that criminal organizations generating forged passports have marketed their products towards terrorist groups.

A third linkage between criminal and terrorist groups is found in the front companies and other organizations that obfuscate the illicit nature of terrorist and organized crime groups. Such front companies provide mechanisms to ship goods around the globe, give credibility to the movement of personnel, and can even serve as another node in the laundering of money. Private security firms are one of the fastest growing economic sectors and are garnering the increased interest of criminals and terrorists alike. Researchers have explored numerous examples of criminal and terrorist organizations using private security firms as cover for their operations.[33] One example is that Abu Bakr Naji's al-Qaida strategy document *Management of Savagery* cites private security companies as a target for infiltration and a potential vulnerability in the security apparatus fighting terrorism.

Regardless of the way it occurs, convergence is resulting in hybrid crime-terror organizations. Since only anecdotal evidence of these organizations exists, researchers are not able to say how frequently these organizations are forming and operating. However, forming they are. An example of one of these hybrid organizations is Dawood Ibrahim's D-Company, which started out as a smuggling operation in the late 1970s and grew into a major transnational organized crime syndicate operating out of Dubai in the 1980s. It was in the mid-1980s that D-Company, at the behest of Pakistan's Inter-Services Intelligence agency, began smuggling weapons to militant and terrorist groups in Afghanistan, Kashmir, Bangladesh, and India. A series of anti-Muslim events led D-Company to augment its criminal operations with a radical Islamic ideology. By 1993, D-Company began to undertake terror attacks of its own, including a series of explosions that rocked Bombay on March 12th of that year and killed 257. In sum, while rare, the existence of these hybrid organizations undermines the utility of the "methods, not motives" argument.

Transforming: The Blending of Criminal and Terrorist Activities

A second way that the analysis of transnational organized crime and terrorism is growing more complex is that each organization is operating in ways that mimic the other. Researchers continue to discuss this transformation of terrorist groups into organized crime outfits. As they continue to engage in organized crime over time, terrorist groups grow more likely to shift their raison d'être from political to economic goals. Likewise, some researchers have documented how organized crime groups have undertaken campaigns of violence that more closely resemble that of terrorist groups. This transformation leads to a blending of motives that further undermines the parsimony of the "methods, not motives" argument.

One of the first to discuss this transformation thesis was Dishman.[34] In his analysis, he noted that a small number of transnational criminal organizations such as the Medellin Cartel and the Sicilian Mafia had engaged in campaigns of violence for political ends that approached if not met the definition of terrorism. Likewise, terrorist organizations like the Provisional IRA, the Liberation Tigers of Tamil Eelam (LTTE), and the Kurdistan Workers' Party (PKK) were increasing their participation in organized crime activities. While he incorrectly concluded that the motives of crime and terror organizations precluded their long-term collaboration, he presciently noted that "terrorists and guerrilla groups who view their cause as futile, might turn their formidable assets towards crime—all the while under a bogus political banner."[35]

A number of studies have supported the observations found in Dishman's transformation theory. In one study, Roth and Sever explore the extensive organized crime portfolio of the PKK.[36] Noting that the PKK turned to organized crime when they lost access to state sponsors, the case study demonstrates the rather significant investments the PKK made in organized crime. The PKK's perpetration of drug trafficking, arms smuggling, human smuggling, extortion, money laundering, counterfeiting, illegal cigarettes, and trafficking in blood products garnered it close to $86 million annually in the 1990s. A telling quote from an unnamed Turkish security officer notes the impact of such large investments in organized crime: "The cooperation between the PKK and Kurdish criminal clans has been similar to the cooperation among Sicilian mafia families."[37]

Another case study in transformation is the Islamic Movement of Uzbekistan (IMU). Analysts often explore the IMU as a terror organization, but others have begun to model them as a major drug trafficking organization in the Central Asia region. For example, Cornell notes that the primary reason for this significant engagement in drug trafficking is in order to secure funds for the IMU's campaigns of violence.[38] Yet the case study also demonstrates the IMU adjusting its tactics to meet the requirements of its criminal enterprises. For example, the study notes that the timing of a series of IMU attacks in Kyrgyzstan and Uzbekistan created instability and confusion sufficient to smuggle recently processed Afghan heroin through strategic mountain passes in these countries.

Transformation is promoting collaboration between crime and terror organizations, and thus serves to reinforce the process of convergence. Makarenko, for example, plots the depth of crime-terror interaction along a spectrum that captures both organizational and operational facets of the relationship.[39] At the outer limits of the spectrum are terror groups engaging in limited forms of organized crime and organized crime groups conducting brief campaigns of political violence. As crime and terror groups continue to appropriate the activity of the other, they begin the process of transformation. The separate motives of illicit economic gain and violent political change grow muddled, with political crime on one side and commercial terrorism on the other. Eventually, towards the center of the spectrum, both types of group converge into one group, making it difficult if not impossible to categorize this new group as solely a terrorist or an organized crime entity. Makarenko also notes that organized crime and terrorist groups learn from one another, adding another important dimension into the transformation thesis.

A number of examples demonstrate an evolutionary path that transforms terrorist groups into something closer to organized crime groups. Rosenthal discusses the rise of terrorism-for-profit and how for-profit terrorists change their behaviors to support more their economic as opposed to political ends: "Terrorism-for-profit is criminal activity—kidnapping, banditry, looting, or smuggling—legitimized by an ideological veneer."[40] The article cites three organizational changes that occur when terrorist groups transform into hybrid crime-terror organizations: a degradation of the leadership cadre committed to the political cause; political transformations that undermine the political raison d'être of the group; and opportunities for significant criminal profits. In sum, transformation supports organizational change as was seen in the convergence examples.

Transformation is not limited to terrorist organizations, however. A number of case studies explore the political violence of criminal organizations. Pacheco notes that during the 1980s and 1990s, the drug DTOs in Mexico were nationalistic and thus focused solely on subverting the state, not challenging it.[41] More recently, however, the vast and brutal campaigns of violence have sought to challenge the authority of the state. Through a detailed analysis, Pacheco builds the case that these DTOs and their offshoots are waging terrorism in Mexico. Ironically, the study concludes that one reason for the transformation of these drug trafficking organizations is the Mexican government's successful campaign against the DTOs' leadership. The removal of this cadre of leaders led the DTOs to detach from the state and loosened the already elastic norms that restrained them from lashing out in widespread campaigns of violence against Mexican government and its citizens.

Locating: The Milieus and Drivers of Convergence and Transformation

The final issue driving the complexity of contemporary crime-terror interaction is the formation of spaces that are welcoming to these groups. While there are a significant number of factors driving the formation and continuation of these spaces, the three that arise most often are globalization, authority, and conflict. Globalization is an important factor in the creation of new opportunities for criminal and terrorist organizations to collaborate. The advancements of globalization's architectures (e.g., transportation, financial, trade, and communication) support networked forms of organizations that operate globally from hospitable yet remote locations.[42] Makarenko notes that when globalization, violence, corruption, and/or conflict weaken the state to a significant degree, it can create a "black hole" that will "foster the convergence between transnational organised crime and terrorism, and ultimately create a safe haven for the continued operations of convergent groups."[43]

As a result, it is important for criminal and terrorist organizations to find locations that are advantageous not just from a security standpoint but that also lie astride these globalization architectures. This is not often the "Afghanistan cave" or some other exceedingly remote location. Rather, it is a range of locations that include émigré communities, globalized slums, border regions, and free trade zones. Indeed, Sverdlick notes that one of the primary reasons the tri-border area of Paraguay, Argentina, and Brazil is so attractive to organized crime and terrorists alike is the combination of large émigré communities and the international financial and trade volumes that move through the region daily.[44]

Globalization is not the only consideration for identifying the most hospitable locations for crime-terror convergence. The "space" that exists between government and civil society is equally important as a predictor of locations favorable to threat convergence. Without delving deep into the social theory of the relations between governments and the governed, it is well accepted that when civil society views government as inept, corrupt, and/or illegitimate it will turn to alternate sources of authority.[45] While some of these alternate sources of authority are legitimate, they can also include illicit groups such as gangs and organized crime groups.[46] Arana explores the degree to which the *maras* in Central America have fomented instability and directly challenged the authority of the state, opening a space that other transnational threats such as terrorist organizations can exploit.[47] Likewise, Fernández maps the recent actions of a São Paulo gang, the Primeiro Comando da Capital (First Command of the Capital or PCC).[48] The case study demonstrates that the PCC's campaign of violence was directly aimed at the Brazilian state, and the political ends of this campaign, namely to obtain sole control of one or more *favelas*, met the definition of terrorism.

Globalization plays a role in accelerating this decomposition of the state's authority as well. With the increased volume of international financial and trade flows has come stronger and more frequent calls for decreased regulation and border controls that, from the private sector's point of view, act as a brake on economic activity. As governments respond to these calls and remove regulations, it places burdens on other countries to respond in kind to remain competitive. The combination of increased trade and decreased oversight, which some have called a "retreat of the state," has proven a boon to transnational organized crime and other illicit cross-border activities.[49] Andreas conducts a detailed analysis of the impact of economic liberalization and globalization on the growth of transnational crime and notes that due to liberalization of trade regulations and the containerization of commercial cargo, it has become exceedingly easier to hide illicit goods in legitimate cargo. By the mid-1990s, U.S. Customs was only searching 3% of the 9 million containers that entered the U.S. annually.[50]

Corruption is another contributing factor in the erosion of a state's authority. As corruption or even the perception of it becomes widespread, civil society mistrusts the state and sees it more as a predator than a protector. This decrease in legitimacy leads again to people turning to private sources of protection. It is therefore no surprise to find that organized crime and terrorist groups gravitate towards regions of the globe with high levels of corruption.[51] For example, studies of the crime-terror nexus in the Tri-Border Area often cite high levels of corruption among border guards and other public officials.[52] Pacheco also cites the high levels of corruption in Mexico as contributing to the DTOs and their campaigns of violence.[53]

Whether arising from state weakness, globalized liberalization, corruption, or other factors, both transnational organized crime and terror organizations have leveraged voids in state authority to further their operations. Gambetta's classic study of organized crime in Sicily used a Weberian model to show how organized crime groups, in lieu of the Italian state, sold private protection of property rights to businesses and individuals.[54] Likewise, Pacheco documents how the campaign of Mexican President Salinas and his government to liberalize the country in the late 1980s and the NAFTA reforms of the 1990s resulted in a "chilling impact throughout all segments of society" and resulted in a "power vacuum" that the narco-traffickers were more than happy to fill.[55] Cornell notes the import of these processes when he describes how they are attractive options for some terror organizations: "In this sense, crime and drugs are instrumental in enabling a [terrorist] group to threaten the state at its very foundation—the monopoly on the use of force and control over territory."[56] In sum, a decrease in state legitimacy and authority often leads to an increase in transnational organized crime and increased opportunities for crime-terror interaction.

One location that crystallizes all of these factors and thus serves as a catalyst for threat convergence is found in contemporary conflict zones and those areas recovering from conflict.[57] It is therefore not surprising to find organized crime groups and terrorist organizations moving into these spaces.[58] Brands examines the crisis in post-civil war Guatemala, noting a rapid increase in violent organized crime that has so undermined the legitimacy and authority of the state that the government can no longer control large sections of its territory.[59] Manwaring sees significant similarities between contemporary insurgency, terrorism, and organized crime, concluding that these represent a new form of war that security planners must now consider as a part of their national security studies.[60]

Conclusion: The Role for Science to Promote Evidence-Based Responses

The science examining crime-terror interaction remains incomplete and uneven. In 2010, the National Institute of Justice sponsored an international expert working group to examine the role of science in fighting transnational organized crime. On the topic of crime-terror interaction, the group noted their disappointment with the status of research. The most significant hurdles included the anecdotal nature of evidence used in articles, the lack of datasets upon which to conduct empirical studies of crime-terror interaction, and the failure to develop theories of the phenomenon. Their recommendations included more basic research that details and catalogues these interactions as well as research in areas such as how crime and terror groups trust one another and how they maintain that trust as well as the role of facilitators in forming and maintaining bonds between crime and terror groups.[61] More research is also needed to identify the etiology for convergence and transformation, the potential for harm from hybrid organizations, and assessing the tools employed to interdict them.

What this article highlights is that serious questions remain about threat convergence and it is up to science to substitute evidence-based explanation for anecdotal overgeneralization. The first step in this process is the development of explanatory frameworks of crime-terror interaction and the potential for hybrid organizations. One suggestion on how science can move forward with explaining the convergence of organized crime and terrorism is to adopt an international political economy approach. International political economy explores the relationship between countries and international markets—a relationship that impacts motive and opportunities for crime-terror interaction. It has proven itself a powerful way for exploring important questions about transnational organized crime. For example, an IPE analysis has described how illicit markets arise through state regulation and continued demand for prohibited goods and services.[62] Andreas noted that an IPE approach not only helps pinpoint the involvement of a diversity of actors in transnational criminal activities, it can also bring history into the analysis:

> There is a tendency in much of the popular and criminological literature to categorize these clandestine cross-border flows as "transnational organized crime." This is a frustratingly broad, vague, and fuzzy term, and is too often used as a poorly defined and all-encompassing umbrella category under which all sorts of perceived "transnational threats" are placed. It also tends to focus attention on large mafia-like organizations (often mislabeled as "cartels") and mafia-like leaders (often colorfully described as "kingpins" and "drug lords") rather than on particular market sectors and activities. For the most part, how transnational, organized, and criminal a market activity is depends largely on the commodity involved and the associated legal and financial risks. At base, most "transnational organized crime" involves some form of profit-driven smuggling across borders. And smuggling, of course, is as old as efforts to control borders. "Transnational organized crime," in other words, is in some respects simply a new and flashier (but less clear) term for a long-established clandestine transnational economic practice. Those who use it tend to emphasize the newness of the phenomenon and the growing nature of the threat.[63]

By focusing on the ways in which state laws and regulations form black markets, and by identifying the sources of supply and demand that fuel these markets, researchers can better understand where terror organizations might engage in illicit activity themselves or where it is better to collaborate with crime groups.

Regardless of the method that science adopts to produce analytical frameworks of crime-terror interaction, some important epistemological and methodological caveats are in order. First, if science is to contribute anything to our understanding of crime-terror interaction, it has to remain skeptical of the existence of these linkages. While this might seem counterintuitive, starting studies with an eye towards falsifying examples of crime-terror interaction produce results that have higher levels of scientific rigor behind them since they rarely oversimplify crime-terror interaction. For example, Warde examines the expansion of rules on money laundering and terrorist financing into the Middle East and North Africa and concludes that it has broadened the scope of black markets and driven more financial flows underground.[64] Warde's work reminds us of the unintended consequences of regulation and criminalization and the potential for creating more problems through solutions.

Second, researchers need to consider the historical context of crime-terror interaction, especially since only a few studies have explored the evolution of crime-terror interaction in a historical context. As Stohl notes, "Despite the argument that the new post-cold war environment and the development of a networked organization is at the root of much of the pressure for terrorists to turn to criminals, organizations which have employed terrorism have engaged in clearly criminal activities for many years."[65] Failure to place threat convergence into a historical context risks falling into the analytical trap that the phenomenon of threat convergence is "new" or "novel" or "growing."

Yet a well constructed analytical framework is only half of the puzzle for science. Without reliable sources of data, these frameworks are useless. The data that is needed to conduct a proper analysis of crime-terror interaction is likely to fall into one of three categories. The first is structured, quantifiable data that researchers can use to develop statistics on crime-terror interaction. A number of datasets contain structured data on the incidence of terrorism and forms of transnational organized crime such as trafficking in human beings and drug smuggling. For example, two NIJ-sponsored studies used datasets from the U.S. Departments of the Treasury and Homeland Security to pinpoint the potential for abusing informal value transfer systems and commodities trading for terrorist financing.[66] Scientists need to identify other datasets that might hold some useful data, suggest modifications to existing datasets to improve their utility vis-à-vis crime-terror interactions, and more than likely engage in basic research that results in new datasets.

A related but second set of structured data is geospatial or geocoded data that researchers can use to understand the locations of crime-terror interaction. Likely, this will involve the modification of existing datasets to allow for the use of geographic information system (GIS) mapping software to explore spatial patterns in the data. Most useful in this regard are datasets supporting social network analysis but that also contain GIS coding. Such datasets not only allow for a visual rendering of the links between criminal and terrorist organizations, but could also overlay that network over a map for even more explanatory power. For example, Smith et al. coded GIS tags into the data found in the American Terrorism Study database, allowing them to explore patterns concerning terrorist incidents, preparatory acts or crimes, offender information, and information on associated terrorist groups.[67]

The last type of data that researchers can leverage is ethnographic and other qualitative data. Far too little is known of the perpetrators involved in crime-terror, how they organize, and why they might cooperate. Research questions that drive studies seeking to understand a social phenomenon rather than explain its causation are well suited to the ethnographic tradition. In particular, the combination of qualitative data and case study method is a particularly powerful approach for developing thick descriptions of crime-terror interaction. For example, Felbab-Brown employs a comparative case study approach to explore the links between drug trafficking, insurgency, and terrorism in three countries, while Peters draws on her journalist background to develop a more ethnographic description of the links between heroin trafficking, insurgency, and terrorism in Afghanistan and Pakistan.[68] The development of datasets that retain qualitative data such as interviews, field notes, and case studies of crime-terror interaction will serve as a research base for future studies in this vein.

In the end, science will face a challenge to explain to these policymakers and practitioners how to implement their strategies, policies, and programs in an efficient and effective way. Responses to threat convergence will not arise from a single set of remedies, and therefore the list of stakeholders who can benefit from scientific studies of crime-terror interaction is diverse. Threat convergence requires a comprehensive response that harnesses the broad range of state authorities and marries those to the capabilities of nongovernmental and international organizations as well. In July of 2011, the U.S. government released the *Strategy to Combat Transnational Organized Crime*.[69] The strategy views transnational organized crime as a complex security issue and cites threat convergence with terrorism as one example of this complexity. The strategy concludes that a whole of government approach bringing all elements of national power to bear is required to combat this threat. The strategy not only augments law enforcement authorities but enhances intelligence and information sharing, proffers regulations to protect markets from criminal penetration, and constructs new links with the private sector, nongovernmental organizations, and international organizations. Its numerous recommendations for policy and practice are an excellent example of the whole of government approach, tapping the strengths of numerous agencies in a coordinated way to attack transnational organized crime and threat convergence on multiple fronts.

Encouragingly, science has developed a number of evidence-based recommendations on how to improve the response to crime-terror interaction. Some focus on the need to recognize this complexity for what it is and adjust investigative and intelligence operations accordingly. For example, studies often note that criminality is ubiquitous within the crime-terror overlap and thus counterterrorism specialists in particular would do well to exploit this as a potential vulnerability.[70] Kenney provides one of the more interesting examples of this genre.[71] From a comparative case study of Colombian drug trafficking organizations and Islamist terror cells, he concludes that counterterrorism experts could learn from their peers in the counternarcotics field to overcome the continuous adaptation of terrorist groups:

> Leadership interdiction is clearly a necessary component of the "wars" on drugs and terror. It is not, however, a sufficient one. In focusing overwhelming US military, law enforcement and intelligence efforts on a handful of terrorist groups and kingpins, a counter-terrorism strategy premised on leadership interdiction runs the risk of merely weeding out the most notorious networks and providing opportunities for lesser known, but equally, if not more, sophisticated groups to materialize. This is the most salient lesson of two decades of the war on drugs in Colombia.[72]

The study concludes that what is needed is a comprehensive approach that harnesses military, intelligence, and law enforcement resources to other elements of national power.

Other works have focused on the need to develop closer ties between investigators and intelligence analysts to foster more robust, accurate, and speedy cases of threat convergence. Trim develops the Global Intelligence and Security Environmental Sustainability (GISES) model that forms a communication and collaboration network among government agencies to fight the networks organized crime and terror organizations are forming.[73] This "networks fighting networks" theme is often spoken as a rhetorical jargon, but Trim takes this beyond the whiteboard to craft an architecture that more closely resembles the "whole of government" approach countries are adopting today. Likewise, Scanlan details how government and the private sector must work together to use new regulatory schemes that defeat organized crime's infiltration of the business community while avoiding the smothering of small businesses under heavy-handed regulations.[74]

One final theme in the literature focuses on law enforcement investigators and how to provide them the tools and programs they need to tackle this problem's growing complexity. One suggestion comes from Shelley et al. who create an indicators and warnings system for investigators entitled Preparation of the Investigative Environment (PIE).[75] With a PIE approach, the investigator can more quickly recognize when their organized crime investigation might actually represent an instance of crime-terror interaction and act accordingly. Stohl takes a different approach and focuses on prevention of crime-terror interaction, noting "that the community needs to be engaged in the effort to isolate terrorists both from the organizations to which they have been connected and to assist the process of questioning the methods by which terrorist goals are sought."[76] Last, Bayley and Perito focus on the specific requirements of policing in conflict and post-conflict zones, noting that one of the central requirements for these units is to fight organized crime and terrorists.[77]

Much work remains to develop better explanations of crime-terror interaction and how it drives threat convergence, and science has a critical role to play in this effort. As states move forward with new strategies to combat transnational organized crime and threat convergence, they are wise to include the promotion of scientific inquiry as a part of their action plan. The investments made now will yield benefits in terms of more effective programs in the years to come. The research community across numerous disciplines of inquiry should ready themselves to take up this call for studies. The moment is right for their insights to have the impact they seek.

Notes

1. National Security Council, *A National Security Strategy for a New Century* (Washington, DC: National Security Council, 1997), http://clinton2.nara.gov/WH/EOP/NSC/Strategy.

2. National Security Council, *Strategy to Combat Transnational Organized Crime* (Washington, DC: National Sceurity Council, 2007), http://www.whitehouse.gov/administration/eop/nsc/transnational-crime.

3. Angela Veng Mei Leong, "Chasing Dirty Money: Domestic and International Measures Against Money Laundering," *Journal of Money Laundering Control* 8, no. 1 (2004): 19–36.

4. John T. Picarelli and Louise Shelley, "Methods not Motives: Implications of the Convergence of International Organized Crime and Terrorism," *Police Practice and Research: An International Journal* 3, no. 4 (2002): 305–318.

5. Sylvia Longmire and John Longmire, "Redefining Terrorism: Why Mexican Drug Trafficking is More than Just Organized Crime," *Journal of Strategic Security* 1, no. 1 (2008): 35–51.

6. Longmire and Longmire (see note 3 above), 46–47.

7. Steven Hutchinson and Pat O'Malley, "A Crime-Terror Nexus? Thinking on Some of the Links between Terrorism and Criminality," *Studies in Conflict and Terrorism* 30, no. 12 (2007): 1095–1107, pp. 1099–1103.

8. An example is Donald Cressey, *Theft of the Nation: The Structure and Operations of Organized Crime in America* (New York: Harper & Row, 1969).

9. Picarelli and Shelley (see note 2 above).

10. Longmire and Longmire (see note 3 above).

11. Emma Bjornehed, "Narco-Terrorism: The Merger of the War on Drugs and the War on Terror," *Global Crime* 6, nos. 3&4 (2004): 305–324.

12. David Luna, "Narco-Trafficking: What is the Nexus with the War on Terror?" Remarks at the Southern Command, Miami FL, 8 October 2008, http://merln.ndu.edu/archivepdf/terrorism/state/110828.pdf.

13. David Luna, "Threat Convergence: Subversion, Destabilization and Insecurity." Remarks at George Mason University, Arlington VA, 4 May 2009, http://www.state.gov/p/inl/rls/rm/122662.htm.

14. Phil Williams, "Terrorism and Organized Crime: Convergence, Nexus or Transformation?" in *Report on Terrorism*, ed. Gunnar Jervas (Stockholm: Swedish Defence Research Establishment, 1998), 69–92.

15. Peter Lowe, "Counterfeiting: Links to Organised Crime and Terrorist Funding," *Journal of Financial Crime* 13, no. 2 (2006): 255–257.

16. John Rollins and Liana Wyler, *International Terrorism and Transnational Crime: Security Threats, U.S. Policy, and Considerations for Congress* (Washington DC: Congressional Research Service, 2010).

17. Ryan Clarke and Stuart Lee, "The PIRA, D-Company, and the Crime-Terror Nexus," *Terrorism and Political Violence* 20, no. 2 (2008): 376–395.

18. Picarelli and Shelley (see note 2 above).

19. R. Thomas Naylor, *Wages of Crime: Black Markets, Illegal Finance and the Underworld Economy* (Ithaca, NY: Cornell University Press, 2002), 45.

20. Defense Science Board, *Summer Study Task Force on DoD Responses to Transnational Threats* (Washington DC: U.S. Department of Defense, 1997), 103.

21. George Shambaugh and Richard Matthew, "Sex, Drugs and Heavy Metal: Transnational Threats and National Vulnerabilities," *Security Dialogue* 29, no. 2 (1998): 163–175; Kimberly Thachuk, "Transnational Threats: Falling Through the Cracks?," *Low Intensity Conflict and Law Enforcement* 10, no. 1 (2001): 47–67; Louise Shelley, "The Unholy Trinity: Transnational Crime, Corruption, and Terrorism," *Brown Journal of World Affairs* 11, no. 2 (2005): 101–111.

22. Sam Mullins, "Parallels Between Crime and Terrorism: A Social Psychological Perspective," *Studies in Conflict and Terrorism* 32, no. 9 (2009): 811–830.

23. Anat Berko, Edna Erez, and Julie Globokar, "Gender, Crime and Terrorism: The Case of Arab/Palestinian Women in Israel," *British Journal of Criminology* 50, no. 4 (2010): 670–689.

24. Bjornehed (see note 9 above).

25. James Rosenau, *Turbulence in World Politics* (Princeton, NJ: Princeton University Press, 1990).

26. John T. Picarelli, "The Turbulent Nexus of Transnational Organized Crime and Terrorism: A Theory of Malevolent International Relations," *Global Crime* 7, no. 1 (2006): 1–24.

27. Chris Dishman, "The Leaderless Nexus: When Crime and Terror Converge," *Studies in Conflict and Terrorism* 28, no. 3 (2005): 237–252.

28. Mette Eilstrup-Sangiovanni and Calvert Jones, "Assessing the Dangers of Illicit Networks: Why al-Qaida may be less Dangerous than Many Think," *International Security* 33, no. 2 (2008): 7–44.

29. Michael Stohl, "Networks, Terrorists and Criminals: The Implications for Community Policing," *Crime, Law and Social Change* 50, nos. 1–2 (2008): 59–72, p. 66.

30. Martin Rudner, "Hizbullah Terrorism Finance: Fund-Raising and Money-Laundering," *Studies in Conflict and Terrorism* 33, no. 8 (2010): 700–715.

31. John Horgan and Max Taylor, "Playing the 'Green Card'—Financing the Provisional IRA: Part 2," *Terrorism and Political Violence* 15, no. 2 (2003): 1–60.

32. Martin Rudner, "Misuse of Passports: Identity Fraud, the Propensity to Travel, and International Terrorism," *Studies in Conflict and Terrorism* 31, no. 2 (2008): 95–110.

33. Graham Turbiville Jr., "Outlaw Private Security Firms: Criminal and Terrorist Agendas Undermine Private Security Alternatives," *Global Crime* 7, nos. 3–4 (2006): 561–582.

34. Chris Dishman, "Terrorism, Crime and Transformation," *Studies in Conflict and Terrorism* 24, no. 1 (2001): 43–58.

35. Ibid., p. 56.

36. Mitchell Roth and Murat Sever, "The Kurdish Workers Party (PKK) as Criminal Syndicate: Funding Terrorism through Organized Crime, A Case Study," *Studies in Conflict and Terrorism* 30, no. 10 (2007): 901–920.

37. Ibid., p. 913.

38. Svante Cornell, "Narcotics, Radicalism, and Armed Conflict in Central Asia: The Islamic Movement of Uzbekistan," *Terrorism and Political Violence* 17, no. 4 (2005): 619–639.

39. Tamara Makarenko, "The Crime-Terror Continuum: Tracing the Interplay between Transnational Organised Crime and Terrorism, " *Global Crime* 6, no. 1 (2004): 129–145.

40. Justine Rosenthal, "For-Profit Terrorism: The Rise of Armed Entrepreneurs," *Studies in Conflict and Terrorism* 31, no. 6 (2008): 481–498.

41. Fernando Pacheco, "Narcofearance: How has Narcoterrorism Settled in Mexico?," *Studies in Conflict and Terrorism* 32, no. 12 (2009): 1021–1048.

42. For more, see *inter alia* John Arquilla and David Ronfeldt, eds., *Networks and Netwards: The Future of Terror, Crime, and Militancy* (Santa Monica, CA: RAND, 2001);

Jorg Raab and H. Brinton Milward, "Dark Networks as Problems," *Journal of Public Administration Research and Theory* 13, no. 4 (2003): 413–439; Alain Bauer and Xavier Raufer, *The Dark Side of Globalization* (Paris: CNRS Editions, 2009).

43. Makarenko (see note 37 above), p. 138.

44. Ana Sverdlick, "Terrorists and Organized Crime Entrepreneurs in the 'Triple Frontier' Among Argentina, Brazil, and Paraguay," *Trends in Organized Crime* 9, no. 2 (2005): 84–93.

45. For an extensive treatment, see Rosenau (note 23 above) *inter alia*.

46. John Rapley, "The New Middle Ages," *Foreign Affairs* 85, no. 3 (2006): 95–104.

47. Ara Arana, "How the Street Gangs Took Central America," *Foreign Affairs* 84, no. 3 (2005): 98–110.

48. Luciana Fernandez, "Organized Crime and Terrorism: From the Cells Towards Political Communication, A Case Study," *Terrorism and Political Violence* 21, no. 4 (2009): 595–616.

49. For more see *inter alia* Susan Strange, *The Retreat of the State: The Diffusion of Power in the World Economy* (Cambridge: Cambridge University Press, 1996) or James Mittelman and Robert Johnston, "The Globalization of Organized Crime, the Courtesan State, and the Corruption of Civil Society," *Global Governance* 5, no. 2 (1999): 103–126.

50. Peter Andreas, "Transnational Crime and Economic Globalization," in *Transnational Organized Crime and International Security*, ed. M. Berdal and M. Serrano (Boulder, CO: Lynne Rienner Publishers, 2002): 37–52, p. 42.

51. Leslie Holmes (ed.), *Terrorism, Organised Crime and Corruption: Networks and Linkages* (Cheltenham: Edward Edgar Publishing, 2007).

52. Rex Hudson, *Terrorist and Organized Crime Groups in the Tri-Border Area (TBA) of South America* (Washington DC: Library of Congress, 2010).

53. Pacheco (see note 39 above).

54. Diego Gambetta, *The Sicilian Mafia: The Business of Private Protection* (Cambridge, MA: Harvard University Press, 1993).

55. Pacheco (see note 39 above), p. 1026.

56. Cornell (see note 36 above), p. 625.

57. For more, see Mary Kaldor, *New and Old Wars: Organized Violence in a Global Era* (Palo Alto, CA: Stanford University Press, 2007).

58. Peter Andreas, *Blue Helmets and Black Markets: The Business of Survival in the Siege of Sarajevo* (Ithaca, NY: Cornell University Press, 2008).

59. Hal Brands, "Crime, Irregular Warfare, and Institutional Failure in Latin America: Guatemala as a Case Study," *Studies in Conflict and Terrorism* 34, no. 2 (2011): 228–247.

60. Max Manwaring, *Insurgency, Terrorism, and Crime: Shadows from the Past and Portents for the Future* (Norman, OK: University of Oklahoma Press, 2008).

61. John T. Picarelli, *Expert Working Group Report on International Organized Crime* (Washington DC: National Institute of Justice, 2010), http://www.nij.gov/nij/topics/crime/transnational-organized-crime/working-group.htm

62. Ethan Nadelmann, "Global Prohibition Regimes: The Evolution of Norms in International Society," *International Organization* 44, no. 4 (1990): 479–526.

63. Peter Andreas, "Illicit International Political Economy: The Clandestine Side of Globalization," *Review of International Political Economy* 11, no. 3 (2004): 641–652.

64. Ibrahim Warde, "The War on Terror, Crime and the Shadow Economy in the MENA Countries," *Mediterranean Politics* 12, no. 2 (2007): 233–248.

65. Michael Stohl (see note 27 above), p. 63.

66. Nikos Passas, *Informal Value Transfer Systems, Terrorism and Money Laundering* (Washington DC: National Institute of Justice, 2005), https://www.ncjrs.gov/pdffiles1/nij/grants/208301.pdf.

67. Brent Smith et al., *Geospatial Analysis of Terrorist Activities: The Identification of Spatial and Temporal Patterns of Preparatory Behavior of International and Environmental Terrorists* (Washington DC: National Institute of Justice, 2008), https://www.ncjrs.gov/pdffiles1/nij/grants/222909.pdf.

68. Vanda Felbab-Brown, *Shooting Up: Counterinsurgency and the War on Drugs* (Washington DC: Brookings, 2010); Gretchen Peters, *Seeds of Terror: How Heroin is Bankrolling the Taliban and Al Qaeda* (New York: Thomas Dunne Books, 2009).

69. For more, see http://www.whitehouse.gov/administration/eop/nsc/transnational-crime.

70. Makarenko (see note 37 above).

71. Michael Kenney, *From Pablo to Osama: Trafficking and Terrorist Networks, Government Bureaucracies, and Competitive Adaptation* (University Park: Pennsylvania State University Press, 2007).

72. Michael Kenney, "From Pablo to Osama: Counter-terrorism Lessons from the War on Drugs," *Survival* 45, no. 3 (2003): 187–206, p. 188.

73. Peter Trim, "The GISES Model for Counteracting Organized Crime and International Terrorism," *International Journal of Intelligence and Counterintelligence* 18, no. 3 (2005): 451–472.

74. Gary Scanlan, "The Enterprise of Crime and Terrorists—The Implication for Good Business," *Journal of Financial Crime* 13, no. 2 (2006): 164–176.

75. Louise Shelley et al., *Methods and Motives: Exploring Links Between Transnational Organized Crime and International Terrorism* (Washington DC: National Institute of Justice, 2005).

76. Michael Stohl, "Networks, Terrorists and Criminals: The Implications for Community Policing," *Crime, Law and Social Change* 50, nos. 1–2 (2008): 59–72, p. 70.

77. David Bayley and Robert Perito, *The Police in War: Fighting Insurgency, Terrorism, and Violent Crime* (Boulder, CO: Lynne Rienner Publishers, 2010).

When Politicians Sell Drugs: Examining Why Middle East Ethnopolitical Organizations Are Involved in the Drug Trade

VICTOR ASAL

Department of Political Science, Nelson A. Rockefeller College of Public Affairs & Policy, University at Albany, Albany, New York, USA

KATHLEEN DELOUGHERY

Department of Public Administration, University at Albany, Albany, New York, USA

BRIAN J. PHILLIPS

Division of International Studies, Center for Research and Teaching in Economics (CIDE), Mexico City, Mexico

Political organizations claim they are serving the interests of their constituents—but being involved in the drug trade does not seem to support those claims. Why would political organizations sell drugs then? Most often the question of why organizations engage in the drug trade has been explored in the context of organizations that are either criminal or violent, thus leaving a large hole in the literature about how violence and legality intersect with other exploratory factors. We explore this issue more fully by looking at both violent and nonviolent organizations using the Middle East Minorities at Risk Organizational Behavior dataset, which has data on over 100 ethnopolitical organizations in the Middle East. Very few of these organizations are involved in the drug trade and yet all of those are engaged in violence at the same time. We explore what factors, other than violence, make this rare behavior for political organizations more likely.

Victor Asal is a professor in the Department of Political Science, Nelson A. Rockefeller College of Public Affairs & Policy, University at Albany. Kathleen Deloughery is a professor in the Department of Public Administration, University at Albany. Brian J. Phillips is an assistant professor in the Division of International Studies, Center for Research and Teaching Economics (CIDE).

This material is based upon work supported by the Science and Technology directorate of the U.S. Department of Homeland Security under grant award numbers N00140510629 and 2008-ST-061-ST0004, made to the National Consortium for the Study of Terrorism and Responses to Terrorism (START, www.start.umd.edu). The views and conclusions contained in this document are those of the authors and should not be interpreted as necessarily representing the official policies, either expressed or implied, of the U.S. Department of Homeland Security or START.

Introduction

What explains the organizational decision to sell drugs? There are clear financial incentives to get into this business, which is reportedly the top source of funds for terrorist and criminal organizations.[1] The drug trade is "...among the richest components of the world underground economy, and its raw materials originate from areas in which insurgencies abound."[2] Many groups, though, choose *not* to sell drugs. Political constraints are likely one reason to pick alternate fundraising activities. The sale of illegal drugs is widely condemned, so groups with political goals—such as ethnonationalist groups—should generally avoid it. In spite of this, however, a substantial number of political groups are involved in the drug trade. This suggests a puzzle: Why do some political groups sell drugs, despite the potential of losing political support? This article seeks to address this question, focusing on politically violent ethnonationalist groups. We use the Middle East Minorities at Risk Organizational Behavior dataset, which has data on over 100 ethnopolitical organizations in the Middle East, in order to examine this question. It is important to note that the key advantage of this dataset is that we have both violent and nonviolent organizations. The key constraint in this dataset is that it is limited to ethnic group organizations and only in the Middle East, but we feel the advantage of diverse types of groups using different types of political activities allows us to examine the relationship between political organizations and involvement in the drug trade in a way that has not been explored quantitatively before.

Many subnational political organizations are in the drug business. The literature has tended to discuss this in the context of one of two research areas: the crime-terror nexus, and studies of civil war funding.[3] Regarding the crime-terror nexus, it has been noted that criminal organizations are increasing their use of violence, while violent groups are increasing their use of illicit fundraising methods.[4] Illicit fundraising often includes drug sales. For example, Hezbollah depends on not only state sponsors and donors, but also substantial drug-trafficking revenue.[5]

Regarding the funding of civil wars, a number of studies treat drugs as part of a set of "lootable resources" that fuel sub-state violence.[6] Coca in Colombia and Peru, and poppies in Afghanistan and Burma, seem to have helped violent groups in those states. Resources such as drugs usually do not "cause" the conflict to start, but often play a role as it continues.[7] The drug business helps organizations to survive, as it allows them to continue funding their operations.[8] Researchers have found important links between drugs and political outcomes, but it remains unclear why only some political groups get into the illegal drug business.

Despite the organizational benefits that seem to come from drug trafficking, there are also several reasons *not* to do so, as the dangers—from both the state and other groups—are such a deterrent that even the Mafia has tried to avoid drug sales.[9] Furthermore, illegal drugs are widely considered immoral, regardless of country, region, or society.[10] Drug trafficking is simply viewed by many as "beyond the pale," and the moral condemnation of it is largely viewed as a "truism."[11]

In addition to general risks, drug trafficking by political groups is especially puzzling because it carries substantial *political* risks. Links to drug trafficking can be used to discredit organizations.[12] Even terrorist groups are often reluctant to cooperate with narcotics syndicates, fearing that being seen as simple criminals could hurt their political goals.[13] While politicians are sometimes popularly characterized as being immoral, political actors strive to retain at least the appearance of morality to maintain legitimacy. Kane, for example, argues that a fundamental difference between politics and the market is that in the former, moral judgment is "intrinsic" and "inescapable," and political actors need to keep this in mind.[14]

In spite of these reasons, many subnational ethnic groups—political actors—choose to sell drugs. Why are some groups much more likely than others to do so? The research described below thus addresses an important puzzle by looking at why a political group would engage in drug trafficking when it seems to be contrary to the group's interests to do so. While the literature ties insurgents and terrorists to the drug trade, what is missing from the literature is an examination of *why* political organizations would be involved in the drug trade in the first place. Is the key factor the need for cash? Is it that they are challenging the state with violence, and thus have limited options for raising funds? Are there factors that constrain political organizations' involvement with drug trafficking? As far as we have been able to ascertain, these issues have not been explored in an empirical quantitative fashion. In this article, we explore the choice of being involved in the drug trade within the context of political organizations—both violent and nonviolent—by using the Middle East Minorities at Risk Organizational Behavior dataset, which has data on over 100 ethnopolitical organizations in the Middle East. We use this dataset to explore what factors make political organizations that claim to be representing a larger population decide to engage in the drug trade—something that many see as morally wrong or bankrupt.[15] We argue that the key factor that determines political organizations' involvement in the drug trade is a strong violent rejection of the political order.

Specifically, we find that organizations that are engaged in violence against the state are more likely to violate the norm of not dealing in drugs. Violence against the state and its citizens is not the only type of violence that predisposes organizations to engage in the drug trade. Organizations that use violence against other organizations are also more likely to engage in the drug trade as are organizations that control their own territory—another way of challenging the state as well as a resource if one is going to engage in the drug trade. Violence from the state also makes an organization more likely to be involved with narcotics. We find some support also for the arguments in the scholarly literature that diaspora connections make organizations more likely to be involved in the drug trade, and interestingly having a religious ideology makes organizations less likely to be engaged in drug trafficking.

Overall, we argue that the organizational decision to sell drugs represents a violent rejection of the political order. This is conditioned by perceived need and opportunity, however. The organizations most likely to sell drugs are those that have the need for more funds, greater means to successfully traffic drugs, and are less restricted by the moral codes that deter some groups from selling drugs because they are already rejecting the norms of the state. These arguments are spelled out with specific hypotheses below.

Why Some Ethnopolitical Organizations Sell Drugs

Violence and its Tie to (Im)moral Utility and Resources

Subnational ethnic groups involved in illegal violence should be more likely to sell drugs, for at least two reasons. First, they clearly have rejected the state's authority, and therefore have less of an issue with engaging in illegal activity. Second, illegal violence is an especially costly enterprise, and forces groups to rely on revenue sources that they might otherwise avoid. We focus on two types of violence: subnational groups controlling territory within a state, and groups attacking each other. We emphasize these types of activity because they require more funds than a typical political organization claiming to represent an ethnic group might need—and organizations that have embraced violence will be restricted in the type of "normal" fundraising they are able to engage in within the country where they are located.

Violent subnational ethnic groups are more likely to sell drugs because they have already rejected the authority of the state, and the state's monopoly on the use of force. Involvement in illicit drug trade represents an additional decision to operate outside of legal norms. A culture of anomie, then, contributes to the explanations of both types of activity. Violence is an extreme form of politics, and as Kane argues, "Extreme forms of politics ... deny any intrinsic significance to moral character independently of political action and commitment."[16] Thus we argue that organizations that have crossed the threshold of violence are more likely to be willing to cross the moral line drawn against drug trafficking. Beyond violence generally, political organizations that also occupy territory show a substantial rejection of the state's authority. These groups challenge the legitimacy of the state to control all of its own territory, and indeed show that the state is not able to do so, further indicating that they do not fully accept the state's legal authority. This should also make them more likely to be willing to engage in illegal activity such as drug sales.

Involvement in the drug business is also a function of an increased need for resources. Groups involved in violence, and especially those occupying territory or violently competing with their peers, face substantial costs. First, these groups need to buy arms. Second, they often need to pay a salary to members who fight. This is consistent with arguments in the civil wars literature about the "opportunity costs" of war—individuals likely have to give up their livelihood or make other sacrifices to become fighters, so rebellion is generally more likely when group leaders have funds to pay combatants.[17] Terrorism has a reputation for being inexpensive (and it is, relative to what states pay for counterterrorism), but sustained terrorism campaigns and major attacks can be very costly.[18] Beyond violence generally, the occupation of territory can be especially costly. Groups that occupy territory face a greater need for soldiers, on a full-time basis, so territory-holding groups face an especially acute need for funds.

Ethnic groups engaged in violent competition with other groups should also see a heightened need for funds. In many countries, multiple groups attempt to represent the same ethnic community, competing for donations and recruits. This competition is sometimes violent, with the groups trying to eliminate their competitors—in spite of similar overall political goals. This situation appeared among Sri Lankan Tamil groups in the 1980s, for example, and has occurred between Palestinian groups for decades. Groups with violent competition face an existential threat, and turn to innovative methods to survive. Competition has led to innovations among businesses,[19] and similar dynamics seem to occur with violent competition between terrorist groups.[20] Bloom argues that competition explains terrorist groups turning to the extreme measure of suicide terrorism, and similarly we expect that competition should explain ethnic groups considering financial sources that would otherwise be deemed unacceptable.

As noted earlier, drug production and trafficking is reportedly the top source of income for both organized crime groups and terrorist groups. When facing an unusual need for resources, groups might be able to initially mobilize resources based simply on community support (donations, volunteers, etc.), but in order to sustain an organization in a long-term manner, alternative sources are often sought out. Organizations have more opportunities if they are willing to break the law. Groups can engage in counterfeiting, piracy of goods, or the drug business.[21] Sanderson argues that restrictions on funding terror groups, particularly since 9/11, have caused subnational groups to increasingly use illicit means to raise money.[22] The drug trade provides a way for groups to raise a substantial amount of money, without depending as much on donations, volunteers, or alternate funding sources. Overall, then, groups engaged in violence such as occupying territory or violent competition have rejected the authority of the state, and face a heightened need for funds. This makes them prime candidates for drug trafficking. This suggests the following hypotheses:

> *Hypothesis 1 (H1)*: Subnational ethnic political organizations using violence should be more likely to sell drugs.
>
> *H2*: Subnational ethnic political organizations occupying territory should be more likely to sell drugs.
>
> *H3*: Subnational ethnic political organizations in violent competition with other subnational ethnic groups should be more likely to sell drugs.

Opportunities and Enablers for Drug Trafficking: The Example of the Diaspora Network

A group's decision to sell drugs is not only a function of its demand for funds. Certain groups are in a better position, due to their global connections, to successfully traffic drugs. When a group is connected to a diaspora community, it is better equipped to engage in transnational illicit activity such as the drug trade. Furthermore, the transnational nature of the community could indicate group members are less committed to the country in which they reside, and therefore these groups might be more likely to act outside of the country's laws.

When a group wants to engage in illicit business such as drug trafficking, transnational connections can be quite helpful.[23] One advantage of operating transnationally is that groups can exploit cross-national legal differences. Williams points out that Israel only criminalized money laundering in 2000, and groups from the former Soviet Union in particular took advantage of this during the 1990s.[24] A second advantage is that contacts in other countries can provide safe havens, allowing criminals to avoid prosecution in their own country. Finally, organizations engage in illegal business transnationally for the same reason many licit corporations do: diverse markets mean a better ability to weather financial trouble in one country or region. Hezbollah, for example, reportedly benefits from operations as diverse as the poppy crop in Lebanon's Beka valley to pseudoephedrine smuggling in the American Midwest.[25]

Beyond the benefits stemming simply from the transnational nature of the relationship, the possibilities of successful drug trafficking are further helped by two other factors: a) The ethnic connection between the group and the diaspora, and b) The relationship between the diaspora and its host state(s). Regarding the ethnic connection, shared ethnicity and common experiences can provide a level of trust needed if one is considering partners in illicit business.[26] Paoli argues that the illegal drug industry in particular depends on familial networks, spread transnationally through immigration.[27] Shelley suggests that sometimes members of the diaspora are complicit because they sympathize with the subnational organization, but other times diaspora members are exploited by a group and inadvertently support its activities.[28]

Members of diasporas can also be helpful to drug traffickers because of the relationship a diaspora often has with the states in which it resides. Local law enforcement agencies often have a difficult time thwarting criminal activities by members of immigrant communities. Language differences, and the related difficulty of conducting electronic surveillance, is one problem that European police forces dealing with Albanian speakers have reported.[29] Additionally, police agencies sometimes have trouble getting recent immigrants to cooperate with investigations. This can be related to poor integration in the host country, or perception of oppression.[30] Willingness of some members of the diaspora to help groups traffic drugs, combined with a lower willingness of some diaspora members to cooperate with local authorities, points to a larger issue related to transnationalism and authority.

The very existence of a diaspora, and the transnational community it suggests, indicates a group that might be more inclined to have loyalties divided between several countries. Members of the community might be loyal to a country other than that in which they are living. This could be explained by feeling oppressed in one's country, as discussed above, or it could be the result of lack of identity with the country in which one lives. Indeed, it is argued that networks of West Africans in Europe and the Americas build on a sense of community, harnessing the idea of us vs. them to create an "ideological community" that rationalizes the sale of drugs.[31]

For these reasons, subnational ethnic groups with diaspora support should be *ex ante* better prepared to successfully sell drugs, and the relationship between the diaspora and its host countries could contribute to an environment where state authority is less respected. This suggests the following hypothesis:

> *H4:* Subnational ethnic political organizations with diaspora support should be more likely to sell drugs.

Moral Frameworks and Authority: Religious Subnational Ethnic Political Organizations

In addition to factors that make subnational ethnic groups more likely to sell drugs, there are some factors that reduce the chances. In particular, groups that include religious elements in their political goals are less likely to get into illicit business. This is not to say that all religiously-oriented groups will stick to legal activity; Hezbollah and the Taliban provide counterexamples. However, generally, groups that advocate a role for religion in public life should be more concerned with avoiding activity considered "immoral," and should *generally* be more receptive to authority, state or otherwise. Even organizations that reject the state and embrace the idea that it is moral to kill the "enemy" see themselves as the good guys[32] and, as we have noted, narcotics are often see as immoral. This does not mean that religious organizations will never sell drugs. As Kane points out, morality in politics is often weighed against utility with utility often winning.[33] It does though mean, we believe, that religious organizations should be less likely to traffic in drugs even if they are engaged in a "cosmic war" against evil.[34]

First, groups with religious motivations should be more concerned with "morality" than others. Every society has different ideas of morality, but as discussed above, illegal drug use and especially trafficking are widely considered unacceptable.[35] Religious groups, as they are more concerned with guidelines for human behavior, should be less likely to be involved in activity largely considered by the wider society to be immoral. For example, imams in Afghanistan have declared the cultivation of poppy to be a violation of sharia law.[36] Furthermore, individual members of the groups should be less likely to be involved in behavior considered antisocial or deviant. The criminology literature suggests that the "social control" exerted on individuals by socializing forces such as religion can affect behavior and ultimately reduce the likelihood of antisocial or deviant behavior.[37] This is said to occur through the bonds formed between the individual and his or her society, and the strength of these bonds determine the extent to which the individual internalizes the norms. Other research finds religiosity associated with "ethical behavior" generally.[38]

Religious beliefs seem to lead to less antisocial or deviant behavior generally, and therefore should correspond to more tolerance of the state and its authority. This suggests less chance of violent rejection of the state. This is consistent with research that finds religiosity associated with less illegal behavior generally.[39] Religious groups' goals are not always consistent with the state's, and these groups are not always subservient to the state. Catholic groups in Poland in the 1980s and Muslim groups that want a less secular government are examples. However, a substantial body of research indicates that religious beliefs are generally consistent with respect for authority, including government authority.

Aside from the notion that religious groups should be more concerned about morality and following rules generally, religious groups should also have members that are less likely to be involved with drugs specifically. A number of studies find religiosity associated with decreased likelihood of drug use.[40] Religious individuals are less likely to use drugs, or be convicted of drug-related offenses, and therefore groups motivated by religious goals should be less likely to be involved in the drug business. Overall, this suggests the following hypothesis:

> *H5:* Subnational ethnic political organizations with a religious motivation should be less likely to sell drugs.

Indicators of Rejection of State Authority: Government Attacks on Groups

The above arguments suggest that a group's need, ability, and social constraints should affect the likelihood of its involvement in drug trade. Additionally, all of the hypotheses draw in part on the assumption that a drug-selling group has likely rejected the authority of the state. Here we explore that assumption by looking at conditions that might more directly indicate such a rejection by a group. Sometimes states target subnational ethnic groups with lethal force, and this is likely an indicator of the group's views of state authority. Groups in this situation, for reasons discussed above, should be more likely to also decide to engage in the trade of illegal drugs.

There are two basic scenarios in which a state would attack a subnational ethnic group. First, this could occur in a two-sided manner, where the substate group is also actively attacking state targets, such as in a civil war.[41] In this context, the subnational group is clearly challenging the authority of the state. Indeed, it can be argued that civil war is fundamentally about a challenge to the authority of the state.[42] Tilly argues that civil war results from "dual sovereignty," the idea that authority over territory is claimed by multiple actors.[43] In accordance with the discussion of violence above, these groups have rejected the authority of the state and should therefore be more likely than other groups to sell drugs.

The other possibility is that the state violence is largely one-sided. States sometimes attack subnational ethnic groups outside the context of an insurgency or civil war, such as when government agents attack relatively peaceful protestors. In these situations, the state violence might not necessarily be "caused" by a group's rejection of state authority, but this extrajudicial violence should increase the chance of the group rejecting the state's authority. If some members already doubt the state's authority, the state violence could encourage other members and potential members to have a similar opinion, radicalizing the group. This is consistent with the notion that repression can help with mobilization of dissident groups.[44] The Bloody Sunday killings of unarmed protestors by British military in 1972 were said to be a "recruitment bonanza" for the IRA, for example.[45] If state violence leads to decreased faith in state authority by a group, this should lead to an increased likelihood of the group engaging in illegal activity, including drug trafficking.

We acknowledge that state violence could be caused by an antecedent rejection of state authority by the group, or that the rejection could manifest itself after state attacks.[46] However, state violence against a group could be one indicator of the group's rejection of authority, suggesting a greater likelihood of involvement in the drug trade. This suggests the following hypothesis:

> *H6*: Subnational ethnic political organizations that have been the target of lethal violence by the state should be more likely to sell drugs.

Data and Methodology

The dependent variable of interest in this study is whether or not a political organization is involved in drug production or trafficking. This information is obtained from the Minorities at Risk Organizational Behavior (MAROB) dataset for the Middle East.[47] MAROB contains information on political organizations active in the Middle East and North Africa between 1980 and 2004. The organizations included in this dataset are political in their goals and activities and claim to represent the interests of an ethnic group.[48] The variable is binary and coded as 1 if the group is involved in the drug trade. However, less than three percent of groups ever participate in the drug trade. Due to the low number of observations for which the dependent variable will be coded as a 1, a rare event logit analysis is conducted. A rare event logit must be used in order to ensure that the probability of an organization being involved in the drug trade is not underestimated.[49]

Currently, there are 45 observations of organizations being involved in the drug trade in a particular year. In each of those 45 observations, the organization is also categorized as militant in the same year. Militant organizations are those that commit acts or violence or have the means to commit violent acts. Given that every organization involved in the drug trade is also militant, this measure of violence cannot be included in a logit analysis. Therefore, *H1* is established by correlation. To test *H2*, whether occupying territory matters, information is pulled from MAROB on whether or not the political organization controls movements through a territory. The variable is binary and coded as 1 if the organization controls territory, regardless of whether it has built infrastructure or established governing structures. Since *H2* hypothesizes that controlling territory should increase involvement in the drug trade, we expect the coefficient on this variable to be positive. Hypothesis *H3* examines whether violent competition between groups increases involvement in the drug trade. Two variables are coded to measure the competition between political organizations. First, the total number of active political organizations operating in the same country in the same year is coded as the level of competition for members. This information is garnered using MAROB. Second, another variable from MAROB is used that measures whether or not the political organization is involved in violent conflict with another organization. Both of these variables will be used as independent variables. If competition is related to increased participation in the drug trade, we would expect the coefficient on both variables to be positive. If, however, only violent conflict increases participation in the drug trade, then only the coefficient on inter-organization violence should be positive.

Diaspora support should increase participation in the drug trade according to hypothesis *H4*. MAROB contains information on whether or not the organization has received support from a kindred group in the past year. If yes, this variable is coded as a 1. The expected sign on diaspora support is positive. Hypothesis *H5* states that religious ideology should have a dampening effect on participation in the drug trade. Information from MAROB is used to determine if organizations advocate policies that incorporate religion into public life. Organizations that do advocate for religious incorporation are coded as a 1; other organizations are coded as 0. Given *H5*, the expected coefficient on religious ideology is negative. Finally, *H6* argues that organizations subject to violence from the state should experience increased participation in the drug trade. This variable is coded from MAROB. This variable is coded as 1 if the state does not use lethal violence against the organization, a 2 if the state periodically uses lethal violence against the organization, and a 3 if the state consistently uses lethal violence against the organization. The expected coefficient on state violence is positive.

Other control variables are also utilized in the analysis. First, group age and structure are considered. When ethnically-based groups start, they might be able to sustain themselves with volunteers and donations. However, with time, most institutions develop permanent infrastructure, permanent workers that expect to be compensated, and therefore increased day-to-day operational costs. The drug trade provides a way for groups to raise a substantial amount of money, without depending as much on donations, volunteers, or alternate funding sources. Drugs are also a particularly lucrative funding source. Groups with substantial overhead and organizational costs, regardless of their age, should also face an increased likelihood of getting involved in the drug business. When a group has a more hierarchical leadership structure, there are more people requiring higher salaries, often permanent headquarters and staffs to maintain, and so forth. Groups with a "flat" or more horizontal leadership structure should have lower operational costs. This suggests that more hierarchical groups may be more likely to get into the drug business. Next, year fixed effects are included in the analysis. Changes in opportunity over time, due to weather or war, may lead to fluctuations in an organization's involvement in the drug trade.

Finally, standard errors in the regressions are clustered by country. This clustering allows for the potential that some countries may provide more opportunity for involvement in the drug trade due to their environment.

Results

The results of the rare event logit analysis can be found in Table 1. The results show weak support for *H2, H4*, and *H5*. Stronger support for *H3* and *H6* exists. As expected, the coefficient on controlling territory is positive, but only statistically significant at the 10 percent level. However, the overall impact of territory is large. The average organization that does not control territory has a 0.80 percent probability of being involved in the drug trade. The same organization that does control territory has a 2.96 percent probability of being involved in the drug trade, more than triple the group without territory. Therefore, there is support for Hypothesis *H2*.

Hypothesis *H3* dealt with the level of competition that political organizations face. The coefficient on competition, which measured the number of other active organizations in that country in that year, is insignificant. However, the coefficient on inter-organization violence is positive and statistically significant. Therefore, it is not just competition that leads to involvement in the drug trade, but violent competition. The average organization not involved in inter-organization violence has a 0.86 percent probability of being involved in the drug trade. However, being involved in inter-organization violence doubles that probability to 1.76 percent.

The coefficient on diaspora support is positive, as expected, but statistically significant at only the 10 percent level. Again, the impact of diaspora support is very large. An organization without diaspora support has a 0.86 percent probability of being involved in the drug trade, while the same organization with diaspora support has a 7.96 percent chance of involvement in the drug trade. This is an increase of over 800 percent. Therefore, hypothesis *H4* is supported.

Next, religious ideology is examined. As expected, the coefficient on religion is negative and statistically significant at the 10 percent level. While a religious

Table 1. Rare event logit estimates of involvement in drug trade

Independent variable	Coefficient (Standard error)
Control territory	1.320* (0.782)
Competition	0.034 (0.038)
Inter-organization violence	0.728** (0.304)
Diaspora support	2.300* (1.360)
Religious ideology	−1.700* (0.930)
State violence	0.856** (0.257)
Age	−0.011 (0.018)
Hierarchical structure	−0.363 (0.554)
Year fixed effects	Yes
Constant	−5.980 (0.905)
Total observations	1667

*Significant at $p = .10$, **significant at $p = .05$, ***significant at $p = .01$.

organization only has a 0.27 percent chance of being involved in the drug trade, the same organization that is not religious has a 1.48 percent chance of being involved in the drug trade. While these probabilities are small, this change represents a percentage change of 440 percent. Religion seems to have the largest dampening effect calculated. Only 0.27 percent of religious organizations with other average characteristics are likely to be involved in the drug trade.

Finally, hypothesis *H6* stated that state violence against an organization would increase the likelihood of being involved in the drug trade. As expected, the coefficient on this variable is positive and statistically significant. An organization that never experiences lethal violence from the state has a 0.86 percent chance of being involved in the drug trade; an organization that experiences periodic lethal violence from the state more than doubles that to a 1.97 percent chance. Finally, an organization that consistently experiences lethal violence from the state has a 4.48 percent chance of being involved in the drug trade. Therefore, *H6* is also supported.

Conclusions

The goal of this research was to examine what causes a political organization—that claims to represent the interests of constituents—to become involved in the production or trafficking of drugs. We believe our findings are important as a first effort to go beyond looking at criminal or violent organizations to examine the factors that lead political organizations in general to engage in the drug trade. Our most important finding underlines the necessity of looking beyond violent organizations when examining the behavior of groups engaged in immoral or deviant activities. None of the nonviolent organizations in the MAROB database were engaged in drug trafficking. While we recognize the limitations of our data in that it is restricted only to ethnic organizations and only in the Middle East, we believe that this is very strong support for the argument that there is an essential link between violence and drug trafficking. We believed that the moral opening created by violence, as well as the pull of resource necessities, makes the choice of drug trafficking—one that is likely to alienate constituencies—much more attractive than it might be otherwise. The remaining hypotheses tested garnered either weak or strong support.

Territorial control and diaspora connections clearly enable organizations to pursue illegal activities tied to transnational relations. Violence with other organizations and violence from the state are positively related to drug trafficking and underline the importance of violence as part of the pattern that we find with this criminal activity by political organizations. Finally, morality rears its head again with religious organizations being less likely to engage in the drug trade. Considering that other studies have found religious groups to be more violent than others,[50] one reason our results are interesting is that they show that religious motivations have divergent effects on different types of illegal activity (drugs vs. catastrophic violence, for example). This raises questions about morality and justifications of criminal activity. Overall, we are cognizant that this is only an initial foray into this area of research and we intend to collect data that will allow us to explore this issue in wider contexts. This study shows that a diverse set of factors are associated with political groups selling drugs, and this should encourage further research on the subject.

Notes

1. Louise I. Shelley and John T. Picarelli, "Methods Not Motives: Implications of The Convergence of International Organized Crime and Terrorism," *Police Practice and Research* 3, no. 4 (2002): 305–318.

2. R. T. Naylor, *Wages of Crime: Black Markets, Illegal Finance, and the Underworld Economy* (Ithaca, NY: Cornell University Press, 2004), 70.

3. There are studies of why criminal organizations sell drugs, but since our focus is on political groups, these are substantially different. See for example Diego Gambetta, *The Sicilian Mafia: The Business of Private Protection* (Cambridge, MA: Harvard University Press, 1996) and Brenda C. Coughlin and Sudhir Alladi Venkatesh, "The Urban Street Gang after 1970," *Annual Review of Sociology* 29 (2003): 41–65. Research on the crime-terror nexus and civil war funding is discussed below.

4. For example, Chris Dishman, "Terrorism, Crime, and Transformation," *Studies in Conflict and Terrorism* 24, no. 1 (2001): 43–58; Tamara Makarenko, "The Crime-Terror Continuum: Tracing the Interplay Between Organised Crime and Terrorism," *Global Crime* 6, no. 1 (2004): 129–145; Shelley and Picarelli (see note 1 above); Alex P. Schmid, "Drug Trafficking, Transnational Crime, and International Terrorist Groups," in *Organized Crime: From Trafficking to Terrorism,* ed. Frank G. Shanty (Santa Barbara, CA: ABC CLIO, 2007), 342–345; Phil Williams, "Illicit Markets, Weak States, and Violence: Iraq and Mexico," *Crime Law and Social Change* 52, no. 3 (2009): 323–336. On differences between studying crime and studying terrorism see Gary LaFree and Laura Dugan, "How Does Studying Terrorism Compare to Studying Crime?," in *Criminology and Terrorism*, ed. Mathieu DeFlem (Oxford: Elsevier, 2004), 53–74.

5. Matthew Levitt, "Hezbollah: Financing Terror Through Criminal Enterprise," Testimony before U.S. Senate Committee on Homeland Security and Governmental Affairs (May 25, 2005), http://www.investigativeproject.org/documents/testimony/313.pdf.

6. Paul Collier, "Rebellion as a Quasi-Criminal Activity," *Journal of Conflict Resolution* 44, no. 6 (2000): 839–853; Phillipe Le Billon, "The Political Ecology of War: Natural Resources and Armed Conflicts," *Political Geography* 20, no. 5 (2001): 561–584.

7. Michael L. Ross "What Do We Know About Natural Resources and Civil War?," *Journal of Peace Research* 41, no. 3 (2004): 337–356; Michael L. Ross, "How Do Natural Resources Influence Civil War? Evidence from Thirteen Cases," *International Organization* 58, no. 1 (2004): 35–67; Svante E. Cornell, "The Interaction of Narcotics and Conflict," *Journal of Peace Research* 42, no. 6 (2005): 751–760.

8. James D. Fearon, "Why Do Some Civil Wars Last So Much Longer than Others?" *Journal of Peace Research* 41, no. 3 (2004): 271–301; Naylor (see note 2 above), 72.

9. Gambetta (see note 3 above), 234–244.

10. Mark S. Gaylord and Harold Traver, "Introduction," in *Drugs, Law, and the State*, ed. Gaylord and Traver (Hong Kong: Hong Kong University Press, 1992), 6; Shane Blackman, *Chilling Out* (New York: Open University Press, 2004), 45.

11. Andrew F. Sunter, "The Harm of Drug Trafficking: Is There Room for Serious Debate?," *Manitoba Law Journal* 32 (2007): 174–212 (quotes are on pp. 175 and 176, respectively).

12. For example, see Stuart Horsman, "Themes in Official Discourses on Terrorism in Central Asia," *Third World Quarterly* 26, no. 1 (2005): 199–213.

13. Dishman (see note 4 above), 46.

14. John Kane, *The Politics of Moral Capital* (Oxford, UK: Oxford University Press, 2001), 11.

15. Gonzalo A. Vargas, "Drugs, Hearts and Minds: Irregular War and the Coca Economy in South Bolivar, Colombia (1996–2004)," *Civil Wars* 13, no. 1 (2011): 21–39.

16. Kane (see note 14 above), 14.

17. Paul Collier and Anke Hoeffler, "Greed and Grievance in Civil War," *Oxford Economic Papers* 56, no. 4 (2004): 563–595.

18. For example, see Matthew A. Levitt, "The Political Economy of Middle Eastern Terrorism," *Middle East Review of International Affairs* 6, no. 4 (2002): 49–65.

19. Michael E. Porter, *Competitive Advantage* (New York: Free Press, 1985).

20. Mia A. Bloom, *Dying to Kill: The Allure of Suicide Terror* (New York: Columbia University Press, 2005). See also Kim Cragin, Peter Chalk, Sara A. Daley, and Brian A. Jackson, *Sharing the Dragon's Teeth: Terrorist Groups and the Exchange of New Technologies* (Santa Monica, CA: RAND, 2007).

21. Gregory F. Treverton, Carl Matthies, Karla J. Cunningham, Jeremiah Goulka, Greg Ridgeway, and Anny Wong, *Film Piracy, Organized Crime, and Terrorism* (Santa Monica, CA: RAND, 2009).

22. Thomas M. Sanderson, "Transnational Terror and Organized Crime: Blurring the Lines," *SAIS Review* 24, no. 1 (2004): 49–61.

23. For example, see John Arquilla and David Ronfeldt, *Networks and Netwars: The Future of Terror, Crime, and Militancy* (Santa Monica, CA: RAND, 2001).

24. Phil Williams, "Transnational Criminal Networks," in Arquilla and Ronfeldt (see note 23 above), 61–97; see 71–72.

25. See Levitt (note 5 above), 10.

26. See Williams (note 24 above), 72.

27. Letizia Paoli, "The Paradoxes of Organized Crime," *Crime, Law and Social Change* 37, no. 1 (2002): 51–97.

28. See Shelley and Picarelli (note 1 above), 308.

29. Letizia Paoli and Peter Reuter, "Drug Trafficking and Ethnic Minorities in Western Europe," *European Journal of Criminology* 5 (January 2008): 13–37, 24.

30. See Paoli and Reuter (ibid.), 13, 25.

31. Emmanuel Akyeampong, "Diaspora and Drug Trafficking in West Africa: A Case Study of Ghana," *African Affairs* 104, no. 416 (2005): 429–447.

32. Mark Juergensmeyer, *Terror in the Mind of God: The Global Rise of Religious Violence* (Berkeley: University of California Press, 2003).

33. See Kane (note 14 above), 14.

34. See Juergensmeyer (note 32 above), 149.

35. See Sunter (see note 11 above), Horsman (see note 12 above), and Vargas (see note 15 above).

36. This has clearly not deterred the Taliban from drug involvement, but it is one of many religious-based groups. See Lowry Taylor, *The Nexus of Terrorism and Drug Trafficking in the Golden Crescent: Afghanistan* (Master's Thesis, U.S. Army War College, 2006).

37. For example, see Travis Hirschi, *Causes of Delinquency* (Piscataway, NJ: Transaction, 2002).

38. Gary R. Weaver and Bradley R. Agle, "Religiosity and Ethical Behavior in Organizations: A Symbolic Interactionist Perspective," *Academy of Management Review* 27, no. 1 (2002): 77–97.

39. Michael R. Welch, Charles R. Tittle, and Harold G. Grasmick, "Christian Religiosity, Self-Control, and Social Conformity," *Social Forces* 84, no. 3 (2006): 1605–1623.

40. Stephen J. Bahr, Suzanne L. Maughan, Anastasios C. Marcos, and Bingdao Li, "Family, Religiosity, and the Risk of Adolescent Drug Use," *Journal of Family and Marriage* 60, no. 4 (1998): 979–992; Rick Linden and Raymond Currie, "Religiosity and Drug Use: A Test of Social Control Theory," *Canadian Journal of Criminology and Corrections* 19 (1977): 346–355; Michael D. Newcomb, Ebrahim Maddahian, and P. M. Bentler, "Risk Factors for Drug Use Among Adolescents: Concurrent and Longitudinal Analyses," *American Journal of Public Health* 76, no. 5 (1986): 525–531.

41. Civil wars can be classified by whether the substate actor aims to capture the state center or capture a segment of territory. Either type of civil war directly challenges the authority of the state.

42. Stathis Kalyvas, *The Logic of Violence in Civil War* (Cambridge: Cambridge University Press, 2006), 18.

43. Charles Tilly, *From Mobilization to Revolution* (New York: McGraw Hill, 1978).

44. See for example Ted Robert Gurr, *Why Men Rebel* (Princeton, NJ: Princeton University Press, 1970) and Patrick M. Regan and Daniel Norton, "Greed, Grievance, and Mobilization in Civil Wars," *Journal of Conflict Resolution* 49, no. 3 (2005): 319–336.

45. Louise Richardson, "Britain and the IRA," in *Democracy and Counterterrorism: Lessons From the Past*, ed. Robert J. Art and Louise Richardson (Washington, DC: United States Institute of Peace, 2007), 69.

46. We are agnostic regarding the temporality between state violence and rejection of state authority. Furthermore, states do not only attack groups that have rejected their authority, and not all groups attacked by the state respond by rejecting its authority.

47. Minorities at Risk Organizational Behavior Data and Codebook Version 9/2008 online: http://www.cidcm.umd.edu/mar/data.asp

48. Ibid.

49. Gary King and Lanche Zeng, "Logistic Regression in Rare Events Data," *Political Analysis* 9, no. 2 (2001): 137–163.

50. Victor Asal and Karl R. Rethemeyer, "The Nature of the Beast: Organizational Structures and the Lethality of Terrorist Attacks," *Journal of Politics* 70, no. 2 (2008): 437–449; Juergensmeyer (note 32 above); and Bruce Hoffman, *Inside Terrorism* (New York: Columbia University Press, 2006), 88.

The Opium Trade and Patterns of Terrorism in the Provinces of Afghanistan: An Empirical Analysis

JAMES A. PIAZZA

Department of Political Science, Penn State University, University Park, Pennsylvania, USA

Contemporary terrorist movements in Afghanistan are frequently alleged to be fueled, in part, by the country's voluminous opium trade. Experts argue that terrorist groups currently active in Afghanistan, like the Afghan Taliban, the Islamic Movement of Uzbekistan, Hizbul Islami, and various al-Qaeda affiliates, use drug trade profits to recruit and pay cadres, acquire weapons and equipment, and bribe officials while becoming more powerful, and deadly, in the process. This study empirically examines the relationship between the opium trade and terrorism in Afghanistan by conducting a series of negative binomial regression estimations on terrorist attacks and casualties in the 34 Afghan provinces for the period 1996 to 2008. The analysis also considers various economic development, infrastructure, geographic, security, and cultural factors when examining causes of terrorism in the provinces. The study determines that, across all model specifications, provinces that produce more opium feature higher levels of terrorist attacks and casualties due to terrorism, and that opium production is a more robust predictor of terrorism than nearly all other province features. Furthermore, tests indicate that the direction of causation runs from opium production to higher rates of terrorism, not otherwise. The study concludes with a brief discussion of the policy implications of the findings.

Currently Afghanistan produces around 90 percent of the world's supply of illicit opium[1] and nearly 85 percent of global supplies of heroin and morphine originate in Afghanistan.[2] Opium is Afghanistan's largest cash crop. In 2006 local export revenues from opiates totaled over U.S. $3 billion—constituting nearly 35 percent of the country's gross national product that year—while opium production employed 500,000 Afghan households or nearly 14 percent of the population, including seasonal farm workers.[3] Furthermore, while indicative gross income per hectare from wheat in Afghanistan languished at U.S. $546 in 2007, indicative gross income per hectare from opium poppy was U.S. $5,200. The total area of farmland under opium cultivation in Afghanistan now exceeds the total hectares of coca cultivation in all Latin American countries, while the burgeoning "opium economy" has created a nouveaux riche class of producers.[4] Afghanistan solidified its status as the top world opium producer—holding what the United Nations Office of Drug Control

James A. Piazza is an associate professor of political science at Penn State University.

(UNODC) refers to as a "near monopoly" on the illicit opiate trade—after the 2001 United States ouster of the Taliban movement, though Makarenko explains that opium has deep roots in Afghanistan.[5] Poppy has been indigenously cultivated in Central Asia since ancient times, but the 1979 Soviet invasion and the turbulent three decades thereafter nurtured the illegal opiates industry by providing opportunities for trans-border trafficking and by degrading Afghan living conditions, social and political institutions, and policing capacity. This legacy has left Afghanistan as ground zero for the heroin, morphine, and opium trade, supplanting the Golden Triangle in Southeast Asia.

Today the illicit opiate trade in Afghanistan is widely portrayed by politicians, policy analysts, academics, and media commentators as an important contributor to terrorist activity in the country.[6] A 2001 report to the U.S. Congress written shortly after the 9/11 terrorist attacks in New York and Washington, DC reflects this consensus, maintaining that the Afghan Taliban movement—as well as the Northern Alliance, which the U.S. would eventually decide to support—used opiate drug revenues to fund themselves, primarily by taxing drug crop cultivation and stocks of harvested poppy and refined products, and by charging drug traffickers for protection.[7] The Hizbul-Islami (HI) movement led by Gulbuddin Hekmatyar has a long history of involvement in the narcotics trade in Afghanistan, and HI's reliance on illicit drugs to finance its activities has become increasingly more pronounced with the 2001 toppling of the Taliban regime.[8] Northern Alliance factions—particularly the Shura-i Nazar faction and Jumbush-i Milli[9]—and figures such as Muhammad Fahim, Abdul Rashid Dostum, and Burhanuddin Rabbani, all of whom were later appointed to ministerial positions in the Karzai government, are also alleged to have been fueled by narcotics smuggling and protection rackets.[10]

The Taliban briefly curtailed poppy cultivation with remarkable effectiveness in 1994–95 in the territory it controlled, ostensibly to conform to Islamic prohibitions against narcotics, and later in a bid to gain greater international recognition banned all opium production throughout Afghanistan in 2000. Because of this, many commentators came to depict the Taliban as a force dampening the Afghan drug trade.[11] However, other scholarship observes that Taliban officials continued to tax storage of opiates during the brief prohibition periods and that the movement's capacity to recruit and launch attacks even benefitted from the higher prices caused by eradication efforts.[12] The 2001 CRS report also claimed that the Taliban used drug revenues to finance the Islamic Movement of Uzbekistan, inserting an international dimension to the illicit drugs–terrorism nexus in Afghanistan.[13] Other scholars draw similar transnational linkages, arguing that the drug trade sustains both domestic terrorist movements in Afghanistan, such as the Taliban, and international terrorist movements like the Al Qaeda network, as well as jihadist groups active in Central Asia, the Middle East, Eastern Africa, and Western Europe.[14]

The significance of the opium economy to terrorism and insurgent activity in Afghanistan also drives U.S. coalition and Afghan government security policy in the country. The strategy of enhancing counterterrorism efforts by using counternarcotics tools is a frequent theme in U.S. Afghan security policy briefings.[15] NATO and United Nations analyses note that Afghan provinces with high levels of opium poppy cultivation, such as Helmand, Kandahar, Nimroz, Oruzgan, and Zabul, are also those with the highest levels of terrorist and insurgent attacks.[16] In early 2010, NATO forces collaborated with the Afghan National Army to conduct a joint military offensive called *Moshtarak* ("unity" in Pashto) in Helmand to clear the province of Taliban forces, which had set up quasi-governing institutions, and to strengthen Kabul's control over the area. A key component of Moshtarak was the disruption of Taliban taxation of poppy cultivation and opiate trafficking, which constituted the mainstay of Taliban revenues in Helmand and helped finance arms purchases and payment for Taliban footsoldiers.[17] *Time* magazine correspondent Tim McGirk depicts Operation Moshtarak as the largest counternarcotics operation in history.[18]

The argument that Afghanistan's drug problem fuels terrorism is, therefore, buttressed by substantial qualitative observation, and seems to have imprinted itself in U.S. counterterrorism policy. But can this popular contention withstand empirical scrutiny? More specifically, do patterns of illicit drug production in Afghanistan predict patterns of terrorist activity? Also, given that experts root the origins of the Afghan drug trade in the economic, social, and political disruption brought on by the Soviet invasion and three subsequent decades of domestic turmoil and foreign occupation[19]—a factor discussed in greater detail below—to what degree might any observed relationship between drugs and terrorism in Afghanistan be complicated by spuriousness or questions about direction of causation? That is to say, do the underlying security, socioeconomic, or political problems of Afghanistan drive both the drug industry and terrorism and does terrorism, as a source of instability, help to sustain or increase drug activity, rather than the other way around?[20] These are the main research questions of this study. The results of the study help to fill an important gap in the empirical literature on the root causes of terrorism. With the exception of one preliminary study indicating that opiate cultivation and opiate product wholesale prices in the Western markets are significant positive predictors of global terrorist attacks,[21] and scant ancillary findings that opium production is a positive predictor of the onset of civil wars and internal armed conflicts[22] or that narcotics extend the duration of conflicts,[23] the effects of illicit drugs on terrorist groups and terrorist activity have not been empirically studied and are poorly understood.

The rest of the article proceeds in the following order: The next section discusses in more detail how the opiate drug trade might increase terrorist activity in Afghanistan. In particular, this section examines both direct links between the illegal opium industry—for example, whereby illicit drug profits enable terrorist groups to recruit cadres and purchase weapons—and more indirect and complex relationships. Following this, the article lays out the hypotheses tested and the empirical models and results. The concluding section summarizes the scholarly and policy implications of the findings.

Opium and Terrorism in Afghanistan

How exactly does the illicit drug trade in Afghanistan drive terrorist activity? The illegal opium economy has both direct and indirect effects on terrorist group vitality and behavior. In terms of direct effects, the trade in illicit narcotics generates enormous revenues: monies that terrorist movements can use to recruit, train and pay members, acquire weapons and equipment, set up networks of safe houses or establish training and command bases, bribe officials and obtain fraudulent legal documents, travel, forge alliances with other terrorists and, ultimately, become more effective and deadly.[24] Scholars examining civil wars observe a similar relationship between the availability of "lootable" natural resources and the onset and duration of internal armed conflicts.[25] There is quite a bit of controversy over exactly how profitable the global drug trade is—UNODC figures estimate it to generate between U.S. \$300 and \$500 billion in sales per year[26] while a much more conservative estimate of U.S. \$20 to \$25 billion is derived by Reuter and Greenfield[27]—but even lower estimates position illicit drugs as a promising, and growing, source of financing for armed movements, including terrorist groups.[28] This is especially so as the post-Cold War period has seen a dramatic reduction in the amount of state financial support available to terrorist movements,[29] which has compelled groups to seek alternative sources of funding and has enabled them to act more autonomously.[30]

Moreover, in addition to being lucrative, the nature of the product traded in illicit narcotics markets easily lends itself to exploitation by terrorist movements in places like Afghanistan. In examining the influence of different types of natural resources on the onset and intensity of internal armed conflicts, Ross finds that natural resources that are easily "lootable," that are not "obstructable," and that are illegal are more centrally linked to political violence.[31] Narcotics are like alluvial diamonds, according to Ross, in that they have a high monetary value but are compact and easy to appropriate, store, and transport by small movements like terrorists, thereby proving to be convenient financial resources. Unlike timber or oil—which have been used by rebel movements in Burma and most recently in Libya—and which require more complicated and involved extraction methods, illicit drugs require little control over infrastructure or time to process and are therefore simpler to exploit by terrorist groups. Finally, the illegality of narcotics is suited to movements that already occupy the sphere of illegality. This provides a relative strategic advantage to terrorist movements that face states unable to benefit from the drug trade due to international legal prohibitions and norms. Illegal activities, like engagement in the drug trade, enable terrorists to challenge the state's monopoly over the projection of force and its control over territory and individuals.[32]

The direct effects of the illicit drug trade on patterns of terrorism are observable in Afghanistan, where due to the prevalence of the opium economy and low levels of internal security terrorist movements are especially well-positioned to insert themselves into the drug trade and take advantage of drug trade revenues. The actual growing of opium poppy and trafficking of opiate products outside of Afghanistan to consumer markets is largely conducted by impoverished peasants and apolitical drug gangs—though Peters makes a controversial claim that since 2001 the Taliban has become more directly engaged in growing, producing, trafficking, and sales of opiates.[33] Groups like the Taliban, the Northern Alliance during the 1990s, and Al Qaeda levy taxes, known locally as *ushr*, on producers, storage agents, and traffickers.[34] Afghanistan's failed legal, security, and economic institutions, severely destabilized by more than thirty years of internal armed conflict, provide the opportunity for these practices. Peters argues that the illicit drug industry is the primary source of revenue for the Taliban and Al Qaeda in Afghanistan. These groups rely upon drug revenues for the recruitment and payment of foot soldiers.[35] A 2006 *New York Times* article claimed that the Taliban derived an estimated 70 percent of their revenue from opium protection rackets[36] and an *Atlanta Journal-Constitution* piece reported that drug profits allowed Taliban commanders to pay cadres U.S. \$200 per month in a country where monthly police salaries averaged \$70 per month.[37] This, presumably, enables terrorist movements to recruit and maintain the loyalty of relatively high-quality segments of the impoverished Afghan labor market.

But in addition to direct effects—providing easy revenue—illicit drug markets also affect terrorist groups and terrorist activities through more indirect means by generally fostering an environment favorable to terrorist activity but challenging for effective counterterrorism policies. There are multiple indirect factors by which the Afghan drug trade fuels terrorism. First, the opium economy contributes to the weakening of state capacity to police territory, guarantee internal security, and to conduct effective counterterrorism. The drug trade increases the scope of domestic criminal activity, taxing state security resources that could otherwise be used to fight terrorism, while "softening" targets for terrorist attacks.[38] For Afghanistan, and many other countries, interpreting such a relationship is complicated by the fact that a priori state weakness and poor domestic security itself fueled the development of the opium economy,[39] and that state weakness and state failure itself has been shown to be a robust predictor of terrorist activity.[40] However, there is evidence that cross-nationally the illicit drug industry drives terrorist activity independent of the effects of state weakness and state failure.[41] I therefore conduct appropriate tests below to control for the security picture in Afghanistan when evaluating the effects of the opium economy on terrorism.

Second, the Afghan opium economy fuels secondary illegal markets in weapons, illegal documents, illegal cross-border movement in persons, money laundering, and financial transactions that are exploited by terrorist movements.[42] The presence of these markets ensures that terrorists have ready access to cheap supplies of the tools they need to thrive.

Third, the drug trade is a destabilizing force that contributes to the weakening of political, civil, financial, and judicial systems and the increase of corruption in countries, thereby degrading popular legitimacy and eroding public trust. This alienates the Afghan population from government authorities and erodes the authority of the state. It leaves civilians prey to radicalization and increases their tolerance for armed movements fighting against the status quo.[43] For example, popular dissatisfaction with the Rabani government during the 1989–1996 period of extreme corruption and poor security—within which the burgeoning opium trade played a significant part—is widely credited as helping push the Afghan people into the arms of the nascent Taliban movement.[44] The Afghan narcotics economy also results in the degradation of healthy legal, civic, and economic infrastructures. This creates the opportunity for terrorist movements to substitute their own structures. For example, Felbab-Brown discusses at length the importance of money laundering, informal black market credit, and illegal transnational financial transactions to the vitality of the Al Qaeda movement in Afghanistan. While the Taliban concentrates on taxation and protection rackets to extract resources from the Opium economy, according to Felbab-Brown, Al Qaeda launders drug money through its network of *hawala* (sometimes called *hundi*) international financial transfer systems. These are traditional informal networks of creditors, found throughout the Islamic world, that allow customers to transfer funds transnationally without relying on written records or formal reporting. The absence of reliable banking, credit, wire transfer services, enforceable contracts, and communications has led to the prevalence of hawala networks, which are ripe for use by drug traffickers.[45]

Hypotheses

The argument that the illicit drug trade in Afghanistan fuels terrorism—an argument raised in the body of qualitative case studies, policy and journalistic work, and theoretical and academic works—lends itself to empirically testable proposals. To test the purported relationship between drugs and terrorism in Afghanistan, this study analyzes annual levels of opium production and terrorist activity in the 34 provinces of Afghanistan for the period 1994 to 2008, the full range of years for which data is available. The design of the study employs Afghan province-years as the unit of analysis, in contrast to a more traditional cross-national analysis[46] involving multiple countries or a time series study of Afghanistan at the national level.[47] This yields three advantages. First, it allows a more complex and nuanced view into how the illegal drug industry might fuel terrorism in ways that could be obscured from view in other types of analyses. The utility of a design using subnational units is evidenced in work by Holmes, Gutierrez de Pineres, and Curtin[48] on human rights abuses, coca production, and FARC (Revolutionary Armed Forces of Colombia) guerilla activity in Colombia. Holmes et al. conduct sets of regression analyses to determine the effects of department-level (state-level) coca production, coca eradication efforts, displaced persons, government security spending, crime, and various economic development indicators on patterns of human rights abuses by guerrilla forces. They make an intriguing finding that would not otherwise reveal itself in a national or cross-national analysis: that local drug production does not predict patterns of guerrilla human rights violations within Colombia, but that homicides, department gross domestic product, and higher security spending and policing trends do. Holmes et al. also produce the highly counterintuitive finding that coca eradication efforts actually seem to worsen the human rights picture at the department level.

Second, it is a good remedy for omitted variable bias and other specification inefficiencies. Chhibber and Nooruddin, in their study of party politics and government delivery of public goods in the Indian states, argue that interpreting results produced in cross-national analyses is often complicated by highly specific institutional features of the individual cases in the study. Though these effects can be ameliorated by selection of proper control variables, or by using country-level fixed-effects, examining sub national units allows one to hold constant country-unique institutional features.[49] Chhibber and Nooruddin justify the effectiveness of sub-national analysis by pointing to Robert Putnam's work on the development of democracy in Italy.[50] This design strategy has also been used by scholars to examine terrorism and civil war.[51]

Third, the nature of opium production and terrorism within Afghanistan is well-suited to this analytical framework. The provinces of Afghanistan provide a unique opportunity to investigate the relationship between the opium economy and terrorism. This is illustrated in the data in the following tables. Table 1 ranks the Afghan provinces by their average annual hectares of opium production from 1994 to 2008 while also listing their average annual rates of terrorist attacks and casualties due to terrorism for that same period. Table 2 publishes the summary and descriptive statistics for the Afghan provinces, including total levels of opium production and terrorism and population, geographic statistics, levels of socioeconomic and infrastructure development, and dominant cultural-linguistic features.

What Tables 1 and 2 demonstrate is that the Afghan provinces are highly diverse in terms of opium production, prevalence of terrorism, level of social, infrastructure, and economic development, as well as geographic, demographic, and security features. This diversity permits cross-province analysis to determine which subnational features might predict terrorism. The data in Table 1 preliminarily suggest a link

Table 1. Annual opium production and terrorism in the Afghan provinces, 1994–2008

Province	Avg. annual opium production (hectares)	Production compared to average (high or low)	Avg. annual terrorist attacks	Avg. annual terrorist casualties
Helmand	42,400	High	9.6	58.2
Nangahrar	14,230	High	3.8	25.8
Kandahar	7,367	High	16.4	122.6
Badakhshan	5,951	High	2.4	17.4
Oruzgan	5,410	High	0.5	3.3
Farah	4,273	High	3.1	10.2
Daykundi	2,677	High	0.1	0.0
Balkh	1,929	High	1.4	4.3
Ghor	1,239	High	0.4	2.4
Nimruz	1,202	High	1.8	15.8
Zabul	1,068	High	1.1	6.8
Faryab	1,067	High	4.6	19.0
Baghlan	765	High	0.5	1.0
Bagdis	735	High	0.7	12.8
Jowzjan	681	High	0.3	1.1
Kunar	679	High	2.9	17.7
Sar-e Pol	590	High	3.0	16.2
Herat	558	High	0.3	0.9
Samangan	523	Low	0.1	0.1
Takhar	508	Low	0.3	2.2
Nurestan	502	Low	0.9	1.2
Laghman	500	Low	1.3	5.1
Kapisa	180	Low	0.6	1.6
Kabul	119	Low	10.6	86.8
Parwan	89	Low	0.7	8.1
Bamiyan	83	Low	0.1	0.2
Paktia	83	Low	3.8	17.9
Kunduz	72	Low	1.7	7.1
Wardak	70	Low	1.5	5.4
Khost	61	Low	8.6	45.8
Ghazni	23	Low	5.2	19.1
Logar	14	Low	1.7	10.2
Paktika	0	Low	4.2	13.2
Panjshir	0	Low	0.1	0.4
Median	574		1.5	7.6
Avg. for high (above median) opium production provinces	5,427		3.1	20.0
Avg. for low (below median) opium production provinces	199		2.5	13.0

Table 2. Summary statistics for provinces of Afghanistan, 1994–2008

Province	Opium cultivation (avg. hecs)	Terrorism incidents (total)	Terrorism casualties (total)	Population (1000s)	Mountainous (%)	Literacy rate	Access to drinking water (%)	Below min. calories (%)	All-season roads (%)	Under 5 mortality (out of 1000)	Pashtun majority	Foreign troops (yr. avg.)
Badakhshan	5,733	7	50	739.4	75.7	25	13	40	25	210	No	1,225.0
Bagdis	779	17	103	499.4	43.7	9	15	40	33	300	No	1,000.0
Baghlan	784	11	193	741.7	38.2	20	19	33	42	300	No	1,225.0
Balkh	2,058	21	65	1,123.9	42.0	37	31	33	38	230	No	1,225.0
Bamiyan	89	2	3	343.9	77.5	24	8	25	21	270	No	4,256.2
Daykundi[1]	2,655	2	0	477.5	89.7	16	3	52	7	300	No	5,193.7
Farah	3,731	47	153	493.0	39.2	15	37	17	49	200	Yes	1,000.0
Faryab	816	7	15	833.7	33.7	18	23	27	43	250	No	1,225.0
Ghazni	25	78	287	1,080.8	41.0	29	35	25	38	240	Yes	4,256.2
Ghor	1,322	6	37	635.3	68.9	15	14	23	12	260	No	1,000.0
Helmand	40,572	144	874	1,441.8	15.8	4	28	49	62	190	Yes	5,193.7
Herat	593	45	244	1,762.2	25.4	29	31	33	56	180	No	1,000.0
Jowzjan	727	5	16	427.0	22.4	27	24	19	45	250	No	1,225.0
Kabul	119	160	1303	3,314.0	34.6	57	65	24	68	155	Yes	1,225.0
Kandahar	6,538	246	1839	913.0	2.6	13	64	33	77	200	Yes	3,593.7
Kapisa	193	9	24	358.3	37.0	32	27	9	58	240	No	4,256.2
Khost	65	129	687	638.8	47.4	23	34	28	59	240	Yes	4,256.2

Kunar	713	44	266	413.0	78.7	27	24	9	39	190	Yes	4,256.2
Kunduz	78	26	106	820.0	3.7	22	25	26	68	270	Yes	1,225.0
Laghman	524	19	77	382.3	42.2	12	39	42	61	270	Yes	4,256.2
Logar	15	25	154	322.7	21.3	17	45	27	78	190	Yes	4,256.2
Nangahrar	15,159	58	388	1,342.5	35.7	27	43	25	54	180	Yes	4,256.2
Nimruz	1,253	27	237	118.0	0.0	15	38	66	61	210	No	5,193.7
Nurestan	536	13	19	131.0	96.6	14	2	40	10	270	No	4,256.2
Oruzgan	5,733	37	262	320.6	47.2	7	8	38	61	300	Yes	5,193.7
Paktia	89	57	269	415.0	47.4	15	34	28	59	240	Yes	4,256.2
Paktika	0	63	199	809.8	31.9	2	28	42	33	220	Yes	4,256.2
Panjshir[1]	0	2	6	128.6	77.8	27	16	11	33	220	No	4,256.2
Parwan	96	11	121	491.9	56.8	30	32	9	61	250	No	4,256.2
Samangan	559	2	1	378.0	58.8	13	7	12	28	250	No	1,225.0
Sar-e Pol	595	4	14	442.3	14.2	11	45	46	12	260	No	1,225.0
Takhar	542	4	34	830.3	33.3	12	29	26	43	250	No	1,225.0
Wardak	75	23	81	529.3	63.4	21	22	41	27	180	Yes	4,256.2
Zabul	1,062	69	285	244.9	22.7	1	38	38	39	260	Yes	5,193.7
Median	594.0	22.0	113.5	496.2	40.1	17.5	28.0	28.0	42.85	240	16/34	0/1,749

[1]Province created in 2004, data from 2004–2008.

between drugs and terrorism in Afghanistan. The provinces ranked at the top of the list—designated as "high" opium producing provinces on a year-to-year basis—such as Helmand, Nangahrar, Kandahar, and Badakhshan also experience higher annual rates of terrorist attacks and terrorist casualties. At the lower ranks of the list on Table 1, provinces like Bamiyan, Samangan, and Panjshir produce little to no opium annually and also experience much lower levels of terrorism annually. Of course, there are also outliers: Oruzgan and Daykuni are major opium-producing provinces but have seen low levels of terrorism while opium production is low in Khosht and Gazni, but terrorist activity is robust during the period examined. When province data is aggregated, however, a pattern is more clearly visible. Overall, high opium production provinces—those with annual hectares of poppy cultivation over the median—experience 3.1 terrorist attacks per year and suffer 20 terrorism casualties while low opium producing provinces average 2.5 terrorist attacks and 13 terrorism casualties annually. Also, Pearson's R coefficients for opium production and terrorist incidents and terrorism casualties are .406 and .374 respectively, suggesting a significant correlation.

Given this preliminary evidence, and the theoretical and qualitative work on drugs and terrorism in Afghanistan noted in the literature review, the study tests the following as its main hypothesis:

> *Hypothesis 1 (H1)*: Afghan provinces characterized by higher levels of opium production are more likely to experience higher levels of terrorist activity.

I also hypothesize that opium production is a robust predictor that *independently* contributes to terrorism in the provinces of Afghanistan. The study, therefore, evaluates opium as a predictor of terrorism while holding other potentially important socioeconomic, geographic, demographic, geographic, and security factors constant.

Previous cross-national studies of terrorism have identified macro-structural factors such as level of social and economic development as important factors determining patterns of terrorist attacks globally.[52] The theory underlying this proposed relationship is that poverty and poor socioeconomic development produce grievances within deprived populations that makes them more likely to support terrorism,[53] though there is considerable disagreement among terrorism experts surrounding the relationship between poverty and terrorism globally.[54] Qualitative case studies examining motivating factors for insurgency and terrorism in Afghanistan likewise identify poor economic development and socio-economic deprivation as important components in the origins, development, and sustenance of the Taliban movement, and as explanatory variables for the different levels of terrorism in parts of Afghanistan.[55] Others point to demographic, geographic, physical, and logistical features of the Afghan provinces—for example, the size of the population, the physical terrain and patterns of uneven infrastructure development—as determinants of terrorism and insurgency, and as impediments to counterinsurgency activites.[56] Furthermore, scholars have noted that the Taliban insurgency and the Al Qaeda terrorist movement has been mostly embedded in the Pashto-speaking population of Afghanistan, and that terrorist activity has been partially fueled by cultural and religious practices characteristic of the Afghan Pashtun community—for example, xenophobic tendencies in Deobandi Islam or within the cultural code of *Pashtunwali*.[57] This may explain the prevalence of terrorist violence and poor security in the Pashtun-majority Southern provinces of Afghanistan, while other regions have experienced quiescence. Finally, scholars have also argued that foreign occupations and the stationing of foreign troops in countries like Afghanistan have consequences for terrorist activity.[58]

I recognize that all of these factors are likely significant predictors of terrorism in Afghanistan, but also expect that the drug trade remains a significant predictor of terrorist attacks and terrorist casualties while holding these constant. Therefore, I test as a second hypothesis:

> *H2*: The positive relationship between opium production and terrorist activity in the Afghan provinces is independent of, and robust to the inclusion of, social, economic, demographic, geographic, religious/cultural, and security factors that predict terrorism.

Finally, the study has an expectation regarding the direction of the causal arrow in the relationship between opium production and terrorism in the Afghan provinces. It posits that the essential nature of the relationship is that opium cultivation and production produces conditions under which terrorism is more likely to occur, and to result in higher casualties, rather than the other way around. It expects that opium production causes terrorism rather than terrorist activity making a province more likely to subsequently host opium production. Reversing the direction of the causal arrow is, of course, a logical possibility. Provinces plagued by a lot of terrorism and political violence could see their political, economic, and security status erode to the point that they become a more convenient locale for drug production because they have vast unpoliced territories and an impoverished, desperate peasantry. Indeed, scholars have argued that the erosion of stability in Afghanistan, due to the aftermath of the Soviet invasion and internal armed conflict of the 1990s, fueled the "relocation" of opiate production from more stable countries like Turkey, Iran, Thailand, and Burma.[59] However, I suspect that the drug trade in Afghanistan, though "created" by the long period of instability and mass political violence after the Soviet invasion, now is a sustaining force for terrorism, which is a smaller-scale and more specifically defined manifestation of political violence. A key issue here is the definition of terrorism used in the study—violence perpetrated by non-state actors against *civilians* with the intention of communicating a political message or influencing an audience—and how it differs from types of violence suffered in Afghanistan after the Soviet invasion during the period 1989 to 1996. This leads to the final hypothesis tested:

> *H3*: The relationship between opium production and terrorist activity in the Afghan provinces is causally linked, rather than merely correlational.

Analysis

To test these hypotheses, the study employs three different types of statistical tests that evaluate opium poppy production as a predictor of terrorist incidents at the Afghan provincial level: a set of six negative binomial regression estimations testing the main relationship between opium and terrorism in Afghanistan; Monte Carlo simulations of first difference substantive effects comparing opium production to other predictors of terrorism used in the study; and differently specified reruns of the core regression estimations and Granger causality tests which are used to shed light on the causal direction of the relationship between opium production and terrorism. Terrorist activity is measured using two dependent variables, both of which are derived from the Global Terrorism Database (GTD). The first is an annual count of all terrorist incidents sorted by province in which the attack took place and the second is a tally of the total casualties due to terrorism—persons killed, wounded, or kidnapped in the course of a terrorist attack—each province-year. The purpose of fitting models with two dependent variables is to examine the effects of the Afghan opium economy on both the frequency and the intensity of terrorism at the province level. The GTD allows researchers to set criteria for type of terrorist events downloaded from the database. For the study, only terrorist events that are classified as "unambiguous" in terms of open source evidence, that are clearly aimed to achieve a "political, economic, religious or social goal"—sifting out attacks motivated by nonpolitical criminal intentions—that are conducted with the intent of communicating a message to a larger audience, and that are "outside the context of legitimate warfare activities" are included in the data.[60] Furthermore, only terrorist attacks that target civilians are included in the analysis. This helps to weed out events, such as attacks against on-duty U.S. or coalition forces, that might be more properly classified as interstate war or civil war events. Robust standard errors clustered by province are calculated for all coefficients.

The opium economy or illicit drug trade in Afghanistan—the main independent variable—is measured using the only available indicator of opiate activity at the province level: the scope of cultivation of opium poppies. The main independent variable is therefore the hectares of opium poppy production in the province, transformed into a natural log and derived from statistics published in various years of the United Nations Office of Drug Control's (UNDOCS) *World Drug Report*. The study is limited to the years 1986 to 2008, the full range of years for which data on opium production in the Afghan provinces is available.

Because the dependent variables are both count indicators with highly skewed distributions, both temporally and spatially, for which observations may not be independent of one another—terrorist attacks and terrorist casualties in one province in one year might be a predictor of attacks in a neighboring province or in a subsequent year—the study employs a negative binomial estimation technique.[61] Under or over-reporting bias is also likely to be minimal in the study, given that reporting on terrorism is unlikely to differ as dramatically from province to province as might be the case in a cross-national analysis. This further underscores the suitability of a negative binomial, rather than a zero-inflated negative binomial, modeling technique.[62]

The analysis also includes several covariates which facilitate the testing of the second hypothesis and comprise a sampling of the political, cultural, demographic, geographic, security, and socio-economic factors discussed previously as contributors to terrorism in Afghanistan and other countries. The first set are demographic and physical features of the province. These include the natural log of the physical size of the province in square kilometers, the natural log of its population, the percentage of its territory described as mountainous, and the percentage of its roads that are passable during all seasons. All of these factors are identified as precipitants of terrorist activity in Afghanistan,[63] and many are indicators that Eyerman[64] and Wade and Reiter[65] test as predictors of terrorism in their cross-national empirical studies. The expectation is that physically large, populous, and mountainous provinces with poor transportation infrastructures (few all-season roads) experience higher levels of terrorism as these provinces are more difficult to police and pose more serious challenges for counterterrorism authorities.

Also included are a set of social and economic development indicators to determine the role played by poverty, socioeconomic underdevelopment, poor education, and poor public health in prompting terrorism in Afghanistan.[66] These include the literacy rate in the province, the percentage of the population with access to safe drinking water, the percentage of the population subsisting below the median caloric intake level, and the mortality rate of children under five years of age. The expectation is generally that Afghan provinces with low literacy, poor access to safe drinking water, higher levels of malnutrition, and high child mortality rates will experience more terrorist activity.

The study also controls for provinces with Pashtun majorities, with the expectation that these provinces will experience more terrorism than provinces dominated by the other major Afghan ethnic groups, the Tajiks, Uzbeks, and Hazara. The Taliban movement itself is a Pashtun-dominated movement that is embedded in the Pashtun-majority provinces in the Southern part of the country, and its ideology is attuned to the puritanical Deobandi interpretation of Islam familiar to Pashtun populations throughout South Asia.[67]

Finally, the study also controls for deployment of foreign troops within provinces. Highly specific and detailed statistics on foreign troop presence on a province-year basis is not available, partially due to security classification barriers. Because the study begins in 1994, no measurements of Soviet troop deployment are included in the analysis. NATO-supported ISAF (International Security Assistance Force) troops that constitute the sole foreign troop presence were originally limited to Kabul after the 2001 invasion—which mostly made use of indigenous Afghan Northern Alliance troops backed by NATO air support—and were then extended to the provinces in 2003. NATO and ISAF troops have since then been incrementally rotated between four zones, East, North, West, and finally South, and are tasked to counterinsurgency, counterterrorism, and patrol duties within provinces in these four zones. The specific location of activities of NATO and ISAF troops within these zones fluctuates throughout the year. Therefore, to operationalize foreign troop levels at the province level, I use figures for general troop deployments in the four zones per year divided by the number of provinces in each zone. This provides a rough estimate of typical foreign troop presence within a province in a given year.

The sources for the socioeconomic, demographic, infrastructural, and cultural indicators are the Afghanistan Ministry of Rural Rehabilitation and Development series of *Provincial Development Reports*[68] and the Afghanistan *Provincial Overviews* published online by the Naval Postgraduate School, Program for Culture and Conflict Studies.[69] Data for foreign troops was derived from a Brookings Institute report entitled *Afghanistan Index*.[70] Descriptive statistics for all variables used in the study are summarized in Table 2.[71]

Results

The results of the main regression models are presented in Table 3.

The analysis fits six models to illustrate the robustness of the core finding: that opium production at the provincial level in Afghanistan is a significant predictor of both terrorist attacks and casualties due to terrorism, regardless of model specification. Models 1 and 2 show provincial opium production to be a significant, positive

Table 3. Regression analysis results: Opium cultivation and terrorism in the provinces of Afghanistan, 1996 to 2008

Characteristic	(1) Terrorist attacks	(2) Terrorist casualties	(3) Terrorist attacks	(4) Terrorist casualties	(5) Terrorist attacks	(6) Terrorist casualties
Opium cultivation (log hectares)	.113 (.044)*	.173 (.048)***	.106 (.026)***	.150 (.038)***	.099 (.023)***	.144 (.038)***
Province population (log)	.675 (.141)***	.776 (.190)***	.621 (.164)***	1.178 (.250)***	.515 (.141)***	1.153 (.240)***
Province area (log)	−.116 (.209)	−.232 (.238)	.370 (.155)*	.253 (.232)	.316 (.134)*	.294 (.229)
Percent mountainous			−.000 (.007)	.009 (.010)	−.000 (.006)	.009 (.010)
Literacy rate			.018 (.013)	.000 (.017)	.014 (.011)	−.008 (.017)
Access to safe drinking water			.020 (.099)*	.031 (.016)	.011 (.009)	.029 (.017)
Percent below min. calories			−.001 (.010)	.012 (.013)	−.000 (.007)	.011 (.013)
Percent all-season roads			.003 (.008)	.027 (.009)**	.004 (.007)	.029 (.229)**
Under 5 mortality rate			.006 (.003)	.006 (.005)	.004 (.003)	.005 (.005)
Pashtun majority			.974 (.322)**	.168 (.351)	.909 (.266)**	.216 (.348)
Foreign troops			.000 (.000)***	.000 (.000)***	.000 (.000)***	.000 (.000)***
Previous terrorism					.042 (.020)*	−.000 (.002)
Constant	−7.442 (2.854)**	−6.258 (3.482)*	−16.363 (2.886)***	−23.106 (4.568)***	−13.558 (2.672)***	−23.053 (4.586)***
Wald χ^2	32.47***	27.98***	431.41***	298.85***	418.18***	346.09***
n	490	490	490	490	458	458

All models are negative binomial regressions, robust standard errors clustered by province in parentheses.
$^*p \le .05$; $^{**}p \le .01$; $^{***}p \le .000$.

predictor of terrorist attacks and casualties, while controlling only for the basic provincial demographic and physical indicators, province population and area. In these first two models, provinces that produce higher levels of opiates experience higher levels of terrorism and suffer higher civilian casualty rates due to terrorism, regardless of the population or physical size of the province. In models 3 and 4, the full compliment of covariates are added to the model and in these opium production remains a significant positive predictor of both attacks and casualties despite the fact that some of the covariates—especially the level of foreign troops present—are highly significant. In models 5 and 6, an indicator for previous incidents of terrorist attacks and casualties due to terrorism in the province is included. This variable is simply a one-year lag of the dependent variable and is included to underscore the robustness of the core findings, that opium production is a significant positive predictor of province-level terrorism, and to help to address questions of temporal autoregression. In models 5 and 6, opium production remains significant and the overall results remain much the same.

Few of the covariates in the models are consistently significant; the prominent exceptions being province population, which is significant in all model specifications and bears large coefficients, and the average number of foreign troops present in the province, which is significant but which has a small coefficient. In some model specifications, province area, access to safe drinking water, percent of province roads categorized as "all season," and Pashtun majority are significant positive predictors of terrorist attacks and casualties.

When they are significant, all have coefficients that are in the direction hypothesized with the exception of "access to safe drinking water" and "all season roads," which are positive rather than negative. This latter finding is curious in that it suggests that terrorist activity is more acute in provinces with better road transportation infrastructure. Rather than being a signifier of lower levels of economic development—thereby working as a motivation for terrorist support by increasing socioeconomic grievances among the locals as expected by Ross[72]—or an impediment to good policing and counterterrorism/counterinsurgency efforts, good road infrastructure seems to boost terrorist activity. I can suggest two explanations for this unanticipated finding: a) good road infrastructure might increase terrorist activity by serving as an efficient conduit for terrorist activity, such as transportation of cadres, weapons, and equipment in much the same way superhighways in developed and developing countries facilitate the movement of infectious diseases and criminal activities; b) or, conversely, provinces with good roads merely present terrorist groups with better targeting opportunities. However, as with the other covariates mentioned, the percentage of all-season roads in a province is not significant across all model specifications, though it is significant in models 5 and 6, which include all covariates. The issue of transportation infrastructure as a predictor of terrorism in Afghanistan begs further scrutiny in future studies.

Substantive Effects

In Figure 1, the results of Monte Carlo simulations of first-difference substantive effects of selected model predictors are graphed to show the amount of terrorist activity that opium economy in the Afghan provinces produces per year. Using the *Clarify* software package developed by Tomz, Wittenburg, and King,[73] I calculate and graph the effects of one quartile increases in raw hectares of opium poppy cultivation on the dependent variables and compare them with corresponding unit

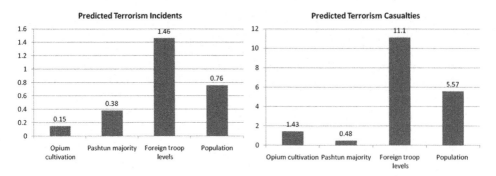

Figure 1. Substantive effects simulations. *Monte Carlo simulations of the substantive effects of one quartile or one unit increases of the independent variable on dependent variables.

increases in three of the most robust covariates in the model: whether or not the province is Pashtun majority, foreign troop presence, and province population. In the simulations, I hold all other covariates in the model constant to their appropriate measures of central tendency—mean for interval indicators and median for ordinal indicators—or at zero if the indicator is a dummy variable.

The results of the substantive effects simulations indicate that while opium production is a significant contributor to terrorist activity at the provincial level, and is highly robust when controlling for other province factors, the local opium economy produces modest amounts of terrorism relative to other significant contributors, thereby supporting hypothesis two. While increasing the number of hectares of opium production in one year by 25 percent yields 0.15 more attacks and 1.43 more casualties due to terrorism annually on average, merely being Pashtun majority ensures that the province experiences 3.8 more terrorist attacks per year and suffers more than .48 more casualties per year. The most substantive contributor to terrorism in the Afghan provinces is the presence of foreign troops. For each quartile increase in NATO-ISAF troops in a province, terrorist attacks increase by 1.46 events while casualties increase by 11.1. This even outstrips province population size as a substantive predictor. Increasing the population of a province by 25% yields .76 more attacks and produces 5.57 more casualties due to terrorism.

I make a couple of comments about the findings in the substantive effects simulations. First, given the potentially strong effects that foreign troop presence may have on terrorism in Afghanistan, I am more confident in my core result that opium production increases terrorism than I would have been if troop presence were omitted from the models. The inclusion of foreign troops to the estimations makes the findings all the more robust. Second, the direction of causation between foreign troop presence and terrorism in Afghanistan is unclear. Theoretically, presence of foreign troops might stimulate terrorist activity, particularly in highly independent and xenophobic Pashtun areas or where such presence is accompanied by human rights abuses or offenses against local customs. However, it also stands to reason that foreign troops are more likely to be deployed to areas where terrorist activity is high and security is poor. Further statistical tests fail to clarify the endogenous nature of troop presence and terrorism in the provinces. For example, lagging by one period troop presence produces the same results as in the core model, suggesting that troops in one year (t_1) predict terrorism in the subsequent year (t_2). However, leads of foreign troop presence are also significant. Furthermore, when the models

Table 4. Direction of causation, regression models with lagged IV opium cultivation and terrorism in the provinces of Afghanistan, 1996 to 2008

Characteristic	(7) Terrorist attacks		(8) Terrorist casualties		(9) Terrorist attacks		(10) Terrorist casualties	
One-year lag, opium cultivation (log hectares)	.120	(.025)***	.177	(.039)***	.112	(.023)***	.178	(.040)***
Province population (log)	.608	(.174)***	1.147	(.242)***	.518	(.151)**	1.159	(.241)***
Province area (log)	.354	(.149)*	.282	(.199)	.288	(.131)*	.285	(.197)
Percent mountainous	.001	(.007)	.015	(.011)	.000	(.006)	.015	(.011)
Literacy rate	.015	(.013)	.003	(.016)	.013	(.021)	.003	(.016)
Access to safe drinking water	.021	(.008)	.040	(.015)**	.015	(.010)	.041	(.015)**
Percent below min. calories	−.000	(.008)	.021	(.015)	.000	(.007)	.021	(.015)
Percent all-season roads	.006	(.008)	.025	(.009)**	.005	(.007)	.025	(.009)**
Under 5 mortality rate	.005	(.003)	.007	(.004)	.004	(.003)	.007	(.004)
Pashtun majority	.997	(.297)**	.322	(.294)	.919	(.264)**	.324	(.296)
Foreign troops	.000	(.000)***	.000	(.000)***	.000	(.000)***	.000	(.000)***
Previous terrorism					.039	(.019)*	−.000	(.002)
Constant	−16.081	(2.855)***	−24.088	(4.406)***	−13.569	(2.582)***	−24.388	(4.322)***
Wald χ^2	364.27***		367.16***		351.33***		460.98***	
n	458		458		458		458	

All models are negative binomial regressions, robust standard errors clustered by province in parentheses.
$*p \leq .05$; $**p \leq .01$; $***p \leq .000$.

Table 5. Direction of causation: Results of Granger causality tests

1, 2 and 3-year lags	Combined model χ^2
Opium cultivation granger causes terrorist incidents	13.61**
Opium cultivation granger causes terrorist casualties	6.15*
Terrorist incidents granger cause opium cultivation	4.79
Terrorist casualties granger cause opium cultivation	2.39

All coefficients are combined tests of one, two and three-year lags.
**$p \leq .01$; *$p \leq .05$.

are respecified to predict foreign troop levels rather than terrorism, both terrorist incidents and terrorist casualties in provinces significantly predict foreign troop presence. These results suggest a complex, endogenous relationship whereby foreign troops are allocated to terrorism-plagued provinces in order to foster security, but in doing so exacerbate terrorist activity.

Direction of Causation Between Opium and Terrorism

Finally, in line with the previous discussion, the study employs two means to further increase confidence in the direction of causation of the relationship between opium production and terrorism at the provincial level and to test for the influence of endogeneity. First, the core negative binomial regression models are refitted using a one-year lagged version of the main independent variable. This allows a test of the effects of opium production in t_1 on terrorist attacks and terrorism casualties in t_2. The results of these models are presented in Table 4.

Across all specifications, lagged opium production is a significant predictor of terrorism. This includes models 9 and 10 where the lagged dependent variable—which is highly significant and adversely affects the level of significance of other covariates in the model—is included. These results provide partial support for hypothesis three, demonstrating that opium production is causally linked to terrorism in the Afghan provinces, and is not a mere correlate.

The results of the second test to determine causation also supports hypothesis three. Table 5 shows the results of a set of Granger causality tests using one, two, and three-year lags of both the independent and dependent variables.

Table 5 demonstrates that opium cultivation Granger-causes terrorist incidents and terrorist casualties in the Afghan provinces, but that incidents and casualties do not Granger-cause opium production. Both Tables 4 and 5 suggest that while opium production produces conditions favorable to the vitality of terrorist groups and their activities, the experience of terrorism does not precipitate opium production; for example, by eroding security to a point that opium producers move in to take advantage of poor policing, or by destroying alternative employment opportunities for locals.

Conclusion

The empirical results of this study are preliminary, but they provide evidence that opium production is an important driver of terrorism in Afghanistan's provinces, that provinces that feature opium cultivation are at a significantly higher risk of experiencing terrorist attacks and of seeing their citizens harmed in terrorist incidents, that opium production is likely a cause of rather than an effect of terrorism, but that poppy cultivation is by no means the only substantive root cause of terrorism at the provincial level. At the very least, the results justify the consideration of the illicit drug market as a crucial contributor to the terrorism threat in Afghanistan and to the larger security picture in that country.

The study also paves the way for several future research directions on the relationship between illicit drugs and terrorism in Afghanistan. First, the study is limited to the 34 provinces of Afghanistan while the Taliban engagement in the opiate trade is known to transcend the border with Pakistan. Furthermore, the type of analysis featured in this piece could be extended to other countries in which illicit drugs are commonly believed to be a driver of terrorist activity—such as Colombia and the Philippines—or regions of the world, like North and West Africa, that have become important transit points for the international drug trade. Second, the study provides a framework within which empirical examination of the effectiveness of U.S. and Afghan government counternarcotics strategies might be assessed. Though analysts and policymakers nearly universally regard the drug trade as a sustaining force for terrorism in the country, and though drug crop eradication and drug interdiction strategies have become staple components of U.S. counterterrorism policy, these strategies are still controversial, with some experts charging that they are counterproductive and may even drive Afghan peasants into support for the Taliban.[74] The effectiveness of counternarcotics efforts in Afghanistan could be similarly evaluated in a province-year framework similar to the one employed in this study.

Notes

1. India is the lead licit opium producer, with its crop used to produce medicinal opiates. See Victoria Greenfield, Victoria A. Letizia Paoli, and Peter Reuter, "Is Medicinal Opium Production Afghanistan's Answer?: Lessons from India and the World Market," *Journal of Drug Policy Analysis* 2, no. 1 (2009): 22–38.

2. UNODC, United Nations Office on Drugs and Crime, *2010 World Drug Report* (Vienna: UNODC, 2010).

3. John A. Glaze, *Opium and Afghanistan: Reassessing U.S. Counternarcotics Strategy*, (Carlisle, PA: Strategic Studies Institute, U.S. Army War College, 2007), http://www.strategic studiesinstitute.army.mil/pdffiles/pub804.pdf.

4. UNODC, United Nations Office on Drugs and Crime, *Afghanistan Opium Survey 2007: Executive Summary* (Vienna: UNODC, 2007).

5. Tamara Makarenko, "Crime, Terror and the Central Asian Drug Trade," *Harvard Asia Quarterly* 6, no. 3 (2005), http://asiaquarterly.com/2006/01/28/ii-88/.

6. Gretchen Peters, *Seeds of Terror: How Heroin is Bankrolling the Taliban and Al Qaeda* (New York: Thomas Dunne Books, 2009); "Afghan Leader Warns of Terrorism," *Los Angeles Times*, October 13, 2006, A9; Henry J. Hyde and Mark Steven Kirk, "Letter to Secretary of Defense Donald Rumsfeld Regarding the Opium Crisis in Afghanistan," October 12, 2006, http://www.internationalrelations.house.gov/archives/press.htm; Svante E. Cornell, "The Interaction of Narcotics and Conflict," *Journal of Peace Research* 42, no. 6 (2005a): 751–760; Svante E. Cornell, "Narcotics, Radicalism and Armed Conflict in Central Asia: The Islamic Movement of Uzbekistan," *Terrorism and Political Violence* 17, no. 4 (2005b): 619–639; Rohan Gunaratna, *Inside al-Qaeda: Global Networks of Terror* (New York, NY: Hurst and Company, 2002); Asa Hutchinson, "Narco-Terrorism: The International Connection Between Drugs and Terror," Address of Drug Enforcement Agency Director before the Heritage Foundation, April 2, 2002, http://www.justice.gov/dea/speeches/s040202.html; Frank Cillufo, "The Threat Posed from the Convergence of Organized Crime, Drug Trafficking, and Terrorism," Director, Counterterrorism Task Force, Center for Strategic and International Studies. Address before

U.S. House Judiciary Subcommittee on Crime, 2000, http://csis.org/files/media/csis/congress/ts001213cilluffo.pdf; Raphael Perl, "Taliban and the Drug Trade," CRS Report for Congress, 2001,http://fpc.state.gov/documents/organization/6210.pdf; Ahmed Rashid, "The Taliban: Exporting Extremism," *Foreign Affairs* 78, no. 22 (1999): 22–35.

7. Perl and Goodhand claim that the Taliban levy a 10 percent tax on cultivation of poppy and a 10 to 20 percent tax/fee on stored product and for trafficking rights. Raphael Perl, "Taliban and the Drug Trade," Congressional Research Service Report for Congress, 2001, http://fpc.state.gov/documents/organization/6210.pdf; Jonathan Goodhand, "From Holy War to Opium War?: A Case Study of the Opium Economy in Northeastern Afghanistan," *Central Asian Survey* 19, no. 2 (2000): 265–280.

8. Hamida Ghafour, "Poverty and Terrorism Fuel Booming Drug Trade in Afghanistan," *Daily Telegraph*, August 24, 2004, http://www.telegraph.co.uk/news/worldnews/asia/afghanistan/1470090/poverty-and-terrorism-fuel-booming-drug-trade-in-Afghanistan.html; John K. Cooley, *Unholy Wars: Afghanistan, America and International Terrorism* (London: Pluto Press, 2002); Ikramul Haq,"Pak-Afghan Drug Trade in Historical Perspective," *Asian Survey* 36, no. 10 (1996): 945–963.

9. According to Cornell (see note 6 above, 2005b), p. 756.

10. Kathy Gannon, "Afghanistan Unbound," *Foreign Affairs* 83, no. 3 (2004): 35–46; Goodhand (see note 7 above).

11. Graham Farrell and John Thorne, "Where Have All the Flowers Gone?: Evaluation of the Taliban Crackdown Against Opium Poppy Cultivation in Afghanistan," *International Journal of Drug Policy* 16 (2005): 81–91.

12. Vanda Felbab-Brown, "Afghanistan: When Counternarcotics Undermines Counterterrorism," *The Washington Quarterly* 28, no. 4 (2005): 55–72; Glaze, *Opium and Afghanistan* (see note 3 above).

13. Perl, "Taliban and the Drug Trade" (see note 6 above).

14. Peters (see note 6 above); Cornell (see note 6 above, 2005b); Gunaratna (see note 6 above).

15. Hyde and Kirk (see note 6 above); Hutchinson (see note 6 above).

16. "NATO To Attack Afghan Opium Labs," *BBC News*, October 10, 2008, http://news.bbc.co.uk/2/hi/south_asia/7663204.stm.

17. "Operation Moshtarak: At a Glance,"*Al Jazeera English*, February 13, 2010, http://english.aljazeera.net/news/asia/2010/02/201021343536129252.html.

18. Tim McGirk, "Afghan Opium: To Crack Down or Not?," *Time*, March 22, 2010, http://www.time.com/time/magazine/article/0,9171,1971405,00.html.

19. Felbab-Brown (see note 12 above); Makarenko (see note 5 above); Rashid (see note 6 above).

20. This is an issue also observed by Cornell, p. 752 (see note 6 above, 2005a).

21. James A. Piazza, "The Illicit Drug Trade, Counternarcotics Strategies and Terrorism," *Public Choice* 149, nos. 3–4 (2011): 297–314.

22. Patrick Regan and Aysegul Aydin, "Weapons, Money and Diplomacy: Intervention Strategies and the Duration of Civil Wars." Paper prepared for the Mapping and Explaining Civil War: What To Do About Contested Datasets and Findings, Human Security Center at the Liu Institute for Global Issues, University of British Columbia, 18–19 August, 2003; Patrick Regan and Daniel Norton,"Protest, Rebellion and the Onset of Civil Wars," Paper prepared for the Mapping and Explaining Civil War: What To Do About Contested Datasets and Findings, Human Security Center at the Liu Institute for Global Issues, University of British Columbia, 18–19 August, 2003.

23. Jeffery Ian Ross, "Structural Causes of Oppositional Political Terrorism: A Causal Model," *Journal of Peace Research* 30, no. 3 (1993): 317–329; Michael L. Ross, "What Do We Know About Natural Resources and Civil War?," *Journal of Peace Research* 41, no. 3 (2004a): 337–356; Michael L. Ross, "How Do Natural Resources Influence Civil War?: Evidence from Thirteen Cases," *International Organization* 58, no. 1 (2004b): 35–67; Michael L. Ross, "Oil, Drugs and Diamonds: The Varying Roles of Natural Resources in Civil War," in *The Political Economy of Armed Conflict*, ed. Karen Ballentine and Jake Sherman (Boulder, CO: Lynne Rienner, 2003).

24. Peters (see note 6 above); Mark A. R. Kleiman, "Illicit Drugs and the Terrorist Threat: Causal Links and Implications for Domestic Drug Control Policy," Congressional Research Service Report for Congress RL32334 (Washington, D.C.: The Library of Congress, 2004.)

25. See, for example, Ross (note 23 above, 2004a and 2004b).

26. UNODC, United Nations Office on Drugs and Crime, *2010 World Drug Report* (Vienna: UNODC, 2010).

27. Peter Reuter and Victoria Greenfield, "Measuring Global Drug Markets: How Good Are the Numbers and Why Should We Care About Them?," *World Economics* 2, no. 4 (2001): 159–173.

28. Paul R. Kan, "Webs of Smoke: Drugs and Small Wars," *Small Wars and Insurgencies* 17, no. 2 (2006): 148–162; Angel Rabassa and Peter Chalk, *Colombian Labyrinth: The Synergy of Drugs and Insurgency and Its Implications for Regional Stability* (Santa Monica, CA: RAND Corporation, 2001).

29. Walter Enders and Todd Sandler, "Is Transnational Terrorism Becoming More Threatening?: A Time-Series Investigation," *Journal of Conflict Resolution* 44, no. 3 (2000): 307–332.

30. Gunaratna (see note 6 above); David Tucker, "What's New About the New Terrorism and How Dangerous Is It?," *Terrorism and Political Violence* 13 (2001): 1–14.

31. Ross (see note 23 above, 2003).

32. Cornell (see note 6 above, 2005a); Karen Ballentine, "Beyond Greed and Grievance: Reconsidering the Economic Dynamics of Armed Conflict," in *The Political Economy of Armed Conflict*, ed. Karen Ballentine and Jack Sherman (Boulder, CO: Lynne Rienner, 2003).

33. Peters (see note 6 above).

34. Goodhand (see note 7 above); Felbab-Brown (see note 12 above).

35. Peters (see note 6 above).

36. "NATO Shifts Afghan Focus to Drug Lords," *New York Times*, July 30, 2006, 1, 6.

37. Don Melvin, "The Taliban Are Winning," *Atlanta Journal-Constitution*, December 14, 2006, http://www.military-quotes.com/forum/taliban-winning-t29840.html.

38. Kleiman (see note 24 above).

39. Cornell (see note 6 above, 2005b).

40. James A. Piazza, "Incubators of Terror: Do Failed and Failing States Promote Transnational Terrorism?," *International Studies Quarterly* 52, no. 3 (2008): 469–488.

41. James A. Piazza, "The Illicit Drug Trade, Counternarcotics Strategies and Terrorism." Paper prepared for the Fourth Annual Terrorism and Policy Workshop, University of Texas at Dallas, May 2011.

42. Kleiman (see note 24 above).

43. Ibid.

44. Rashid (see note 6 above).

45. Felbab-Brown (see note 12 above).

46. As previously mentioned, however, Piazza's cross-national panel time series analysis of 170 countries for the period 1986 to 2006 produces results that are consistent with the core findings of this study: that illicit drug production is a positive predictor of terrorist activity. Piazza (see note 41 above).

47. However, national levels of opium production in Afghanistan—coded as annual totals for all provinces for the period 1980 to 2008—are highly correlated with national annual totals of terrorist attacks and numbers of terrorist casualties. Pearson's r values for opium production and terrorist incidents is 0.84 and for opium and casualties is 0.81.

48. Jennifer S. Holmes, Sheila Amin Gutierrez de Pineres, and Kevin M. Curtin, "A Subnational Study of Insurgency: FARC Violence in the 1990s," *Studies in Conflict and Terrorism* 30 (2007): 249–265; Jennifer S. Holmes, Sheila Amin Gutierrez de Pineres, and Kevin M. Curtin, "Drugs, Violence and Development in Colombia: A Department-Level Analysis," *Latin American Politics and Society* 48, no. 3 (2006): 157–184.

49. Pradeep Chhibber and Irfan Nooruddin, "Do Party Systems Count?: The Number of Parties and Government Performance in the Indian States," *Comparative Political Studies* 37, no. 2 (2004): 152–187.

50. Robert Putnam, *Making Democracy Work: Civic Traditions in Modern Italy* (Princeton, NJ: Princeton University Press, 1993).

51. Siri Camilla Aas Rustad, Halvard Buhaug, Ashild Falch, and Scott Gates, "All Conflict is Local: Modeling Sub-National Variation in Civil Conflict Risk," *Conflict Management and Peace Science* 28, no. 1 (2011): 15–40; James A. Piazza, "Terrorism and Party Systems in the States of India," *Security Studies* 19 (2010): 99–123.

52. Sarah Jackson Wade and Dan Reiter, "Does Democracy Matter?," *Journal of Conflict Resolution* 51, no. 2 (2007): 329–348; Alberto Abadie, "Poverty, Political Freedom and the Roots of Terrorism," *American Economic Review* 96, no. 2 (2006): 159–177; Quan Li,"Does Democracy Promote or Reduce Transnational Terrorist Incidents?," *Journal of Conflict Resolution* 49, no. 2 (2005): 278–297.

53. See Ross (note 23 above, 2003).

54. James A. Piazza, "Does Poverty Serve as a Root Cause of Terrorism?: No, Poverty is a Weak Causal Link," in *Debating Terrorism and Counterterrorism: Conflicting Perspectives on Causes, Contexts and Responses*, ed. Stuart Gottlieb (Washington, DC: Congressional Quarterly Press, 2009); Karin Von Hippel, "Does Poverty Serve as a Root Cause of Terrorism?: Yes, Poverty is an Important Cause," in *Debating Terrorism and Counterterrorism: Conflicting Perspectives on Causes, Contexts and Responses*, ed. Stuart Gottblief (Washington, DC: Congressional Quarterly Press, 2009).

55. Karin Von Hippel, "A Counterradicalization Strategy for a New U.S. Administration," *The Annals of the American Academy of Political and Social Science* 618, no. 1 (2008): 182–196; Cooley (see note 8 above); Rashid (see note 6 above).

56. Seth G. Jones, *Counterinsurgency in Afghanistan* (Santa Monica, CA: RAND, 2008).

57. Abdulkader Sinno, "Explaining the Taliban's Ability to Mobilize the Pashtuns," in *The Taliban and the Crisis of Afghanistan*, ed. Robert D. Crews and Amin Tarzi (Cambridge, MA: Harvard University Press, 2009); Thomas H. Johnson and M. Chris Mason, "Understanding the Taliban Insurgency in Afghanistan," *Orbis* 51, no. 1 (2006): 71–89.

58. See for example Robert A. Pape, "The Strategic Logic of Suicide Terrorism," *American Political Science Review* 97, no. 3 (2003): 343–361.

59. A. Feldman and M. Perala, "Reassessing the Causes of Nongovernmental Terrorism in Latin America," *Latin American Politics and Society* 46, no. 2 (2004): 101–132; Makarenko (see note 5 above).

60. For more information about the criteria researchers may select when downloading GTD data, see http://www.start.umd.edu/gtd/search/. The criteria selected for the data in this study are "criterions 1, 2 and 3" and "exclude ambiguous cases."

61. Patrick T. Brandt, John T. Williams, Benjamin O. Fordham, and Brian Pollins, "Dynamic Models for Persistent Event Count Time Series," *American Journal of Political Science* 44, no. 4 (2000): 823–843; Adrian Colin Cameron and P. K. Trivedi, *Regression Analysis of Count Data* (Cambridge: Cambridge University Press, 1998); Gary King, "Statistical Models for Political Science Event Counts: Bias in Conventional Procedures and Evidence for the Exponential Poisson Regression Model," *American Journal of Political Science* 32, no. 3 (1988): 838–863.

62. See Konstantinos Drakos and Andreas Gofas, "The Devil You Know but Are Afraid to Face: Underreporting Bias and Its Distorting Effects on the Study of Terrorism," *Journal of Conflict Resolution* 50, no. 5 (2006): 714–735.

63. Jones (see note 56 above).

64. Joe Eyerman, "Terrorism and Democratic States: Soft Targets or Accessible Systems," *International Interactions* 24, no. 2 (1998): 151–170.

65. Wade and Reiter (see note 52 above).

66. Von Hippel (see note 55 above); Cooley (see note 8 above); Rashid (see note 6 above).

67. Sinno (see note 57 above); Johnson and Mason (see note 57 above).

68. Available online at: http://www.mrrd.gov.af/nabdp/.

69. Available online at: http://www.nps.edu/Programs/CCS/ExecSumm.html.

70. Ian S. Livingston and Michael O'Hanlon, *Afghanistan Index: Tracking Variables of Reconstruction and Security in Post 9/11 Afghanistan* (Washington, DC: Brookings Institution, 2011), http://www.brookings.edu/~/media/Files/Programs/FP/afghanistan%20 index/index.pdf.

71. Complete data for province-year indicators are available from the author.

72. Jeffery Ian Ross, "Structural Causes of Oppositional Political Terrorism: A Causal Model," *Journal of Peace Research* 30, no. 3 (1993): 317–329.

73. Michael Tomz, Jason Wittenburg, and Gary King, "CLARIFY: Software for Interpreting and Presenting Statistical Results," *Journal of Statistical Software* 8, no. 1 (2003), http://www.jstatsoft.org/v08/i01/paper.

74. Felbab-Brown (see note 12 above).

Surreptitious Lifelines: A Structural Analysis of the FARC and the PKK

VERA ECCARIUS-KELLY

Department of Political Science, Siena College, Loudonville, New York, USA

The Armed Revolutionary Forces of Columbia (FARC) and Kurdistan Workers Party (PKK) have both demonstrated an uncanny ability to transform themselves and adapt to changing environmental conditions. Integral to the groups are webbed criminal enterprises, cross-border sanctuaries, and internationally-oriented advocacy networks. Both organizations avoided catastrophic breakdowns through a combination of organic survival mechanisms and precise organizational restructuring. Since 2008, the FARC moved away from a centralized wheel structure model toward a system of multiple decision-making nodes. Guerrilla units now operate in an atomized manner since they are often disconnected from the central leadership. This encouraged a growing number of FARC commanders to focus on narco-profits rather than the organization's ideological goals. Meanwhile, the PKK functions in an octopus-like manner, extending its tentacles into neighboring countries and Europe. However, the process of democratization in Turkey and improved international law enforcement collaboration increased internal as well as external pressure on the PKK to restructure. As a result the PKK is struggling to keep its far-reaching tentacles coordinated. The PKK misjudged its ability to manage political groups which weakened its ideological grip, yet the organization's control over criminal and guerrilla branches continues to be as fierce as ever. The FARC's and the PKK's organizational changes suggest that security agencies in Colombia and Turkey need to adapt their counterterrorism strategies also.

Why have decades of counter-insurgency strategies, economic development plans, and political pressure campaigns failed to incapacitate Colombia's and Turkey's foremost guerrilla organizations?[1] Among the often lamented causes are weak democratic structures along with failures to implement substantive socio-economic reforms, and an overreliance on military power.[2] In the mid-1990s, scholarly attention shifted to another cause, namely the emerging nexus between organized crime

Vera Eccarius-Kelly is an associate professor of political science at Siena College in Loudonville, New York. She earned her PhD from the Fletcher School of Law and Diplomacy at Tufts University (2002). Her areas of interest are comparative politics, security studies, and revolutionary movements in Latin America and the Middle East. She is the author of *Militant Kurds: A Dual Strategy for Freedom* (Praeger, 2011).

The author would like to thank the anonymous reviewers for valuable feedback.

cartels and guerrilla groups. The ability of insurgents to benefit from an unprecedented boon of resources through their participation in the illicit drug trade offered a plausible explanation for the resilience of particular guerrilla groups.[3]

With the rise of narco-terrorism it would also make sense to expect guerrilla organizations to transform and mutate their structures to circumvent intensifying counter-insurgency and anti-crime efforts. Yet few scholars theorize about internal reorganizational processes or structural changes within such guerrilla organizations.[4] This article focuses on conceptualizing the consequences of structural mutations[5] within two distinctive guerrilla groups that have become more assertive, adaptable, and pluralistic in the past 8 years. By critically analyzing and revising established models depicting typical guerrilla structures and their criminal networks, it is possible to devise more effective policy responses to that nexus, and ultimately weaken it.

The selection of the FARC and the PKK for a structural analysis may seem unusual, but three criteria contextualize the underlying rationale for the case studies more clearly: (a) both groups operate in partial (or fragile) democratic environments in which the conduct of military forces has been inconsistently constrained; (b) both groups have engaged in classic insurgent strategies that focused on providing an alternative to state structures by temporarily holding sovereignty over territory or populations; and (c) both groups emerged during the Cold War period, benefited from state sponsors until 10 years ago, and framed their ideological motivations as left-wing revolutionary or ethno-nationalist. Among their motivations were changes to the nature of society through the redistribution of resources and demands for increased local autonomy or separation.[6] Today, the FARC and the PKK are considered fully self-funded organizations.

This article suggests that the Colombian FARC and the Turkish PKK avoided catastrophic breakdowns through a combination of organic survival mechanisms and precise interventions.[7] Organic survival mechanisms include the mobilization of alternative resources such as the production and trafficking of illicit drugs. In contrast, interventions involve the deliberate design of multiple specialized and independently thinking control centers, and a network of organizational nodes. In concrete terms, the FARC and the PKK have demonstrated uncanny abilities to transform themselves and adapt to changing environmental conditions. Among the familiar lifelines to the groups are webbed criminal enterprises, cross-border sanctuaries, and internationally-oriented advocacy networks. Equally significant, but frequently overlooked, are surreptitious mechanisms spawned to safeguard the organizations from internal collapse or decapitation.[8] The FARC's and the PKK's structural mutations, although distinctive from each other, have not only sustained the insurgencies, but made the guerrilla groups more elastic and pluralistic by spinning off a range of hybridized subsidiaries.

The FARC and the PKK in a Snapshot

The FARC has operated as an insurgent force since 1964, when initial conflict-related casualties were recorded. Today the FARC is the longest surviving and most entrenched revolutionary group in all of the Americas, once controlling more than a third of the country's territory.[9] In the aftermath of significant leadership losses in the late 2000s, the FARC now predominantly operates in the southern and eastern provinces of Colombia. Its top leadership remained dogmatic and unbending, in particular septuagenarian Manuel Marulanda, who had been disinclined to adjust his perspectives even though the organization experienced a tremendous loss of credibility. In 2008, at the time of Marulanda's death of an apparent heart attack, only about one percent of Colombia's urban populations held positive views of the FARC.[10] The guerrilla group was next headed by its new *máximo líder*, Alfonso Cano, widely perceived as more of an ideologue than a skillful military tactician.[11] In contrast to Marulanda's peasant roots, Cano's background as a formally educated, urban person was rumored to have created a rift with segments of the FARC.[12] Cano was killed in a shoot-out following a bombing raid in early November 2011, when military units targeted his remote encampment in Cauca province (southwestern Colombia).[13]

In 1984, twenty years after the FARC emerged, the PKK publicly initiated its guerrilla operations (although the group was formed in 1978—just shortly before Turkey's *coup d'état* of 1980). Under Abdullah Öcalan's leadership the PKK initially pursued a traditional leftist ideology to increase its regional profile and relevancy. The guerrilla group quickly reshaped its revolutionary principles to appeal to the Kurdish minority by integrating an ethno-national emphasis. In essence, the PKK pledged to liberate the Kurdish minority from Turkish domination by establishing an ethnic homeland called Kurdistan. This ideological change significantly improved the PKK's capacity to recruit young people in rural areas and expanded its logistical support networks into neighboring Iraq and Syria. Both the PKK and the FARC effectively appealed to marginalized populations and relied predominantly on impoverished and disillusioned young recruits to enlarge their rank-and-file.[14] Since Öcalan's capture and imprisonment in 1999, the PKK reorganized itself by adding an emphasis on transnational political campaigns, which have been orchestrated by multiple PKK branches.

The Wheel, the Star, and the Octopus

The FARC's organizational structure is often conceptualized in the shape of a wheel, a hub, or a star. These classic models express three analogous and accurate observations; (a) the FARC's Leninist ideology has long favored a centralized command structure and a hierarchical system based on the concept of democratic centralism; (b) the FARC's intelligence passes through a clearly identified chain of command; and (c) autonomous pursuits by field commanders have been curtailed through slightly overlapping assignments and specialization by region (such as producing or trafficking narcotics, for example). The hub and the star model often imply visual perimeters suggesting that the FARC has been contained domestically, but that impression would be misleading. With the FARC's growing involvement in the illicit drug trade, its operatives have been found in Venezuela, Ecuador, Brazil, Nicaragua, France, and elsewhere. Figure 1 depicts a classic version of a wheel or hub guerrilla structure.

In recent years, innovative descriptors have been added to explicate the FARC's structural changes. The guerrilla group is now perceived as increasingly hybridized, multidimensional, and networked to reflect its emphasis on narcotics trafficking.[15] For instance, a member of the U.S. military portrayed the FARC as having a dual structure that "closely resembles a classic flat wheel structure, but in other instances exhibits more hierarchy in vertical arrangements."[16] In essence, the FARC is still perceived as operating within an established wheel structure, although its spokes that reach the outer perimeter have become more self-directed.

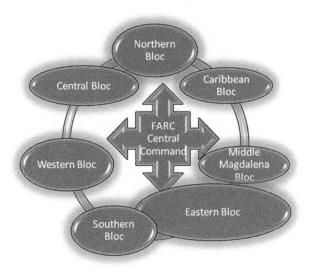

Figure 1. The FARC's wheel structure.

The PKK's emphasis on transnational operations contributed to that group's description as hydra-headed or, more accurately, as an octopus that extends its numerous, probing tentacles into neighboring countries and beyond.[17] Both descriptive models offer several significant and accurate insights; (a) the PKK's ethno-nationalist ideology has long favored a centralized command structure; (b) the PKK gathers intelligence through its tentacles and creates the impression of a roving chain of command; and (c) criminal, political, and guerrilla tentacles frequently vary direction to obscure the organizational structure. Observers of the PKK often use terminology that emphasizes organizational webbing and networking to portray its sinuous modus operandi.[18] Specialized PKK units carry out guerrilla ambushes, networked branches transport drugs to Europe, and affiliated political actors pursue semi-autonomous activities on a transnational and particularly European level.

Time and again it seemed that internal discord and dissension dominated interactions between guerrilla branches of the PKK and its political offspring. But the lack of a clearly articulated and shared vision among more autonomous tentacles could also serve as a protective layer against state intervention and guard against a resurgence of the PKK's guerrilla wing among Kurdish political circles in Europe.[19] Turkish Army LTC Abdulkadir Onay referenced remarks by Frank Urbancic, at that time Deputy to the Coordinator of the U.S. Office of Counter-terrorism, who depicted the PKK in the following manner: "the PKK has an octopus-like structure carrying out criminal activity, including drug and people smuggling [with] fronts that provide cover to the organization's criminal and terror activities."[20] Figure 2 depicts one version of an octopus-shaped guerrilla organization that is deeply entrenched in criminal activities. The tentacles extend and retreat in response to government anti-crime and counter-insurgency measures. This model has a slightly disordered appearance, which is a tactic used to obscure and camouflage the PKK's hierarchical structure of its criminal and guerrilla tentacles. The political branches, however, operate increasingly independently of the command center. In particular the

Figure 2. The PKK's octopus structure with transnational tentacles.

European political networks interact and communicate less frequently with the other PKK tentacles, and thereby challenge the established hierarchical patterns.

Resource Mobilization

The FARC and the PKK have long been categorized as "self-funding organizations," a term that epitomizes a group's capacity to operate without receiving support from powerful state patrons. Europol's *EU Terrorism Situation and Trend Report 2011* described both as mutating guerrilla groups with an increasing inclination to embrace criminality.[21] Fluid interactions between guerrilla groups and criminal networks tend to advance the interests of both types of organizations. At times guerrilla groups and criminal organizations pursue symbiotic relationships to diversify their skill sets.[22] Guerrillas gain advanced knowledge about smuggling operations, they acquire techniques for the transshipment of illicit products, and they learn about money laundering systems and communications technologies. Meanwhile, criminal networks benefit from accessing a wider range of weapons, receive specialized military training, and benefit from the use of safe houses. Occasionally, guerrilla groups and criminal networks agree to cooperate within the same territory, share intelligence information, rely on the same corrupt government officials, and use fraudulent passports and customs documents for joint operations. There are no indications that members of the FARC and the PKK share expertise or intelligence with each other. But plenty of available information outlines the FARC's and the PKK's respective collaborative relationships with regional criminal networks (and their ferocious battles against them when they compete). The U.S. Department of State's *Country Reports on Terrorism 2009* highlighted increasing patterns of self-funding activities by the FARC and the PKK.[23] Annual reports issued by NCIS (British National Criminal Intelligence Service), and the DEA (U.S. Drug Enforcement Administration) use similar language to characterize criminal activities pursued by the FARC and the PKK. Increasingly, both guerrilla groups are also classified as networked "full-service" organizations because their criminality has graduated from taxing and extortion schemes to managing aspects of production and international sales of illicit drugs.

During the 1960s and 1970s, the FARC collected so-called revolutionary taxes from landowners and peasants to raise money for supplies, food, and of course weapons. By the 1980s, FARC units started to profit from the illicit drug trade predominantly by imposing taxes or *gramaje* on coca farmers and emerging narco-traffickers. Guerrilla units charged both local peasants and traffickers between 10 and 15 percent of the value of each shipment, earned substantial amounts of money from extortion schemes that targeted oil companies and multinational corporations, and benefited from its kidnap-for-ransom operations.[24] During the 1990s, FARC units intensified demands on drug traffickers by expecting payments in exchange for the use of land for cultivation, the construction of labs as well as landing strips in the jungle, and imposed standardized shipping charges. The FARC imposed its authority by enforcing rules and behaving like a shadow government in parts of Colombia.[25]

While difficult to confirm, estimates suggest that the FARC earned hundreds of millions of U.S. dollars annually (the street value of cocaine is significantly higher, of course).[26] In 2009, the U.S. Government Accountability Office (GAO) suggested that the FARC benefited from about 60 percent of all of the processed cocaine that entered the U.S. market. In August 2010, the FBI's New York Field Office announced the conviction of an extradited FARC leader who also operated as a major cocaine production manager. In its press release, the FBI asserted that FARC "is responsible for the production of more than half the world's supply of cocaine and nearly two-thirds of the cocaine imported into the United States, and is the world's leading cocaine manufacturer."[27] As a "full-service" guerrilla organization, the FARC is involved in all stages of production, processing, and trafficking of illicit drugs. Obviously, Colombia's domestic security situation has been threatened by various narco-trafficking, paramilitary, and guerrilla organizations, and not exclusively by the FARC.[28] According to the U.S. Department of State, Colombia's defense expenditures more than tripled from $2.6 billion in 2001 to over $9 billion in 2009 and continued to rise to more than $11 billion in 2010 (inching close to four percent of Colombia's GDP).[29]

Already in 1997 the U.S. government labeled both the FARC and the PKK as Foreign Terrorist Organizations, yet the groups were not simultaneously designated under the Foreign Narcotics Kingpin Act. The FARC was added to the list of Narcotics Kingpins in 2003, while the PKK received its designation much later in 2008. The underlying reasons for the disparity in timing hinted at a range of political concerns expressed in European capitals and in the U.S.[30] While ethnic Kurdish grievances gained traction in Europe for a variety of reasons, the U.S. government expressed an interest in stabilizing Iraq.[31] U.S. military commanders focused on collaborating with the emerging KRG (Kurdistan Regional Government) in the north of Iraq, pushing concerns related to the PKK aside for the time being.[32] Iraqi-Kurdish political figures and Kurdish *peshmerga* forces maintained webbed relationships with PKK encampments in the Qandil Mountains of Iraq, which complicated efforts to designate the PKK under the Kingpin Act. Once a modicum of stability and security existed throughout all provinces of Iraq, and after the Turkish government improved its relationship with the KRG, the PKK was added to the list in 2008.

Since then, Turkey's defense expenditures have risen from about $12 billion in 2008 to $15.6 billion in 2010 (or 2.7 percent of its GDP).[33] The country's newest national security assessments reflect concerns beyond the threats posed by the PKK. Pockets of instability in Northern Iraq in addition to the growing Syrian volatility related to that regime's brutal repression of popular protests have triggered broader security concerns.[34] A variety of networked criminal gangs are likely to benefit in the long run from the regional chaos.[35] Similarly, the PKK may be poised to take advantage of weakening state structures in Syria by pursuing webbed relationships with Arab and Kurdish refugee communities, just as it did with Kurdish refugees after the establishment of the Northern Iraqi Makhmour encampment in the late 90s.[36] Today, some of the PKK's most ideologically committed activists operate out of Makhmour camp, a development that has convinced Turkish security experts that "a growing Syrian refugee crisis could create unpredictable challenges for Turkey years down the road."[37]

As a self-funded organization, the PKK strategically pursues emerging opportunities for resource mobilization. Estimates suggest that the PKK can rely on up to $100 million annually in terms of its total resource collection (these numbers do not reflect the street value of opiate derivatives).[38] According to an analysis released by *Jane's Intelligence Review* in March 2008, General Ergin Saygun, Turkey's Deputy Chief of the General Staff, stated that "the PKK gathers some USD 615-770 million annually, whereas a 2007 NATO Terrorist Threat Intelligence Unit report puts the number at a more modest, and perhaps more credible, USD50-100 million annually."[39] Members of the Turkish high command may be motivated to submit higher estimates for resources gathered by the PKK since they have a vested interest in accessing significant resources to fund Turkey's counter-insurgency campaigns.

Despite such disagreements, several details are well-known about the PKK. The organization is involved in both illicit and legitimate fundraising operations, which are predominantly set up among diaspora networks. Operatives in these networks assist the PKK by intermingling money laundering and smuggling ventures, drug trafficking, and extortion schemes with running legitimate cultural centers, döner kebab restaurants, and pizza shops.[40] While the PKK does not manage large multinational business ventures in Europe, it exercises significant influence through cultural festivities, online magazines, and ROJ-TV, a media outlet with a fundraising arm.[41] Estimates suggest that the PKK collects about a third of its annual budget through imposing taxes on business earnings as well as on salaried positions (alternatively, these "solidarity taxes" can be called extortion payments). Of course, the organization claims that the contributions are voluntary donations from diaspora communities, but some are clearly not. Smaller amounts are also collected by the PKK through ticket sales to cultural events, the peddling of newspapers and journals, and other propaganda materials. Pooled earnings are used for the procurement of weapons and ammunition and to cover a multitude of organizational expenses related to propaganda activities.

The PKK benefits greatly from the drug trade according to KOM, Turkey's Department of Anti-Smuggling and Organized Crime, which publishes regular reports indicating the PKK's involvement in all phases of smuggling, production, and sales.[42] Already in 1998, Germany's former federal state prosecutor Kay Nehm argued that the PKK behaved like a criminal rather than a terrorist (or guerrilla) organization.[43] Yet, as several scholars have pointed out, the PKK does not appear to be in the same "narco-league" as the FARC. Both van Bruinessen and Robins have long suggested that the PKK's classification as the foremost organization that manages and controls the drug trade into Europe is a distortion, an "oversimplification," and even fails to be borne out by the evidentiary documentation.[44]

Van Bruinessen asserted that drug profits are widely shared among regional criminal networks, various police and military forces, political actors, and of course, the PKK. In effect, he proposed that an analysis of the nexus between the state's security apparatus and various criminal enterprises would provide a more convincing body of evidence than unsubstantiated assertions suggesting that the PKK controlled the drug market. Eight years later, Robins maintained that an examination of the PKK's transnational character would help to contextualize complex cross-border connections between various players involved in the illicit drug trade in Turkey.[45] Since one of the main supply routes for opiates into Europe passes through Iran and Syria as well as other transit countries before it even reaches Turkey, it is more than likely that many groups along the way take *rüşvet* (bribe in Turkish), or, to use a more descriptive Latin American colloquialism, a *mordida* (to take a "bite" out of profits). Are security analysts and law enforcement agencies providing ambiguous information about the PKK? Or are both the FARC and the PKK increasingly transforming themselves into hybrid enterprises that rely on terror and criminal tactics for operational purposes?[46] The answer, not surprisingly, is as complex and multifaceted as the structural mutations devised by guerrilla organizations.

Revisiting the Transformation Spectrum

A decade ago, intelligence analyst Chris Dishman advanced a persuasive theory that situated terrorist and guerrilla groups on a transformational spectrum that ranged from ideologically committed to criminally motivated. He proposed that guerrilla groups increasingly pursued alternative resource opportunities once regional state sponsorships faded away. Yet, Dishman also cautioned, that cooperation between guerrilla groups and transnational criminal enterprises appeared to be a sporadic phenomena or represented a temporary strategic partnership rather than a permanent convergence of interests for most terrorist groups.[47]

Despite improved international anti-terror cooperation and information sharing, it is still extremely difficult to pinpoint where on such a spectrum from political violence to criminality the FARC and the PKK should be located today. In part, the lack of certainty is a reflection of the secretive nature of guerrilla groups and their affiliated networks, which often effectively obfuscate their operations. It is also a result of the proliferation of communications technologies that have become widely available to such groups. Evaluating conviction records of FARC and PKK affiliated drug dealers provides some insights, but also highlights problems. Police organizations from various countries share only selected information with each other and often work with dissimilar standards for convictions. It is particularly cumbersome to prove a linkage to the PKK without irrefutable evidence as many countries publish records on Turkish citizens caught up in crimes, but do not disseminate separate data on ethnic Kurds (of Turkish or European citizenship).[48] Similarly, successful interdiction efforts and the monitoring of seizure amounts over time provide a limited perspective. Despite the increased availability of international statistics, it is a herculean task to attempt to identify whether the FARC and the PKK are morphing into criminal enterprises or if they are predominantly ideologically motivated yet access as many resources as possible to continue their operations in pursuit of political causes.[49]

While the FARC and the PKK cause significant harm with their involvement in criminal activities, their use of political violence (or terrorism) is equally lethal. Three interrelated and commonly employed forms of political violence create tremendous damage to Colombian and Turkish societies. In general, guerrillas tend to: (a) make use of campaigns of annihilation (a term that describes the killings of political figures, representatives of the state and its bureaucracy, and internal dissidents); (b) employ conspiratorial terror techniques through systematized hostage taking and abductions; and (c) rely on lethal contestations (such as ambushes, road blocks, the use of landmines or IEDs (Improvised Explosive Devices), car bombs, etc.).[50] Since the 1980s, the FARC consistently incorporated all three of these elements into its tactical operations (as did the right-wing paramilitary units focused on eradicating the FARC), while the PKK favored regular campaigns of annihilation as well as an emphasis on lethal contestations. The PKK rejected the practice of habitual abductions of public officials and did not engage in mass hostage taking in civilian areas or the practice of systematic executions of long-term hostages, in contrast to the FARC. The PKK, however, made use of abductions during earlier operational phases and held several German hikers hostage as late as 2008 to make a political point in Europe.[51]

Reliable and up-to-date comparative data for the FARC and the PKK are remarkably difficult to find because their collection requires lasting commitments by government agencies and research foundations. The most comprehensive cross-group data set that includes information about both the FARC and the PKK is available from the Israeli International Institute for Counter-Terrorism (ICT) collected between 1980 and 2002. While the ICT data offers no insights into either group's drug trafficking habits, it provides a window into patterns of criminality by measuring involvement in hijacking, kidnapping, and hostage taking as a means of resource mobilization. In Gupta's work on the linkages between terrorism and organized crime, he evaluated ICT data related to ten different groups.[52] Table 1 relies on Gupta's display of the ICT data, but limits it to selected information that serves this comparative case study of the FARC and the PKK. The data provide an effective starting point for an analysis of where on the transformation spectrum, ranging from ideological commitment to criminal entrepreneurial activity, the selected guerrilla groups were located by 2002—at about the same time that Dishman advanced his transformation theory.

A typology of four separate categories is used in this article to measure similarities and differences between the two guerrilla groups.[53] Category I includes the use of suicide bombings, shootings, and hand grenades, which require the highest levels of ideological commitment by guerrillas. Individual group members must demonstrate a willingness to either sacrifice themselves for the cause or accept a high likelihood of suffering dreadful injuries. Based on the Gupta data displayed above, 31 percent of the PKK's activities fit that description, while the FARC's percentages are negligible at 2.6 percent. Between 1980 and 2002, the PKK was significantly more ideologically oriented than the FARC.

Table 1. ICT data, 1980–2002

	Percent of total activities: FARC	Percent of total activities: PKK
Category 1: Level of ideological commitment		
Suicide bombings	0	13.8
Shootings	2.6	13.8
Hand grenades	0	3.4
	Sub-total: 2.6%	Sub-total: 31.0%
Category 2: Specialized technical skills		
Bombings	7.9	27.6
Car bombs	5.3	0
Mortar attacks	5.3	0
Rocket attacks	2.6	0
	Sub-total: 21.1%	Sub-total: 27.6%
Category 3: Involvement in criminal activities		
Hijacking	2.6	3.4
Hostage taking	7.9	0
Kidnapping	65.8	20.7
	Sub-total: 76.3%	Sub-total: 24.0%
Category 4: Popular mobilization		
Incendiary devices	0	10.3
Vandalism	0	3.4
Arson	0	3.4
	Sub-total: 0	Sub-total: 17.1%

Category II examines the groups' reliance on bombings, car bombings, and mortar and rocket attacks. The use of such tactics indicates that guerrillas have received specialized training and expert skills through collaborative relationships with other groups. In this category, it is noticeable that both the FARC and the PKK have been able to acquire such training. The FARC obtained its wide range of specialized skills from contacts with the IRA and ETA, for example.[54] The PKK, which exclusively relied on the use of bombings according to the available information, obtained its professional knowledge through Middle Eastern connections in the Bekaa Valley in Lebanon (at that time under Syrian control).[55]

Category III displays the guerrillas' involvement in criminal activities, although it offers no information on resource mobilization through in-house capabilities related to the production and trafficking of illicit drugs. Despite this caveat, it is significant to notice that between 1980 and 2002 the FARC engaged in hijacking, hostage taking, and kidnapping some 76 percent of the time, while the PKK attained a notably lower 24 percent in the third category. Again, this result indicates that the PKK was more ideologically oriented than the FARC between 1980 and 2002. The FARC appears to be very focused on fundraising through criminal activity, even without considering data beyond its involvement with extortion and kidnapping operations.

Category IV offers one more observation that plays a particularly significant role for the PKK, namely its ability to motivate affiliated or networked sub-groups that are willing to engage in unskilled and often amateurish violence. This category includes the use of incendiary devices (such as Molotov cocktails, etc.), arson, rock-throwing, and various forms of vandalism (i.e., property damage, etc.) Part of the reason for the PKK's extensive use of this fourth category relates to its nature as an ethno-nationalist group that inspires violent protests among supporters in the region as well as in the diaspora. Based on the data below, the FARC has been unable to rely on such networks either domestically or abroad. This difference hints at one of the most significant structural differences between the FARC and the PKK; the Colombian guerrilla organization has not created a reliable political network of support and appears to rely predominantly on its militant and criminal hubs.

Socio-Political Causes for Conversions

The ICT data indicates that the Colombian guerrilla group is located on the right of Dishman's transformation spectrum (i.e., at an acute level of criminality).[56] This is also confirmed by observations that the FARC appears to be significantly less ideologically committed than the PKK. It seems logical then to place the PKK somewhere in the mid-section of Dishman's transformation spectrum since this particular guerrilla group operates in similar ways to many other organizations that blur the lines between terrorism and organized crime.[57] So far, most of the evidence provided by government officials and various police organizations suggests that the FARC is increasingly aggressive in its criminal conduct. Information about the PKK gives the impression that the Kurdish guerrilla group is more interested in advancing symbiotic relationships with various criminal operations to advance its ideological aims. An analysis of three additional socio-political factors provides further insights into why the PKK may be pursuing a divergent path from the FARC. Comparisons of the following factors advance this discussion: (a) Location and Opportunity, (b) Cultural Context, and (c) Democratization and Transnational Politics.

Location and Opportunity

The FARC pursued criminal opportunities for the purpose of resource mobilization early on. Its initial involvement in extortion schemes and kidnapping on a mass scale soon included the trade of illicit drugs for much higher rewards (despite growing anti-drug campaigns by government forces and competition from paramilitary groups). In recent years, the FARC transitioned from involvement with the transshipment of cocaine and its derivatives to managing production hubs.[58] But in addition to becoming a dominant player in the cocaine trade, the FARC also extorts money through hostage taking and widespread destruction of oil pipelines. Multinational corporations, including those involved in oil extraction and gold and silver mining, as well as in fruit and palm oil plantations, often pay *vacuna* or "vaccination fees" that protect their employees and facilities.[59] The FARC will likely continue to pursue standard extortion schemes in addition to strengthening its involvement in the cocaine trade.

Until the late 1990s the FARC's disciplined, rural, and communal orientation advanced its strategic position. Filling a power vacuum, the FARC marketed itself by providing protection against abusive rural elites and offered sorely missing social services such as basic health care and education to agrarian communities. In 1998

Colombian President Pastrana attempted to negotiate with the FARC to end the bloodshed. He granted the guerrillas a vast "demilitarized zone" (an area of 42,000-square-miles free of military encampments) in the Meta and Caquetá departments (in central and southern Colombia), which traditionally had been jungle strongholds for the guerrillas.[60] However, the Pastrana administration failed to achieve a negotiated resolution, and instead the situation worsened when guerrillas used the zone to prepare for large scale ambushes against state forces and staged kidnapping operations from there. In 2002, the Colombian army reentered the demilitarized zone to directly confront the FARC guerrillas.

Massive U.S. support for Colombian anti-narcotics operations has reduced the production of coca in the south-central provinces of the country, yet cultivation migrated to the Pacific regions of Colombia and across the border into Peru—a process that often is referred to as the balloon effect.[61] It is highly likely that FARC units currently interact with splinter *Sendero Luminoso* (Shining Path) guerrillas in Peru. Both share an interest in taking advantage of resource mobilization opportunities, but they may also compete with each other in the near future.[62] Pressure from the Colombian state has forced the FARC to adjust its centralized wheel structure model to allow regional commanders to operate more independently of the control hub. The government should now increasingly focus on a range of anti-crime rather than counterterrorism strategies, and emphasize measures to strengthen the state's legitimacy by reforming the country's legal system.[63]

The PKK has benefited from a distinctive geographical advantage in comparison with the FARC. Turkey borders eight countries and offers ideal transshipment conditions for heroin from Southwest Asia and the Middle East into Europe. Some of its networked representatives in Europe established concentrated heroin distribution centers in addition to managing human smuggling operations. Innovative and deeply entrenched transfer nodes also help to move other illegal products through Europe, adding to the challenges experienced by law enforcement agencies. The PKK's networked criminal branches suggest a centralized and hierarchical modus operandi, but the widespread use of communication technologies—including texting, social networking sites, and full-feature smart phones—simultaneously disperses control. Criminal branches of the PKK have endorsed the use of multiple control nodes which creates new challenges for agencies that aim to interrupt the high-speed flow of information.

The PKK's early embrace of transnational operations pushed its leaders to develop a more sophisticated grasp of emerging regional opportunities and a clearer understanding of European political dynamics. European PKK branches learned to obscure their financing operations by adding legal businesses and spawning political networks (YEK-KOM, for example). The PKK also benefited from aggressive marketing campaigns through ethno-portals and satellite TV outlets such as Med-TV, later called Medya-TV, and more recently broadcasting as Roj-TV.[64] In sum, the PKK as an organization gained significant international experience, used its emerging opportunities as a springboard to integrate modern technological capabilities, and set up symbiotic relationships with regional criminal networks. Over time these innovations transformed the PKK's organizational configuration. The "head" of the octopus structure manages criminal and guerrilla tentacles, but the political branches behave in an increasingly divergent manner, and in particular those ensconced in Europe. This development suggests that the Turkish government should emphasize varied and complex measures to address the PKK, end the nationalist framing of the so-called Kurdish question, and abandon the notion that multiculturalism represents an existential threat to the integrity of modern Turkey.

Cultural Context

While guerrilla groups earn staggering profits from their involvement with the production, distribution, and sale of illicit drugs, they also pay "costs" in terms of their cultural resonance and political legitimacy. While the FARC worries less about cultural resonance and political legitimacy, the PKK demonstrates concern about such factors because of its complex transnational character. Within the PKK's regional context, both in a cultural and in a religious sense, the consumption of illicit drugs is customarily rejected (although opium has been consumed in the region for centuries along with stimulants such as coffee, tea, and tobacco). Kurdish communities, and religiously conservative Kurds in particular, are incensed by broad generalizations that describe the entire ethnic group as involved in the drug trade—an idea occasionally advanced by nationalist fringe groups in Turkey.[65]

Patterns of smuggling, however, are not necessarily perceived as criminal activity by everyone in the border regions spanning Turkey, Iraq, Iran, Syria, Bulgaria, Azerbaijan, etc. It has been common practice in Turkey's southeastern provinces and across the border to engage in a wide range of smuggling activities to supplement family earnings or to make a living.[66] Segments of the population engage in smuggling as a profession, circumvent abusive government controls, or support the Kurdish insurgency. Since criminal and military branches of the PKK operate similarly to a shadow government in some provinces, the organization has gained an enhanced reputation as a powerful regional actor. The PKK generally denies its involvement in the production and transport of drugs, but its operatives have been convicted of involvement in the transshipment of heroin derivatives through PKK dominated regions into Europe.[67] From the perspective of law enforcement officials, the PKK engages in hideous criminal enterprises and sanitizes its activities by denying that it functions like a drug cartel.[68] In the diaspora, the PKK tends to be significantly more defensive about its reputation as a drug dealing organization. Kurdish nationalist media outlets carefully monitor and respond to accusations that portray the organization or its political leaders as deeply entrenched in the drug trade.[69] With planned regularity, bloggers dispute the PKK's involvement in the dissemination of drugs and instead suggest that Turkish intelligence operatives are involved in a conspiracy against Kurds.[70] Interestingly, Turkish political circles have vacillated between denying Turkey's role as a major heroin transshipment country and blaming the Kurdish insurgency for the rise of the drug trade.[71] Some members of the Turkish ruling party, the socially conservative and religious AKP (Justice and Development Party), appear to believe that "Islam provides an effective barrier against the erosion of society," and that this could organically weaken the narcotics trade and the consumption of drugs.[72] However, recent wikileaks disclosures related to Iran, Pakistan, and Afghanistan clearly demonstrate that the transshipment of heroin derivatives and its consumption is not curtailed in any way by religious values in Muslim countries.[73] If such perceptions accurately reflect the thinking in segments of the Turkish political structure, it could undermine international coalitions that aim to disrupt drug shipments through Turkey.

In Colombia the cultural context in relation to drugs is different, particularly in regards to the production and use of coca leaves, although the chemical processing of such leaves to produce cocaine is clearly illegal. Indigenous communities along the Colombian-Ecuadorian and Colombian-Peruvian border regions traditionally chew coca and produce coca drinks, and cultivation of coca plants for personal consumption is permitted in *resguardos* (indigenous reservations). Drug cartels have taken advantage of these cultural practices. Awa indigenous Colombians in the province of Nariño (on the border to Ecuador) have long been repressed by FARC and ELN guerrilla units as well as by the Rastrojos, a virulent drug gang with trafficking connections to Central America. Frequently, Awa members are threatened and murdered by roving bands of militants. Guerrillas, paramilitary groups, and members of drug gangs move through indigenous reservations to harvest coca and extort local farming communities. In addition, farmers are plagued by anti-personnel mines used by competing factions against each other and the Colombian military.[74] The FARC has been so discredited in vast segments of Colombia that the organization now seems less concerned about its reputation than with shoring up support from remote farming communities in its remaining jungle strongholds.

Democratization and Transnational Politics

Growing and persistent social and political inequalities raise the revolutionary potential in countries, which over time increases the entanglement of guerrilla groups with criminality. In democracies that are not fully consolidated or institutionalized, or at least incomplete in their transitions, resistance tends to manifest in very violent ways.[75] Such violence often includes assassinations of opponents, extortion schemes, abductions, forced taxations, intimidation, and involvement in a variety of criminal enterprises. In Colombia and Turkey, although both countries hold regular elections and increasingly support economic reforms, the political systems are only partially open for some segments of society.[76] This reality in combination with limited political accountability has encouraged violent dissent among various embittered constituencies over time.

The PKK has routinely encouraged regionally based Kurdish riots against Turkish authorities, pursued propaganda activities, and promoted acts of economic sabotage. During the 1990s, the PKK initiated a parallel European strategy that was carried out by Kurdish political refugees and militants who settled in Europe (predominantly in Germany, Belgium, and the Netherlands, but also in France, Scandinavia, and the UK).[77] There, PKK operatives and sympathizers emphasized collective protest action, extortion schemes, and bombings of commercial Turkish interests abroad.

From 1994 until the capture of PKK leader Öcalan in 1999, the group implemented a more conciliatory political phase in Europe using extensive pressure campaigns spearheaded by radical elements within the Kurdish diaspora. Political activism became an effective long-term strategy for launching a transnational Kurdish agenda. Instead of openly seeking an independent homeland, Kurdish activists started to push for the recognition of minority status for Kurds in Turkey. European government officials, while considering Turkey for membership in the European Union, demonstrated limited support for Kurds to be recognized as a separate ethnic group in Turkey.[78] EU parliamentary committees began to investigate human rights violations in the Southeastern provinces of Turkey, and sent fact-finding missions to speak with representatives of Kurdish civil society. Since 2003, PKK elements in Europe have pursued a complex political strategy that utilizes protest and civil disobedience campaigns but also employs political lobby-ing.[79] PKK operatives and diaspora Kurdish political activists frequently pursue political goals in a less rigid and coordinated manner, especially since many sym-pathizers simultaneously belong to numerous overlapping networks of Kurdish activists. The PKK has lost full control over the political process as various net-works linked to the original political tentacles are participating in legitimate civil society activities. Occasionally, the PKK attempts to re-unite the diaspora through "Save Öcalan" campaigns, but such efforts usually speak to more radicalized seg-ments of the diaspora.[80] However, as soon as the Turkish government engages in a targeted effort to repress Kurdish political activism, the PKK improves its position.

It also is to be expected that European-born Kurds will increasingly stage pro-tests in an autonomous fashion in order to loosen the grip of the PKK. The result will be diminished political controls by the PKK and a more pluralistic political agenda among ethnic Kurds. The goals of European Kurdish political activists clearly has shifted away from vigilante action toward increasing the pressure on European governments to insist that Turkey grant full minority status to Kurds prior to Turkey's full inclusion in the EU.

Meanwhile in Colombia, the FARC can neither count on a reliable propaganda machine nor on an extensive network of sympathizers in neighboring countries. Some of the FARC's blocs traditionally relied on protective havens across the bor-ders in Ecuador and Venezuela. But since Colombia sent missiles into Ecuadorian territory in 2008 to eradicate a large FARC encampment, the level of uncertainty only increased for the guerrillas. After Colombian officials apologized for the incur-sion into Ecuadorian territory, the two governments have come to specific anti-terrorism agreements, which made it hazardous for FARC leaders to meet up in Quito, the capital of Ecuador. In June 2011, Quito police arrested two FARC members, including the leader of the 48th front, and quickly extradited them to Colombia. Venezuela also extradited a captured FARC member to Colombia in 2011, but the relationship between Chavez' Venezuela and consecutive Colombian governments has been troubled. Venezuela provided safe havens for the guerrillas, the FARC acquired arms in Venezuela, and some FARC members may have been hired as professional hit men by Venezuelan forces.[81] In addition, a Spanish court issued arrest warrants for ETA members (Basque separatists) who lived in Venezuela and trained FARC members in their encampments in Venezuela.[82]

The FARC failed to establish a parallel political network like the PKK and now faces growing military pressure at the center and the south of the country. The Pacific provinces are considered awash in cocaine money, especially in Nariño, which borders on Ecuador. It appears that the FARC's wheel structure is fragment-ing into autonomously operating fronts for two simple reasons: (a) communication has been disrupted between the center and the outlying areas, and (b) specialized fronts involved in the drug trade—with access to greater resources and a lack of ideological commitment—operate more effectively than units that focus on carrying out ambushes.[83] As a result of growing regional pressure and weak transnational network connections, the FARC is likely to splinter into various regional subunits that increasingly mutate into predatory criminal operations with linkages to Central American and Mexican cartels. Such atomized units use political agendas as a mere veneer, as argued by Makarenko, requiring a significant adjustment in the state's counterterrorism policies to the FARC.[84]

Conceptualizing Mutations

The FARC has moved away from the centralized wheel structure model toward a system of multiple decision-making nodes. Guerrilla units disconnected from central control as their political destinations became unfocused following the losses in 2008 of Marulanda and Raúl Reyes (commander of the southern bloc), Mono Jojoy's killing in 2010 (top military tactician of the FARC), followed by Cano's death in 2011. Political justifications for the use of narcotics revenues shifted to pursuing personal financial gains. Since the FARC's 2010 and 2011 leadership losses, regional bloc commanders have increased their operational flexibility and local commanders initiated atomized operations to pursue personal interests. Colombian newspapers such as *El Tiempo* reported that corruption is on the rise among FARC commanders, weakening the guerrillas' organizational discipline and shared ideological goals.[85] In addition, the increased turnover rates among commanders due to killings, captures, and defections have allowed inexperienced, self-interested, and ideologically disoriented regional commanders to rise.[86] Based on such assessments, the familiar wheel model, even one with an elevated hub, is no longer applicable for the FARC today. Bloc commanders are now increasingly motivated by profits from the narcotics business and operate independently and sometimes in opposition to the central command. What emerges now is a runner or stolon structure[87] that organically produces a horizontal extension of cells by adding additional nodes. This development presents the Colombian state and its neighbors with a particularly daunting challenge. The attrition of ideological FARC leaders has produced an atomized structure with increasingly aggressive and profit-oriented identities. Leaders of narcotics nodes systematically seek out corrupt officials and take advantage of every weakness in the state's bureaucracy, its legal system, and the overbearing security apparatus. While the traditional guerrilla insurgency is coming to an end in Colombia, atomized gangs of cocaine traffickers are exceedingly difficult to eradicate in the jungle zones of a country that continues to grapple with a significant gap in the distribution of income and a persistent urban-rural divide.

The PKK's organizational configuration also has changed but its mutations have not resulted in an atomized structure. The PKK operates like an octopus under intense internal as well as external pressure to keep all of its far-reaching tentacles coordinated. In the mid-1990s the PKK orchestrated the formation of parallel political structures in Turkey and in Europe to galvanize as much political support and momentum as possible. Yet the PKK's satellite leadership failed to imagine the consequences of arousing such support. The PKK octopus expected all of its tentacles to function in full coordination with the criminal and military branches, but instead political entrepreneurs pursued unanticipated autonomy. Today, it increasingly fails to manage ethnic Kurdish political activities, which are producing independent and more participatory structures.[88] Over time, this uncoordinated octopus structure has failed to integrate the evolving political interests among dynamic Kurdish networks abroad. Transnational diaspora communities test boundaries, expand their own networks, and reshape their roles. European-educated Kurds contribute diverse competencies to the ideological struggle, including communications, technological, and legal skills, language abilities, and an organic dislike for centralized, hierarchical, and controlling mechanisms. As a consequence, the criminal and guerrilla branches communicate intensively with each other, forging a symbiotic relationship. The PKK faces a new reality. Instead of being able to count on large numbers of ideologically committed operatives in Europe, significant segments of the ethnic-Kurdish communities only occasionally participate as active supporters and many more express mere passive support. Two important observations need to be considered today: (a) political activities carried out by ethnic Kurds do not automatically represent an endorsement of the PKK, and (b) a generational shift is shaping current ethnonational dynamics, presenting a problem for the central command. Younger political entrepreneurs in the diaspora and in Turkey reject a quasi-colonial relationship with the PKK and increasingly refuse to act like satellite branches. (This observation, however, excludes Kurds who are enticed by profits and recruited into the criminal and guerrilla networks.) Inside Turkey, ethnic Kurdish parties also receive support from a budding civil society that prefers to pursue a political solution to the Kurdish struggle rather than a continuation of the insurgency.

The PKK not only miscalculated its ability to manage political groups it originally spawned, but also underestimated the consequences of Turkey's plodding democratization process. This development has diffused the PKK's reach and its organizational capabilities in the past several years. The PKK's grip on civil society activities has been loosened, but its control over military and criminal operations is rigorously enforced. This evolution presents the Turkish state with an opportunity to recognize the separate PKK tentacles and deal with each of them strategically. Turkey ideally would provide democratic space to Kurdish civil society and ethno-national political parties in order to further disrupt communications between political tentacles and criminal/guerrilla tentacles. Security agencies should focus on dangerous narcotics trafficking networks by disrupting routes and communication patterns in coordination with their European counterparts and move away from a militarized counterinsurgency approach.[89]

Concluding Remarks

For about a decade, experts have called for enhanced global intelligence-gathering and improved processes to share information among various police agencies. But despite many improvements on the international and global levels, not enough has been accomplished yet.[90] As a general rule, security analysts, anti-smuggling and crime units, and law enforcement agencies are disseminating similar and long-established assessments of the PKK or the FARC. By nature of their professions, they tend to be intransigent and deeply suspicious of untested ideas, especially since their work revolves around collecting actionable intelligence to weaken malicious organizations.

Theoretical discussions, modeling, and exchanges between security analysts and academics add significant value to advancing a clearer understanding about why and how guerrilla groups mutate, adapt, and evolve. Conceptual ideas are worth considering, especially since they provide a larger story that contextualizes socio-political developments on the ground. It is important to incorporate perspectives and modes of thinking that help to not only understand the genesis and history of organizations like the FARC and the PKK, but also predict what they are becoming and how they may behave in the future. A combination of theory and practice only adds to an improved security dialogue, which must be as innovative and unconstrained as the metamorphosis of multidimensional guerrilla organizations.

Notes

1. See Audrey Kurth Cronin, *How Terrorism Ends* (Princeton, NJ: Princeton University Press, 2009), and "How al-Qaida Ends; The Decline and Demise of Terrorist Groups," *International Security* 31, no. 1 (Summer 2006): 7–48. In her work, Cronin argues that repression failed in the Turkish case because of inept use of military force, the country's fragile state of democracy, and the hypersensitivity of the secular, nationalist state apparatus regarding ethnic Kurdish dissention. See pp. 128–129 for further details.

2. Audrey Kurth Cronin, "Behind the Curve: Globalization and International Terrorism," *International Security* 27, no. 3 (Winter 2002/3): 30–58. Cronin has long argued that an overreliance on military power is a mistake. In "Behind the Curve" she suggests that states often favor military power rather than complex "long-term, sophisticated analysis" because the results are considered "measurable, obvious, and gratifying." See pp. 55–56. Her analysis certainly encapsulates both the Colombian and the Turkish strategies that have relied extensively on military strategies to counterterrorism, but less so on good governance. Michael Kenney concludes that "a body-count mentality among officials that defined 'success' in terms of outputs—the number of traffickers captured, drugs confiscated, assets frozen, 'kingpins' extradited to the United States—while largely ignoring the inputs that sustained the Colombian trafficking system—the number of leaders replaced, networks reorganized, smuggling routes resurrected, drug fields replanted." See *From Pablo to Osama: Trafficking and Terrorist Networks, Government Bureaucracies, and Competitive Adaptation* (University Park, PA: Pennsylvania State University Press, 2007), 225.

3. Colombia's most prominent and feared guerrilla group is known as the FARC-EP or the Armed Revolutionary Forces of Colombia—People's Army (Fuerzas Armadas Revolucionarias de Colombia—Ejército del Pueblo). Estimates suggest that since the mid-1980s at least 50,000 people have died in Colombia as a consequence of the country's lethal conflict between the armed forces, paramilitary units, and insurgent groups. The PKK or the Kurdistan Workers Party (Partiya Karkerên Kurdistan) has been Turkey's most dreaded guerrilla group. In Turkey some 40,000 combatants, civilians, and members of state forces have perished in the country's struggle with the PKK. Both groups are involved in the illicit drug trade today.

4. A notable exception is the following publication for example: John Arquilla and David Ronfeldt, eds., *Networks and Netwars* (Santa Monica, CA: RAND, 2001).

5. The word mutation implies a change in the genetic makeup of an organism, or in this case, a guerrilla organization. The implied argument is that a structural mutation can have a genetically beneficial effect, cause remarkable damage, or be neutral without having any impact at all.

6. Robert J. Art and Louise Richardson, eds., *Democracy and Counterterrorism: Lessons from the Past* (Washington, DC: United States Institute of the Peace Press, 2007). See the editors' categorization of terrorist groups in the introductory section, pp. 1–23.

7. The PKK originated in Turkey, but operates on a transnational level and recruits heavily among ethnic Kurdish communities in Syria and Northern Iraq (and coordinates its campaigns with the Iranian branch known as PJAK). The PKK also attracts European-born Kurds to its encampments in the Iraqi Qandil Mountains.

8. It is important to note that several generations of FARC leaders have been killed in recent years, and that the PKK's leader Abdullah Öcalan was captured in 1999. But neither the FARC nor the PKK was "decapitated" in the process. The PKK's political tentacles in Europe successfully leveraged Kurdish diasporic influences that re-mobilized the organization and the Iraq war in 2003 created geographic space for the PKK to operate in KRG-controlled territory. The FARC lost multiple leaders but focused on pursuing predatory economic tactics to sustain itself.

9. Another note related to terminology in this article: a clear distinction is drawn between the use of "terrorist" and "guerrilla" to indicate several significant differences in behavior. Guerrilla forces often challenge military units directly and engage in ambushes on barracks, convoys, and outposts, while terrorists rarely pursue such direct confrontational tactics. In addition, guerrilla units attempt to control territory and its populations, while terrorists avoid extensive interactions with local populations. These lines of distinction are becoming increasingly hazy, however, because splinter cells of guerrilla groups operate like terrorists in urban environments such as the so-called Freedom Falcons in Turkey. In the

Colombian context, it is important to note that some groups within the FARC have been trained by ETA explosives experts, which also shows that a blurring of lines has taken place.

10. Of interest might be Marulanda's obituary published in the *New York Times* on May 26, 2008. It is available at http://www.nytimes.com/2008/05/26/world/americas/26iht-26marulanda.13202958.html.

11. A most interesting report from inside a mobile FARC unit in the Valle del Cauca department (in the southwestern region of Colombia) was posted by France 24's reporter Romeo Langlois and is available at http://www.france24.com/en/20101001-reporters-colombia-farc-rebels-guerillas-jungle-death-leader-mono-jojoy-freeing-ingrid-betancourt-army.

12. Cano attended the University of Bogotá in the 1970s, participated in the student protest movement there, and then went underground to join the FARC.

13. Two factions of FARC seem to compete for the leadership position now. One option appears to be the narco-rich Southern bloc commander Joaquin Gomez, while an ideologue known under the nom-de-guerre Timochenko is also under discussion. He apparently operates along the Colombian-Venezuelan border region.

14. For more information on the PKK, see Martin van Bruinessen, "Between Guerrilla War and Political Murder: The Workers' Party of Kurdistan," *Middle East Report* 153 (July–August, 1988): 40–42, 44, 46, 50. Bruinessen suggested that many young people from small towns with limited education joined the PKK. For information about the FARC, see Timothy Wickham-Crowley, *Guerrillas and Revolution in Latin America* (Princeton, NJ: Princeton University Press, 1992). His evidence shows that traditional Latin American revolutionary forces recruited among marginalized and often rural youth.

15. For an insightful study consider Michael Kenney's work, *From Pablo to Osama: Trafficking and Terrorist Networks, Government Bureaucracies, and Competitive Adaptation* (University Park, PA: Pennsylvania State University Press, 2007), 25–47. Kenney examines a variety of organizational cartel structures (wheels, chains, and flat networks) in his chapter on "The Architecture of Drug Trafficking." Also, see the following May 2010 article in the *New York Times* entitled "FARC Have Drug Trafficking Networks in Brazil" at http://colombiareports.com/colombia-news/news/9791-farc-have-drug-trafficking-networks-in-brazil.html.

16. MAJ Jon-Paul N. Maddaloni's monograph is helpful here; *An Analysis of the FARC in Colombia: Breaking the Frame of FM 3-24* (Fort Leavenworth, KS: School of Advanced Military Studies, United States Army Command and General Staff College, 2009), 27, http://www.cgsc.edu/sams/media/Monographs/MaddaloniJ-21MAY09.pdf. (FM 3-24 stands for Field Manual 3-24 and addresses U.S. counterinsurgency operations.)

17. I have referred to the PKK as hydra-headed in multiple publications. For example, see Vera Eccarius-Kelly, "Interpreting the PKK's Signals in Europe," *Perspectives on Terrorism* 2, no. 11 (2008): 10–14.

18. Intelligence analysts increasingly study social networks to examine threats. For an excellent discussion on network analysis, see Marc Sageman, *Understanding Terror Networks* (Philadelphia: University of Pennsylvania Press, 2004). Also consider Scott Helfstein and Dominick Wright, "Success, Lethality, and Cell Structure across the Dimensions of Al Qaeda," *Studies in Conflict and Terrorism* 34 (2011): 367–382.

19. For a more detailed discussion of such tactics, see Vera Eccarius-Kelly, "Reframing the Nationalist Perspective," in *Symbiotic Antagonisms: Competing Nationalisms in Turkey*, eds. Ayse Kadioglu and Fuat Keyman (Salt Lake City: University of Utah Press, 2010), 311–315.

20. The U.S. Embassy in Ankara maintains a website that highlights Urbancic's interview with Osman Sert from CNN Türk, February 12, 2008. In the interview Urbancic suggested that the PKK in Europe operated like an octopus, but he also proposed that the U.S. applied an "Al Capone approach" to weaken the PKK's criminal operations. http://turkey.usembassy.gov/urbancic.html. Also, see http://archive.hurriyetdailynews.com/h.php?news=pkk-criminal-networks-and-fronts-in-europe-2008-03-20.

21. http://www.europol.europa.eu/publications/EU_Terrorism_Situation_and_Trend_Report_TE-SAT/TE-SAT2011.pdf. The PKK's extensive fundraising and smuggling activities appear multiple times in the report as does the FARC's relationship with ETA explosives experts in Venezuela.

22. See Tamara Makarenko, "The Crime-Terror Continuum: Tracing the Interplay between Transnational Organized Crime and Terrorism," *Global Crime* 6, no. 1 (February 2004): 129–145. See in particular 131–132.

23. http://www.state.gov/documents/organization/141114.pdf. Both the PKK and the FARC's international connections are discussed in detail.

24. Russell Crandall, *Driven by Drugs: U.S. Policy Toward Colombia* (New York: Lynne Rienner, 2002), 90.

25. Peter Waldmann proposed that the Colombian state needed to reclaim its legitimacy to more effectively address the FARC's parallel governing structures. See "Colombia and the FARC: Failed Attempts to Stop Violence and Terrorism in a Weak State," *Democracy and Counterterrorism: Lessons from the Past* (see note 6 above), 221–260.

26. Vanda Felbab-Brown, for example, suggested the following estimates for FARC in her work: "drug rents represented about 50 percent of the FARC's income. Extortion of oil companies and other large companies generated an additional 34 percent, kidnapping brought in another 8 percent, and cattle rustling another 6 percent." She suggested that estimates for annual profits ranged from a low of $60 million in the early 90s to a high of $600 million in the late 90s. For further details, see Vanda Felbab-Brown, *Shooting Up: Counterinsurgency and the War on Drugs* (Washington, DC: The Brookings Institution, 2010), 81.

27. See the FBI press release at http://www.fbi.gov/newyork/press-releases/2010/nyfo081710.htm.

28. In particular, note Daniel Pécaut's extensive work in which he analyzes how such groups terrorize society. See *Guerra Contra la Sociedad* (Bogota: Espasa Hoy, 2001).

29. Also, see the Center for International Policy's Colombia Program for further information on the country's defense budget allocations at http://www.cipcol.org/?cat=78.

30. For a Turkish security analysis, see Sedat Laçiner, "The West and Terrorism: PKK as a Privileged Terrorist Organization," *The Journal of Turkish Weekly*, 14 May, 2006, http://www.turkishweekly.net/columnist/2089/the-west-and-terrorism-pkk-as-a-privileged-terrorist-organization.html.

31. I would argue that the EU has become increasingly sensitized to minority concerns, while others have suggested that some EU member states are scheming to keep Turkey from becoming a full member state. Such accusations are frequently uttered by Turkish nationalists. See for example remarks made by General Yaşar Büyükanit, the former chief of the Turkish General Staff, which were discussed in *Eurasia Daily Monitor,* a publication by the Jamestown Foundation, on April 7, 2008. The article is available at http://www.jamestown.org/programs/edm/single/?tx_ttnews%5Btt_news%5D=33527&tx_ttnews%5BbackPid%5D=166&no_cache=1.

32. For a captivating analysis of Turkish, KRG, and U.S. interactions, see Karen Kaya, "The Turkish-American Crisis," *Military Review*, July–August 2011, 69–75. Also see Henri Barkey, "Turkey and the PKK: A Pyrrhic Victory?," in *Democracy and Counterterrorism* (see note 6 above), 343–381.

33. Additional details are available from the Stockholm International Peace Research Institute (SIPRI) at http://www.sipri.org/. Of course it is difficult to contrast Colombia's and Turkey's defense expenditures since Turkey's data is based on NATO's definition of such expenditures, while Colombia's expenditures are more obscured and may exclude certain covert operations.

34. For a helpful assessment of Turkish security concerns related to the border with Syria, the growing refugee crisis, and the role of the PKK, see this article in *Southeast European Times* from June 2011 at http://www.setimes.com/cocoon/setimes/xhtml/en_GB/features/setimes/features/2011/06/22/feature-03.

35. For a general newspaper account that addresses human smuggling in Turkey ($500 million annually), see http://www.todayszaman.com/newsDetail_getNewsById.action?load=detay&link=184738. Also, my discussion in Vera Eccarius-Kelly, *The Militant Kurds: A Dual Strategy for Freedom* (Santa Barbara, CA: Praeger Security International, 2011), 44–46.

36. For a broader analysis of the nexus between refugee camps, humanitarian intervention, the presence of militants, and unintended consequences, see Sarah Kenyon Lischer, *Dangerous Sanctuaries: Refugee Camps, Civil War, and the Dilemmas of Humanitarian Aid* (Ithaca, NY: Cornell University Press, 2005).

37. This comment is based on a private conversation with a security analyst who asked for anonymity.

38. For further information, see Lyubov Mincheva and Ted Robert Gurr's case study entitled "Unholy Alliances III: Communal Militants and Criminal Networks in the Middle

East, with a Case Study of the Kurdistan Workers Party (PKK)," presented at ISA, San Francisco, March 28, 2008, http://www.humansecuritygateway.com/documents/ISA_ unholyalliancesIII.pdf.

39. See Michael Jonsson and Svante Cornell, "Kurds and Pay—Examinining PKK Financing," *Jane's Intelligence Review* (2008), http://www.silkroadstudies.org/new/docs/ publications/2007/0803JIR-PKK.pdf.

40. Some cultural centers and restaurants are influenced or managed by supporters of the PKK abroad, but certainly not all. Various Kurdish interest groups and networks struggle with each other over control of such centers and businesses.

41. Henri Barkey's chapter in *Democracy and Counterterrorism* (see note 32 above), 352. The satellite TV station and its predecessors are described as "important consciousness-raising instruments" by Barkey.

42. For a recent article that discusses the PKK's organized crime operations, see Ahmet Pek and Behsat Ekici, "Narcoterrorism in Turkey: The Financing of PKK-KONGRA GEL from Illicit Drug Business," in *Understanding and Responding to the Terrorism Phenomenon: A Multi-Dimensional Perspective*, eds. Ozgur Nikbay and Suleyman Hancerli (Washington, DC: IOS Press, 2007), 140–152.

43. See Nehm's January 14, 1998 comments reprinted in part in the attached article in the German daily *Die Welt*, http://www.welt.de/print-welt/article597228/Nehm_PKK_keine_ Terrorgruppe.html.

44. Martin van Bruinessen's article discusses this issue in detail. "Transnational Aspects of the Kurdish Question," presented at the Robert Schuman Centre for Advanced Studies at the European University Institute, Florence, Italy, 2000, 19. Also, consider Philip Robins, "Back from the Brink: Turkey's Ambivalent Approaches to the Hard Drugs Issue," *Middle East Journal* 62, no. 4 (Autumn 2008): 629, 637–640.

45. Robins (see note 44 above), 349. Criminal operations overlap with the PKK insurgency, but the questions raised relate to the level of control. The PKK has been a transnational group for decades since its leadership was located in Damascus, its early training camps could be found in Lebanon, and its ambushes on Turkish military and police outposts were organized in Iraq, Syria, and Iran, i.e., from across the border.

46. Tamara Makarenko suggested that a growing number of groups engage in hybrid activities in "The Crime-Terror Continuum" (see note 22 above), 141.

47. Chris Dishman," Terrorism, Crime, and Transformation," *Studies in Conflict and Terrorism* 24 (2001): 43–58. In 2004, Tamara Makarenko observed that the distinctions between politically and criminally motivated violence were increasingly blurred. Organized crime groups used terror tactics to advance their operational purposes, while terrorist groups pursued criminal activities for their objectives. Makarenko argued that both types of groups can converge or even change organizational identities and purposes along her crime-terror continuum. See Makarenko, "The Crime-Terror Continuum" (note 22 above), 129–145.

48. A note of clarification here: Kurdish ethnicity does not automatically indicate membership in the PKK nor affiliation with its criminal branches as occasionally seems to be suggested by analysts. Ethnic Turkish criminal groups also regularly collaborate with PKK branches.

49. Makarenko, as others, suggested that the FARC has evolved into a group that is primarily engaged in criminal activity today. According to her analysis, the FARC utilizes political issues as a mere façade to encourage the Colombian government to focus on military measures instead of anti-crime operations. Makarenko, "The Crime-Terror Continuum" (see note 22 above), 136–137.

50. Charles Tilly, *The Politics of Collective Violence* (Cambridge, UK: Cambridge University Press, 2003), 227–228.

51. See Vera Eccarius-Kelly, "Interpreting the PKK's Signals in Europe," *Perspectives on Terrorism* 2, no. 11 (2008): 10–14.

52. Dipak K. Gupta, *Understanding Terrorism and Political Violence* (New York: Routledge, 2008), 78–81.

53. I made some modest changes to Gupta's typology, but in essence relied on his thoughtfully developed work.

54. For details, see the April 24, 2002 "Summary of Investigation of IRA Links to FARC Narco-Terrorists in Colombia" by the Committee on International Relations, U.S. House of Representatives. Also, Russell Crandall (see note 24 above), *Driven by Drugs*, 91.

55. See for example a report filed about German citizens who joined the PKK and trained in Bekaa by Klaus Brinkbäumer and Georg Mascolo, "Die Verlorene Brigade," *Spiegel* 7, February 14, 2000, 58–64.

56. For a comparative, Makarenko's scale of the crime-terror continuum shows that the FARC moved to the area of convergence. Makarenko, "The Crime-Terror Continuum" (see note 22 above), 131.

57. For a discussion on this topic, see Mitchel P. Roth and Murat Sever, "The Kurdish Workers Party (PKK) as Criminal Syndicate: Funding Terrorism through Organized Crime, A Case Study," *Studies in Conflict and Terrorism* 30 (2007): 912–915.

58. For a harrowing insight into the Latin American drug trade, see Peter Chalk's 2011 report published by the RAND Corporation's Project Air Force. A summary of the report is available online at http://www.rand.org/content/dam/rand/pubs/monographs/2011/RAND_MG1076.sum.pdf.

59. Chiquita Brands International, for example, was caught paying extortion fees to both FARC guerrillas and AUC paramilitary units to keep its employees safe. See http://news.bbc.co.uk/2/hi/americas/6452455.stm. Also, see http://www.miamiherald.com/2011/02/07/2055591/tarnished-gold.html.

60. In Colombia the vast area controlled by the FARC was called *zona de despeje* or cleared zone.

61. The United Nations Office on Drugs and Crime indicated in its World Drug Report 2010 that coca cultivation decreased in Colombia in 2009, but increased in Peru and Bolivia. For specific details, see the following report http://www.unodc.org/documents/wdr/WDR_2010/World_Drug_Report_2010_lo-res.pdf. Also, consider this *New York Times* article at http://www.nytimes.com/2010/06/14/world/americas/14peru.html.

62. For studies on the Shining Path, see Cynthia McClintock, *Revolutionary Movements in Latin America: El Salvador's FMLN and Peru's Shining Path* (Washington, DC: USIP Press, 1998) and David Scott Palmer, "The Revolutionary Terrorism of Peru's Shining Path" in *Terrorism in Context*, ed. Martha Crenshaw (University Park, PA: Pennsylvania University Press, 1995), 249–308.

63. See Liam Whittington's December 2011 report "A Legal Wasteland – Lawyers, Murder, Democracy, and Justice in Colombia," prepared by the Council on Hemispheric Affairs (COHA) and available at http://www.coha.org/a-legal-wasteland-%e2%80%93-lawyers-murder-democracy-and-justice-in-colombia/.

64. Insightful articles on TV stations started by members of the Kurdish diaspora can be found from the following authors: Amir Hassanpour, "Satellite Footprints as National Borders: MED-TV and the Extraterritoriality of State Sovereignty," *Journal of Muslim Minority Affairs* 18, no. 1 (1998): 53–72, and David Romano, "Modern Communications Technology in Ethnic Nationalist Hands: The Case of the Kurds," *Canadian Journal of Political Science / Revue Canadienne de Science Politique* 35, no. 1 (March/Mars 2002): 127–149.

65. Recent clashes between nationalist Turkish factions and groups of Kurds who feel misrepresented and attacked are explored in an article titled "Tension simmers in northwestern Turkey in wake of BDP, HEPAR fight," in *Hürriyet Daily News,* June 8, 2011, http://www.hurriyetdailynews.com/n.php?n=tension-between-young-groups-become-political-fight-2011-06-08.

66. See Delphine Strauss, "Smuggling Runs Deep in Blood of Eastern Turkey," *Financial Times* Online, October 7, 2010, http://www.ft.com/cms/s/0/5e2920b0-d230-11df-8fbe-00144feabdc0,s01 = 1.html#axzz1RMg5KB4Z. "Eighteen of my family are in jail," said a man from Van's Baskale district, who thought the government was "punishing this region" for voting for pro-Kurdish politicians by clamping down. But with migrants willing to pay $250 for help across the border, and a single kilo of heroin fetching $5,000 profit, the appeal of smuggling remains. "In one day you can be a billionaire – or you can lose everything," he said.

67. This is a blog post by writer van Wilgenburg based on a *Sabah* article related to the PKK's financial structure in Europe: http://vvanwilgenburg.blogspot.com/2009/06/sabah-germany-plays-central-role-in-pkk.html. Also, see the following article in *Today's Zaman* http://www.todayszaman.com/news-248630-outlawed-pkks-organizational-structure-in-france-exposed.html. Also, see Pek and Ekici, "Narcoterrorism in Turkey" (note 42 above).

68. Emrullah Uslu and Onder Aytac, "War of Paradigms: the PKK, Europe, and Turkey," in *Understanding and Responding to the Terrorism Phenomenon* (see note 42 above), 124–139.

69. See for example the reposting of an EUTCC (EU-Turkey Civic Commission, a European non-profit organization) statement on *Rojhelat News* at http://www.rojhelat.info/english/world/1122-outrageous-unproven-accusations-against-five-kurdish-politicians. The article's first paragraph reads, "Outrageous and unproven accusations and threats of persecution have been directed against five Kurdish politicians by the United States Department of the Treasury Office of Foreign Assets Control (OFAC). The five Kurdish politicians are accused of being actively involved in drug trafficking being financed by the Kurdistan Workers Party (PKK)."

70. This remark is based on my interactions with nationalist Kurds in Germany, who take offense at suggestions that the PKK benefits from the drug trade in Europe.

71. Robins, "Back from the Brink" (see note 44 above), 636, 649–650.

72. Ibid., 649.

73. A German newspaper, *Die Welt*, published an article that exposed Iran's Revolutionary Guards as one of the most influential heroin traders in the region on January 21, 2011. See the article by Boris Kálnoky entitled "Iran ist einer der weltweit größten Heroinhändler." Clearly, Islam has not organically protected Muslim societies from involvement with the drug trade.

74. For a larger indigenous perspective, see Judith Walcott, "Nowhere Left to Run: An Indigenous Ecuadoran Perspective on Plan Colombia (An Anonymous Narrative)," *Cultural Survival* 26, no. 4, Winter 2002, http://www.culturalsurvival.org/publications/cultural-survival-quarterly/colombia/nowhere-left-run-indigenous-ecuadoran-perspective-.

75. I suggest that both in Colombia and in Turkey gaps exist between elite politics and civil society, although those gaps are increasingly closing (in my estimation the process is moving more quickly in Turkey). A continued lack of accountability of the political system to specific constituencies negatively affects both countries. In particular, see Guillermo O'Donnell, "Illusions about Consolidation," *Journal of Democracy* 7, no. 2 (April 1996): 34–51.

76. Eduardo Posada-Carbó wrote a superb analysis of recent electoral developments in Colombia, including on the referendum and the role of the constitutional court. He called the referendum a sign of "the relative vitality of Colombia's key liberal-democratic institutions, even if most scholarly writing on the country undervalues, despises, or ignores them." His article, "Colombia after Uribe," was published in the *Journal of Democracy* 22, no. 1 (2011): 137–151. The above quote is taken from page 150.

77. For a detailed discussion of the Europeanization strategy of the PKK, see Vera Eccarius-Kelly, *The Militant Kurds: A Dual Strategy for Freedom* (Santa Barbara, CA: Praeger Security International, 2010).

78. A fascinating case study is available from Marlies Casier, "Neglected Middle Men? Gatekeepers in Homeland Politics, Case: Flemish Nationalists' Receptivity to the Plight of Turkey's Kurds," *Social Identities* 17, no. 4 (2011): 501–521.

79. See Uslu and Aytac, "War of Paradigms" (note 68 above), 136. The authors suggest that European countries have been reluctant to address the PKK issue because of Kurdish linkages to church-based groups and NGOs.

80. Audrey Kurth Cronin, *How Terrorism Ends* (Princeton, NJ: Princeton University Press, 2009), 21.

81. Consider information published by the *BBC* and the *Economist*: http://www.bbc.co.uk/news/world-latin-america-13343810 and http://www.economist.com/node/11412645.

82. *Semana* reported the following account: "Juez español acusa a Venezuela de amparar colaboración ETA-FARC" at http://www.semana.com/europa/juez-espanol-acusa-venezuela-amparar-colaboracion-etafarc/135676-3.aspx.

83. The 2008 missile attack against the FARC encampment in Ecuador took place in part because satellite phone cables were discovered by informants. FARC members had apparently tied cables to branches to improve the jungle antenna system.

84. Makarenko, "The Crime-Terror Continuum" (see note 22 above), 136.

85. *El Tiempo*, "La corrupción llegó a las filas de las Farc," December 1, 2010, http://www.eltiempo.com/colombia/llano/ARTICULO-WEB-NEW_NOTA_INTERIOR-8497500.html.

86. Paul E. Saskiewicz, *The Revolutionary Armed Forces of Colombia - People's Army (FARC-EP): Marxist-Leninist Insurgency or Criminal Enterprise?* Master's Thesis, Naval Postgraduate School, Monterey, CA, 2005.

87. In standard Botany or Life Sciences textbooks, a stolon is described as a long horizontal stem that grows along the surface of the soil and propagates by producing roots and shoots at the nodes or tip.

88. The influence of social media has in essence "democratized" many of the Kurdish networks. Participation is voluntary and the membership fluctuates depending on the appeal of specific activities.

89. Different foreign policy perceptions in Europe and Turkey present a significant obstacle to such a neo-liberal paradigm according to Uslu and Aytac, "War of Paradigms" (see note 68 above).

90. See for example, Jonathan M. Winer, "Countering Terrorist Finance: A Work Mostly in Progress," *The Annals of the American Academy of Political and Social Science* 618, no. 1 (July 2008): 112–132.

The Terrorism Debate Over Mexican Drug Trafficking Violence

PHIL WILLIAMS

Matthew B. Ridgway Center for International Security Studies,
University of Pittsburgh, Pittsburgh, Pennsylvania, USA

Violence in Mexico related to drug trafficking has expanded enormously, and observers have begun using terms like terrorism, nacro-terrorism, and criminal insurgency to label the violence. However, arguments that Mexico is the victim of growing terrorism are both exaggerated and unconvincing. While there have been many murders of innocent civilians, these killings do not seem to have been motivated by a political, ideological, or religious cause. This analysis seeks to understand the nature of the expanding violence in Mexico. It starts from the premise that the violence is a complex and multi-layered phenomenon with a variety of different rationales and motivations. From this perspective, a pyramidal approach to the violence can be identified. At the base of the pyramid is the notion of drug-related violence as the medium of rational strategic competition in a highly lucrative illicit market. A second layer in the pyramid emphasizes factionalism within the organizations as well as a process of contracting out for much of the violence to youth gangs and specialists. And a third perspective on the violence puts less emphasis on organizations and more on the degeneration of norms and inhibitions.

Introduction

In recent years, violence in Mexico related to drug trafficking has expanded enormously. In 2008, the Mexican government recorded 6,837 drug-related homicides; in 2009 there was almost a 40% increase with 9,614 people killed.[1] In 2010 the number jumped to 15,273, an increase of almost 60%.[2] Even allowing for the possibility that some of these increases simply reflected better recording mechanisms, it is clear that drug-related killings more than doubled from 2008 to 2010. While the overall homicide rate in Mexico remains well below that of countries such as Venezuela and El Salvador, the figures for drug-related homicides are startling. In simple numbers of violent deaths in 2010, Mexico had almost twice as many killings as Iraq and

Phil Williams is the director of the Matthew B. Ridgway Center for International Security Studies at the University of Pittsburgh.

The author would like to thank Guillermo Vasquez Del Mercado for his assistance with some of the research for this article. He would also like to thank James J.F. Forest and the two anonymous reviewers for their helpful comments and suggestions.

Afghanistan combined. The Iraq Body Count (IBC) recorded 4,038 civilian deaths from violence in 2010 (compared to 4,690 in 2009).[3] In Afghanistan in 2010 the United States lost 499 soldiers, the United Kingdom lost 103, and other coalition members lost 109.[4] In the same year an estimated 2,777 Afghan civilians were killed, about 75% of them by insurgent forces.[5]

These are gross figures, of course, and are not really appropriate for cross-national comparisons, which typically use homicide rates per 100,000 of the population. Mexico's population numbers approximately 110 million, while that of Iraq is estimated at 31 million. Population estimates for Afghanistan range from 26 to 30 million.[6] Even if one controls for these population differences, however, it is impossible to avoid the conclusion that Mexican homicide rates in 2010 were not very different from—and probably slightly higher than—those in two war zones.

Against this background, this analysis explores the nature of the violence in Mexico. It considers whether or not labels such as narco-terrorism or criminal insurgency that are increasingly being applied to Mexico are really appropriate. The argument of this article is that they are not. Instead, it is suggested, the violence can be seen in some respects as very typical of organized crime. Drug violence in Mexico resembles Mafia clan violence in Sicily, blood feuds among criminal organizations in Albania, and the upsurge in contract killings in Russia during the 1990s. The thesis here, however, is that while strategic competition among major Mexican drug trafficking organizations explains a lot of the violence, the dynamics of factionalism and outsourcing of violence to gangs provide an additional layer of understanding. Moreover, there has also been a growth in careless or anomic violence. These three interlocking and overlapping dimensions of the violence in Mexico give it an intensity and ferocity that surpass many other cases of organized crime violence and at the same time make it more complex and intractable than terrorist or insurgent violence.

Neither Terrorism Nor Insurgency

It is hardly surprising though, that many observers have made efforts to label the violence (and understand the broader phenomenon to which it is related) in new ways. The notion that the high level of drug-related violence can be simply criminal violence is not readily accepted when casualties are so high, when traffickers routinely torture, kill, and decapitate rivals, when pitched battles are fought between trafficking organizations and the military or police, when gunfights break out in shopping malls, and when police chiefs and local politicians and officials are routinely assassinated. Some commentators have resorted to the old and somewhat overused term, narco-terrorism to describe the violence.[7] Others, however, have enunciated the concept of criminal insurgency to explain what they see as the growing political and coercive power of criminal organizations willing to challenge the Mexican state.[8] The impulse to which both sets of commentators are responding is powerful: the escalation of violence during the last few years has been dramatic, unremitting, and deeply disturbing. Organized crime violence in Sicily during the five decades after the Second World War, or even in Russia during the 1990s, seems to pale in comparison not only with the levels of drug-related violence in Mexico, but also with the barbarity and gruesomeness with which so much of this violence has been carried out.

Even so, arguments that Mexico is the victim of growing terrorism are both exaggerated and unconvincing. While there have been many murders of innocent civilians—including journalists, musicians, priests, and local officials and politicians—these killings do not seem to have been motivated by a political, ideological, or religious cause. Moreover, the essence of terrorism is the indiscriminate killing of innocent people for political purposes. Most of the violence in Mexico has been selective (although, as discussed more fully below, increasingly careless) and not designed to kill indiscriminately. The one exception is the throwing of grenades into crowds during the Independence Day celebrations in Morelia in September 2008.[9] While many observers noted that this was a significant departure that crossed the line from criminal violence to terrorism, the major drug trafficking organizations were both rapid and unequivocal in their denials of responsibility and their denunciations of the attacks. There was clearly an element of game playing in these statements, with several organizations seeking to exonerate themselves while implicating major rivals. Nevertheless, the most significant point about the traffickers' reactions is that they were both uniform and vehement in their condemnation of the grenade attacks. Moreover (and this has been somewhat lost in the concerns about the increased violence since 2008), this kind of action has not been repeated. It is almost as if crossing the line reaffirmed both the importance of the line and the need to refrain from crossing it again. This is not to claim that drug violence has invariably remained selective and focused on particular targets or that the perpetrators have been careful to avoid collateral damage. On the contrary, one of the major themes of this analysis is that the violence has become much more careless. It is argued below, however, that this is a rather different phenomenon from terrorism and one that is not easily and neatly captured under the rubric of terrorist violence. Arguably, the targeting of innocent civilians in Morelia was not the first step of a continued terrorist campaign, but a one-off action that most of the major organizations involved in drug violence were quick to condemn and reluctant to emulate.

Some observers have also pointed to the use of improvised explosive devices to buttress the argument about terrorism in Mexico. It is worth noting, however, that during the 1950s and early 1960s, Youngstown, Ohio witnessed 75 car bombings over a ten-year period.[10] This was rarely, if ever, labeled as terrorism; rather it was seen for what it was—a struggle between rival mafia families and factions. This is not to deny that criminal organizations sometimes carry out terrorist campaigns. The two that stand out most obviously are those by Pablo Escobar in the 1980s and 1990s, which included the bombing of an Avianca plane and explosions in shopping malls, and the Sicilian Mafia's campaign, which included placement of bombs on trains and attacks on some of Italy's historic monuments. There has been no equivalent in Mexico of these systematic campaigns of terror. It is possible, of course, that one or more of the major Mexican drug trafficking organizations will initiate such a campaign in the future. As of this writing, however, this is not the case.

The proposition that the Mexican state is facing a criminal insurgency is perhaps not as quickly or easily dismissed as the terrorism argument. The notion that Mexican drug trafficking organizations en masse are engaged in insurgency is unpersuasive. There is no cohesive, let alone monolithic, effort to challenge and replace the government. And even were the notion of criminal insurgency to be accepted, the implication would be that Mexico confronts not a single cohesive insurgency but rather multiple insurgencies that are competing with one another. Yet, with one exception discussed below, Mexican drug trafficking organizations, by and large, do not appear to have political agendas. There is no evidence that Mexican drug trafficking organizations seek to control the state. In an insurgency, the state is the prize; in Mexico the state is an obstacle or threat to the drug trafficking industry and trafficking organizations seek to constrain the state's ability to interfere with their business operations. In effect, Mexican drug trafficking organizations are trying to carve out operating space within the Mexican state and society, not striving to overthrow, replace, or supersede the state. At times they seek to create the operating space by developing symbiotic or collusive relationships with state structures, ranging from mayors and governors to Federal law enforcement agencies and personnel. These collusive relationships are accompanied (and perhaps strengthened) by the use of violence and intimidation against officials and law enforcement and military personnel.[11]

Perhaps the one drug trafficking organization with more ambitious political aspirations is La Familia Michoacana, which has now split into two factions with one reinventing itself as Los Caballeros Templarios.[12] La Familia was and is a curious organization, combining what appeared to be cult behavior with the operations of a modern transnational drug trafficking organization. Presenting itself as the defender of the state of Michoacan from outsiders, the organization also declared war on the Federal Police while suborning governance structures and co-opting municipal leaders in Michoacan.[13] But even this is not atypical for criminal organizations, which often seek to develop symbiotic relationships with political elites and even law enforcement agencies. Moreover, many criminal organizations exhibit some degree of paternalism. This is not surprising. These organizations benefit considerably from the tacit support of the population, and providing them with services, employment, and protection helps to generate such support. While La Familia was providing alternative governance—which can be understood as an inherent challenge to the state—this is not the equivalent of an insurgency. In effect, La Familia was seeking to delineate and protect operating space for its drug business and develop a sanctuary in Michoacan. Yet, even these efforts were counter-productive. The brazen attacks on the Federal Police, including the killing of 12 federal policemen in one day in July 2009, made La Familia a high priority target. In late 2010 and the first half of 2011 Mexican government forces not only decapitated the leadership structure of La Familia but also weakened the organization through multiple arrests. The killing of the leader, Nazario Moreno González, in December 2010 resulted in a vicious succession struggle. This, along with the arrest of several hundred members in Mexico and about 2,000 members and affiliates of La Familia in the United States, suggests that the organization's agenda for the foreseeable future is likely to be dominated by concerns over self-preservation rather than by ambitious political aspirations.[14]

None of this is intended to deny the seriousness of the challenge faced by the Mexican government and populace as a result of the increasing drug violence. It is merely to argue that labels are important both conceptually and because of their policy implications—and that some of the labels being used are not only potentially misleading but also could result in inappropriate or misguided policy responses.

The Pyramid of Violence

Against this background, this analysis seeks to understand the nature of the expanding violence in Mexico. It starts from the premise that the violence is a complex and multi-layered phenomenon with a variety of different rationales and motivations. Consequently, analysis must be highly eclectic and open to various ways of understanding and conceptualizing trends and developments in both the levels and the forms of violence. Efforts to dissect drug-related violence in Mexico must also identify both the perpetrators and the targets or victims. Indeed, "marked improvement in our understanding... depends critically on more self-consciousness about what observers bring to the analysis. What each analyst sees and judges to be important is a function not only of the evidence about what happened but also of the 'conceptual lenses' through which he looks at the evidence."[15] And no single conceptual lens is sufficient, by itself, to explain or understand a complex phenomenon such as drug-related violence in Mexico. Multiple layers or perspectives are essential with each adding to our overall understanding of the nature and scope of the violence.

Even with multiple perspectives, limitations on the analysis are unavoidable. Many of the killings have no obvious motive, the victims are unknown, and the level of subsequent investigation is generally woefully inadequate. As many observers have pointed out, criminals in Mexico enjoy a high level of impunity.[16] Relatively few perpetrators of violence are caught and, of those who are, even fewer are successfully prosecuted. Without much more detailed and specific knowledge of both victims and perpetrators, the analysis of the drug-related violence is inevitably incomplete. It is not clear, for example, if the *sicarios* (contract killers) who kill members of rival organizations are the same people who kill journalists or other civilians. Nor is it always possible to distinguish between those who are specifically targeted and those who are killed by accident, or between law enforcement personnel who are killed because they are doing their best to combat the traffickers and those who are killed because they have been working with the traffickers and have either committed some transgression or know too much about the business.

With this injunction in mind, this analysis identifies what might be termed a pyramidal approach to the violence. At the base of the pyramid is the notion of drug-related violence as the medium of rational strategic competition in a highly lucrative illicit market. This lens offers a compelling core explanation of much of the violence. It is very similar to the rational actor model that is central to economics and political science. Violence is the result of strategic choices by drug trafficking organizations seeking to enlarge market share, to control routes and markets, and to expand their profits. As Mexican drug trafficking organizations have become the dominant suppliers to U.S. drug markets, so the payoffs have become much larger and the incentives for violence to enhance market position have correspondingly increased. Moreover, as suggested below, government policy has sometimes inadvertently accentuated these incentives.

A second layer in the pyramid suggests an approach that in some respects complements but in others challenges the strategic competition model. The complement is a similar focus on economic incentives; the challenge concerns the nature of the actors responding to these incentives. Whereas the strategic model focuses on coherent organizations involved in a grand strategic competition, this second model emphasizes factionalism within the organizations as well as a process of contracting out for much of the violence to youth gangs and specialists. Both these developments have added elements of viciousness, callousness, and unpredictability to the mix. As opposed to the strategic competition model in which violence is centralized, top-down, and highly purposeful and disciplined, in this perspective violence is diffuse, driven by decision-making at low levels of the organization, and reflects the dissolution rather than the effectiveness of command and control mechanisms and structures. It runs parallel to Graham Allison's notion that governmental actions cannot be seen simply in terms of monolithic bodies making well-informed strategic choices; equally if not more important are the bureaucracies, each of which has its own perspectives and interests that are not necessarily synonymous with those of the political leadership.[17] In drug trafficking organizations, this translates into factions and service providers with their own ambitions, interests, and perspectives that do not invariably coincide with those of the leaders.

A third perspective on the violence puts less emphasis on organizations and more on the degeneration of norms and inhibitions. It also suggests that the violence has taken on a dynamism and life of its own. Tactics such as decapitation, for example, that started as dramatic if brutal forms of strategic communication have become so widely imitated and emulated that they have lost much of their value as messages and become almost routine. This suggests two things. First, it highlights the relevance of notions of tipping points and epidemics of behavior popularized by Malcolm Gladwell.[18] In effect, drug-related violence in Mexico has ceased to be simply a manifestation of rational competition, and has instead become what could tritely be described as a fashion and more accurately as a form of contagion.[19] Second, the violence has not only intensified but also transformed from stable or bounded forms into something that is far less discriminate and predictable.

Indeed, one of the most disturbing features of violence in Mexico is the way it has become both more careless and more callous. The loss of selectivity and care

Table 1. Three models to conceptualize Mexican drug trafficking

	Strategic	**Factionalism and outsourcing**	**Anomic violence**
Objectives	Competitive advantage and control	Greater share of the action Go from service provider to player	Violence as an end in itself
Purpose of violence	Strategic control over routes and warehouses Revise or uphold status quo	Control over local markets Enhanced status	Empower user, imitate and emulate Create reputation
Direction of violence	Top down command and control	Bottom up	Omni-directional-targets of convenience
Impact of the state	Alter balance of power provide competitive advantage	Create internal succession struggles	Provides climate of impunity
Major targets	Rivals, police	Defectors, controllers	Careless and callous

in the use of violence has become pervasive; as a result violence has intruded into locales, taken on forms, and been carried out at levels that go well beyond the norm even for ruthless criminal organizations. In terms of propensity for violence, Mexican drug trafficking organizations have few if any peers, other than Pablo Escobar's organization in Medellin in the early 1990s. Yet, apart from the Independence Day grenade attack discussed above, violence in Mexico has not indiscriminately targeted civilians; the perpetrators of drug-related violence, however, no longer take care and seek to avoid killing innocent civilians. Being in the wrong time or the wrong place has put ordinary citizens in Mexico at risk in ways that, only a few years ago, were unthinkable. This is best understood as resulting from an epidemic of anomic violence. The three models are summarized in Table 1 and developed more fully in the subsequent sections of this article.

Model One: Rational Competition Through Violence and Intimidation

The dominant model of drug-related violence in Mexico is that of rationality and purpose. In effect, criminal organizations are seen as purposeful actors using violence as a continuation of business by other means. Rather like states in the international system, they operate in an anarchic system outside rules and laws. In effect, it is a self-help system involving both the offensive and defensive uses of violence to expand or maintain business interests.[20]

At a fundamental level, the violence in Mexico is primarily about criminal competition and is not very different from Capone's Chicago, the "Wild East" that was Russia in the 1990s, the internecine wars of the Mafia in Sicily, or the feuds between rival Chinese Triads. The competition has become more intense because the stakes have become so high: controlling the entry points into the United States and the strategic warehouses used to store drugs has driven much of the violence along the U.S.-Mexican border, a violence that has its own geography and trajectory.[21] A decade or so ago much of the violence was centered on Tijuana, where the Arellano Felix Organization had imposed transit taxes on other drug trafficking organizations. From 2005 to 2007 the locus of the violence became Nuevo Laredo, as the Sinaloa Federation and the Gulf drug trafficking organization vied for control. Subsequently Juarez became the major flashpoint and the locus of a significant percentage of the drug-related homicides in Mexico. In 2010 and 2011 violence also expanded in Reynosa, Matamoros, and Monterrey as the Gulf organization and its former enforcement arm the Zetas went to war with one another. What is often described as control of the plaza in Mexico's northern cities has become critical to the movement of drugs into the United States and the large, regular, and rapid profits that accrue from the trafficking, distribution, and sale. As such, this control is highly and violently contested.

It is sometimes argued that, from an industry perspective, the violence in Mexico is not rational—it brings unwanted attention and enforcement efforts that, to one degree or another, hurt all the players.[22] Yet, from the perspective of a particular trafficking organization, violence can look very attractive as a means of enhancing territorial control of transshipment points and/or market share. And for those trafficking organizations that are trying to hold on to what they have, defensive violence is an equally rational and logical alternative to being driven out of business. At its core, therefore, the violence associated with drug trafficking in and through Mexico to the United States is not irrational—it is the result of capitalistic competition that is totally ruthless and unfettered by laws or regulations.

There is even a somewhat perverse entrepreneurial quality about the violence. As one astute observer has noted, "the killing has become qualitatively, as well as quantitatively, more grotesque—savage mutilation, tortures to a point of perverse cruelty. All this requires a deviant sense of innovation."[23] If the aim is to eliminate or coerce rival organizations and violence is the means, then adopting ruthless, brutal, and even bizarre forms of violence is a rational and logical approach consistent with the main tenets of the strategic competition model. Even what initially appears to be senseless and gratuitous violence has its own logic and rationale. From this perspective, many of the beheadings, which have become commonplace since 2006, and other grotesque actions such as disfiguring corpses or hanging them from bridges, can be understood as a rational part of a strategic competition designed to intimidate rivals. In effect, the drug trafficking organizations are using what in military parlance is called "strategic communications."[24] Just as deeds often spoke louder than words in the Cold War, so do they in Mexico's criminal world. As several authors have argued, beheadings have become an important component of the competition among drug trafficking organizations. "To accomplish both their strategic and tactical objectives, cartels must keep police and soldiers at bay, out-terrorize rival cartels, silence reporters and eyewitnesses, keep lawyers from prosecuting and prevent investigators from investigating. Beheadings are one of the most effective means by which the cartels accomplish these objectives."[25] Sebastian Rotella made a similar observation well over a decade ago, describing what he termed the semiotics of murder as being about conveying messages. As he noted, "to the outside world, the drug wars were frenzied and murky. For the participants, the violence had very specific codes and objectives, a logic all its own. The choice of the victim, the method and the location were all calculated to make a statement . . . It all has meaning. It is like a language."[26]

While strategic competition in a criminal world that is outside the law (and akin to Hobbes' state of nature) contains an inherent potential for escalation, that potential is not always realized. In some cases, prudence prevails and equilibrium is reached at relatively low levels of violence. In the Mexican case, however, three convergent factors contributed significantly to the increasing levels of violence: a major drug trafficking organization with revisionist and expansionist aspirations; the increasing availability of weapons and the growing involvement in the drug business of former military and police personnel with the knowledge of how to use them; and government policies and strategies that inadvertently created new competitive opportunities and encouraged violence.

The Sinaloa Federation is in many respects (along with the Juarez organization) one of the more traditional drug trafficking organizations, with a relatively narrow portfolio of criminal activities but a high level of competency in managing all aspects of the drug business. It is focused on generating large profits, and although deeply embedded in the society and economy of Sinaloa does not appear to have any political aspirations, beyond the desire to maintain an environment within which it can operate with a high degree of impunity. Yet, the Sinaloa Federation under the leadership of Chapo Guzman has been consistently and even relentlessly expansionist in its approach to the business, exploiting any weakness on the part of other organizations and successively challenging the control of the plazas in Tijuana, traditionally dominated by the Arellano Felix Organization, in Nuevo Laredo dominated by the Gulf organization, and in Juarez, traditionally dominated by the Carillo Fuentes family.[27] In terms drawn from the international politics literature, the Sinaloa Federation is a revisionist power dissatisfied with the status quo in terms of both market share and territorial control, and constantly seeking to alter both these things in its favor. The organization is Clausewitzian in its approach and treats violence as simply a continuation of its business by other means. Just as violence can be used to alter the status quo, however, other drug trafficking organizations can equally well use violence in an effort to uphold the status quo.

Sometimes the strategic competition turns into what might be termed blood feuds. Some of the more traditional Mexican drug trafficking organizations at the core are still family-based enterprises—and killing family members transforms the competitive struggle into something very personal, sparking a cycle of vengeance and vendetta that is very difficult to stop, let alone reverse. The struggle between the Sinaloa Federation and the Arellano Felix Organization in particular took on many of the qualities of a blood feud and lasted for two decades. Even in recent years after the Arellano Felix brothers running the organization were either arrested or killed and the AFO split into rival factions, Chapo Guzman supported the faction headed by El Teo, who was not a member of the Arellano family.[28] While this is perhaps the most dramatic and obvious case of market competition being overlaid by blood feuds, it is certainly not the only one. In a culture characterized by machismo, and in which major narco-traffickers become legendary figures celebrated in narco-ballads, this is hardly surprising. Even though the blood feuds encourage escalation and give conflicts a momentum of their own, however, they ultimately only accentuate and exaggerate the underlying market impulses. Moreover, the blood feuds are hardly a novel feature of the Mexican drug world.

What has made the clash between revisionist and status quo organizations particularly bloody in the last five to ten years is the increasing availability of weapons and of people and organizations adept in their use. Many of the weapons are smuggled into Mexico from the United States, where they are purchased by straw buyers at the poorly regulated weapons shows and sales that are regularly held in border states such as Texas and Arizona. Indeed, Mexican drug trafficking organizations have been able to acquire not only sophisticated weaponry but also large amounts of ammunition. In one seizure in January 2009, for example, over 500,000 bullets were discovered in a disused warehouse.[29] Other seizures have included advanced weaponry. Perhaps even more important than the weapons, however, has been the creation of enforcement arms that act as muscle for criminal organization.

In this regard, the creation of the Zetas in 1997 by then leader of the Gulf drug trafficking organization Osiel Cardenas, gave that organization a competitive edge that other organizations subsequently sought to neutralize by developing similar groups of their own. Cardenas recruited about 30 members and former members of Mexico's Army and Airborne Special Forces Groups (known as Gafes and Gaifes) led by Lieutenant Arturo Guzmán Decenas.[30] After Guzmán Decenas was killed and his deputy captured, Heriberto Lazcano (also known as El Lazca or as Z3) took over the leadership.[31] After Cardenas was arrested in 2003, Los Zetas became more directly involved in the drug business. In 2005 and 2006 the paramilitary forces also played a major role in beating back the attempt by Sinaloa to wrest control of Nuevo Laredo from the Gulf trafficking organization. In the process, Los Zetas developed a formidable reputation for violence and brutality. It subsequently maintained this reputation while broadening its role beyond protection and enforcement to people smuggling, kidnapping, extortion, and arms trafficking. The group also distanced itself from its employer and ultimately emerged as an independent entity or what Samuel Logan termed the Zetas Organization.[32] The organization has a membership that is probably in the thousands, and a reputation for operational military sophistication that is matched only by its ruthlessness.

The emergence and evolution of the Zetas Organization can be understood as both symptom and cause of the militarization of the Mexican drug wars. Not only has the organization been at the heart of much of the violence in Mexico during the last decade, but it also introduced into the violence a military quality that had hitherto been lacking. Other drug trafficking organizations made efforts to emulate and to counter the Zetas by creating similar enforcement and militarized units, and by mobilizing street gangs. The ultimate irony was that, in the early months of 2010, the Zetas organization found itself facing an alliance of the Gulf and Sinaloa organizations and La Familia—one their former employer, the second their traditional enemy, and the third, their protégé—all of whom claimed that the Zetas had undermined and discredited "true drug traffickers."[33]

Ironically, government efforts to combat drug trafficking can also inadvertently exacerbate both the competition and the violence. There are two ways in which the strategic competition has been intensified by the Mexican government's enforcement efforts. In the first place under both Fox and Calderon (and it is important to note the continuity in their policies even though many Mexicans call the offensive against drug trafficking Calderon's War) the effort to target trafficking organizations has simply become more serious and systematic, an effort that has been exemplified in increased reliance on the military, the serious weakening of several important organizations, and more vigorous—if still far from successful—efforts to reduce corruption. These measures have increased the risk and cost of doing business for drug trafficking organizations. In such an environment, competition becomes even more intense and organizations seek to develop greater efficiencies by becoming even more ruthless in challenging their competitors.

The second and more important way in which the government has intensified the competition is through what might be termed sequential rather than simultaneous targeting.[34] Some observers believe that this is deliberate and that the Calderon Administration, in particular, has favored the Sinaloa organization by targeting only its competitors.[35] Another possibility, however, is that enforcement is opportunity driven and that differential enforcement is the result of opportunities being presented rather than a government strategy designed to favor a particular organization. The problem, however, as Richard Friman has brilliantly enunciated, is that whether strategy has the objective of amputation (taking out part of the organization), decapitation (arresting or killing the leadership), or elimination (taking the organization out of the market altogether), it invariably creates "vacancy chains."[36] Rival organizations, particularly those with revisionist aspirations, see in these chains new opportunities for aggrandizement. In other words, vacancy chains encourage what are competitive feeding frenzies. The paradox, therefore, is that government successes lead to increased rather than reduced inter-organizational violence. Drug trafficking organizations weakened by government efforts become vulnerable and attractive targets to their rivals.

This rational competition model provides a high degree of explanatory power. It is not only parsimonious, but also has a tidiness and simplicity that make it compelling. But this tidiness is also part of its weakness. The model assumes very good decision-making and implementation by largely monolithic hierarchical organizations in which the wishes and desires of the leaders are communicated, understood, and carried out with little deviation. The reality, however, is much messier. Although the strategic competition model provides an initial analytic framework for understanding the violence, it does not capture all the subtleties of this violence. Indeed, there is a second perspective that is supplemental rather than an alternative to the strategic perspective, but in some ways qualifies and undermines the former. This model can be described in terms of factionalism and bottom-up violence.

Model Two: Factionalism and Bottom-Up Violence

One of the paradoxes of Mexican drug trafficking organizations is that there are simultaneous tendencies towards consolidation and inter-organizational violence on the one side and towards fragmentation and intra-organizational violence on the other. This second perspective or model of violence in Mexico focuses on the tendencies towards disintegration and on relatively autonomous low-level violence. In effect, it suggests that the violence cannot be understood as simply a strategic competition among highly centralized and monolithic actors with clear strategies and effective command and control arrangements. Instead, Mexican drug trafficking is characterized by the emergence of what Doyle and Sambanis in a different context termed "incoherent factions."[37] This alternative perspective is informed by a recognition of the need for disaggregation, the tendencies towards factional infighting, and the increasing emphasis on contracting out for services, including the provision of violence. Moreover, it recognizes that the high level leadership of the organization does not control much of this violence. Not only is there a high degree of autonomy and independence at lower levels, but this can also take on its own momentum—and, at times, feedback into, and intensify, the strategic competition. At least some of the violence, therefore, can be understood in terms of multiple incidents of micro-violence at local levels rather than macro-violence at the strategic level.

This alternative perspective is based in part on the difficulties faced by large drug trafficking organizations in maintaining a high degree of unity and cohesion given the inherent tendencies towards fracture and fragmentation. This has been exacerbated in recent years by the tendencies to contract out for services. In Juarez, for example, the Carillo Fuentes family (leaders of what traditionally has been termed the Juarez Cartel) hired a youth gang known as La Linea to combat the encroachments of the Sinaloa organization and its local proxies, the Artistic Assassins.[38] La Linea has been responsible for a great deal of the violence in the city and in July 2011 made threats against the U.S. Drug Enforcement Administration, and reportedly was planning bomb attacks on the U.S. consulate in Juarez and the bridges to the United States.[39] On July 29, the leader of La Linea, Jose Antonio Acosta Hernandez, known as El Diego, was captured. Reportedly, he is linked to 1,500 murders and commanded a group of about 45 gunmen aged 18 to 25.[40] He had become a high priority target because of the threats. Although El Diego reportedly worked under the direction of Juan Pablo Ledezma ("el JL") who is close to Vicente Carillo, leader of the Juarez organization, he seems to have exercised a great deal of autonomy, perhaps going far beyond the bounds of what was expected or even permitted.

The implication is that claims about competition among major drug trafficking organizations provide an explanation that is tidy and oddly comforting but ultimately inadequate. One very close observer has suggested that the fighting in Ciudad

Juárez cannot be explained simply in terms of strategic competition among major drug trafficking organizations. His advice is to "forget what you've read and heard about who controls what. Whoever the controllers are, they leave those who remain in the city to fight the battle to the finish that involves the extermination of rivals, and others. This has become crazy warfare, not even necessarily between the... cartels; it is anarchy.... the pyramids have collapsed, and not one of the big bosses in the battle for Juárez has been touched, not one–they are far away. This is a fight between the groups and gangs on the ground that used to work for them, and it has become a massacre."[41] As Vulliamy has argued, such an interpretation is a heresy that subverts the official account of violence as a struggle between the major drug trafficking organizations and "fundamentally challenges the notion of a carefully staged...war on a narco Monopoly board."[42]

Julian Cardona and Ignacio Alvarado Alvarez have identified what they argue is an outsourcing of violence, as a result of which the major trafficking organizations have lost control of the streets.[43] In this assessment, drug trafficking in Ciudad Juárez has become "a formless, horizontal hierarchy," responding not to the desire for control over transnational trafficking routes but to the opportunities provided by the emergence of local consumer markets in Mexico.[44] "As the cartel pyramids collapse, they lose control of the burgeoning domestic market for drugs" with each retail outlet claiming its own turf with the protection of the local gang.[45] In other words, what was once a clear chain of command has been superseded by "an affiliation system of outsourced gangs."[46] In this situation, much of the violence is bottom-up. Foot soldiers or "wannabes" try to establish a reputation for ruthless violence to attract the attention of their superiors (in effect violence becomes a means of career advancement). Assassins kill to justify the continued payments of wages. And existing gang rivalries are intensified by the fact that the control of turf has now become profitable rather than simply being about identity and status.

This second, alternative perspective on drug violence in Mexico moves from the grand strategic level to the micro-level, from directed or top down to emergent or bottom-up behavior. As suggested above, there is also a mid-level equivalent with factional splits becoming commonplace in the large drug trafficking organizations. Indeed, one of the key problems confronted by the major organizations is the growth of appetites by the smaller groups, families, or factions within them. As these factions become aware of the profits that can be obtained, they sometimes become dissatisfied with a subordinate role, preferring instead to branch out on their own as an independent organization.

In some cases, the fracturing comes as a result of a single episode that breaks down what is often a very fragile level of trust. A corrupt law enforcement official working for SIEDO, for example, revealed that the defection from Sinaloa by the Beltran Leyva Organization (BLO) in 2008 came after Arturo Beltran Leyva felt slighted by being left out of a deal between Nacho Coronel and Chapo Guzman.[47] And at this level too a blood feud can quickly develop. Soon after the split, Alfredo Beltran Leyva was arrested; Arturo blamed Guzman and retaliated by killing Guzman's son.[48] The BLO, which had been a major enforcement arm for Sinaloa, found itself at war with the parent organization. The split between the Gulf drug trafficking organizations and the Zetas Organization was more gradual; but after an incident in January 2010 these two organizations went to war against one another.

If these splits have become very familiar, others have been far less publicized. Some reports for example suggest that many of the killings in Durango in early

2011 were the result of internecine fighting within the Sinaloa Federation.[49] According to one Mexican official, a Sinaloa subgroup loyal to Guzmán and known as the Ms has been struggling with two rival groups, the "Canelos" and the "Cabreras," that had broken away from Sinaloa in spite of what Proceso termed "longstanding business ties" to the Federation.[50] The resulting conflict helps to explain the 223 bodies found in seven mass graves in Durango in April and May 2011.[51] This is not surprising. From the perspective of organizational cohesion, this kind of defection has to be met with violence. Indeed, much of what is typically understood as externally directed violence might actually be internally directed. Violence can be used to stop or punish defection, to maintain internal discipline, to impose order, to reinforce loyalty, and to enhance security.

The implication of all this is that the Mexican drug trafficking world is more complex than often acknowledged. It is characterized by an unsettling mix of grand strategic competition and factionalism, a constant struggle between consolidation and expansion on the one side and division and fragmentation on the other. In other words, the escalation of violence that has occurred in recent years is not just the result of intensified strategic competition; it also reflects changing dynamics within organizations and in particular what might be termed the diffusion of violence. Yet the change is not solely in the level of violence; it is also in the character of the violence, the targets, and the victims. And this is something that cannot simply be explained by strategic competition, contracting out, or by factionalism. Consequently, it is necessary to examine an additional perspective that focuses not on organizations but on the breakdown of norms, that sees violence as an epidemic rather than as a strategy, and that focuses upon both growing carelessness and growing callousness.

Model Three: An Epidemic of Anomic Violence

The increase in violence in Mexico between 2007 and 2011 has been startling. Although much of the violence has been concentrated in certain cities and states, it has also taken on some particularly disturbing qualities. While the decapitations and the gruesome nature of some of the killings can be understood initially as a competition in shock tactics, they have become the new norm. Indeed, there are trends in the violence that cannot be explained rationally. Through a mixture of callousness and carelessness, the violence has expanded to include killings of women, children, and at times whole families, as well as illegal migrants. In Juarez, there have been two cases in which gunmen have massacred teenagers at parties. The first occurred on January 2010. A group of gunmen burst into a party, apparently looking for a rival gang member. None of the teenagers attending the party was involved in the drug business and reportedly one of the gunmen said that it was the wrong place and they should leave. Another replied that they were there so they should do it anyway.[52] The result was the killing of 15 teenagers, most of whom were students and athletes. In spite of the outrage created by this incident and promises and reassurances by the government, a very similar event occurred in October 2010, again in Juarez. Gunmen stormed a party in a lower middle class neighborhood and killed 13 people aged from 13 to 32 including 6 women and girls.[53] Others who were wounded included a nine-year-old boy.[54] Reports suggest that the killers were looking for one person.[55]

Another episode that displayed a level of brutality and callousness on an even larger scale was the killing of 72 illegal migrants from Central and South America in August 2010 allegedly by the Zetas.[56] Reportedly, the Zetas were initially trying to recruit the migrants, but when they met resistance simply killed them and dumped the bodies in a mass grave. While this was the most egregious and well-publicized episode of this kind, it is not the only one. An increasing number of illegal migrants have been abducted and held hostage until payments were received from their families. Illegal migrants willing to entrust themselves to human smugglers have always been at risk of abuse; in Mexico during the last several years, however, these risks have increased significantly. Reportedly, Zetas members have also staged crude gladiatorial contests with the winners "recruited and sent on high risk missions in the territory of rival organizations. The losers are simply killed and their bodies buried in mass graves."[57] Although such contests have not been confirmed—and could be no more than an urban myth—they would certainly conform to an emerging pattern in which brutality has become the norm, even if the victims have nothing to do with the drug business.

In this regard, it is worth emphasizing that other targets have included journalists and their families. According to the Committee to Protect Journalists, 42 journalists have been killed in Mexico in the last five years.[58] Mexico's Human Rights Commission puts the number at 50. In 2010, the situation became so bad that *El Diario de Juarez* published a front-page editorial asking the traffickers as "the de facto authorities" to "tell us what you expect from us as a newspaper."[59] In June and July 2011 three journalists working for the Veracruz newspaper *Notiver* were killed. In June columnist Miguel Angel Lopez Velasco was murdered, along with his wife and their son, the newspaper's crime photographer.[60] The victims were killed in their home. In late July, the decapitated body of Yolanda Ordaz de la Cruz was discovered several days after she had been reported missing. According to some sources, she had been investigating the killing of Lopez Velasco.[61] Many other reports reveal that journalists are routinely threatened and warned to back off their investigations or commentaries. Compare this to what Cindy Combs has called a "symbiotic relationship" between terrorists (who seek attention from an audience) and news organizations (which seek dramatic stories to increase their readership and ratings).[62] While criminal organizations have often tried to muzzle the press, it is contrary to the goals of terrorist organizations.

In a growing number of cases in Juarez and elsewhere, mass killings have also occurred at drug rehabilitation centers. In September 2009, 18 people were killed in a drug rehabilitation in Ciudad Juarez;[63] in June 2010, 19 people were killed in a drug rehabilitation center in the city of Chihuahua; in October 2010, 13 people were killed at a similar center in Tijuana;[64] and in June 2011, another 13 victims were killed at a rehabilitation center in Torreon, Coahuila state.[65] Killings with smaller numbers of victims have also taken place. The purpose of such killings is hard to determine: some argue that those in rehabilitation are potential recruits for drug gangs; others claim that the centers themselves are the targets since they are in effect trying to reduce the customer base. Some officials also see the largely unauthorized clinics as venues where traffickers and gang members go to hide. In this view the killings are usually about revenge or retaliation.

Other trends are equally disturbing. Children have regularly become victims of shootouts and families of targeted people are regularly killed in assassinations that have lost the selectivity they once had. Although some of the murders can be understood as intimidation exercises, designed in part for their impact on others, the violence has become both excessive and gratuitous. It is almost as if violence has become an end in itself rather than simply a means to an end. Indeed, it appears that at least some of the violence is morphing from a means to an economic end, into a channel for self-definition and self-assertion: killing provides a sense of power for those who are alienated and disenfranchised and does so whether it is purposeful or purposeless. Machismo, identity, and communication fuse as increasingly gruesome murders become the norm—partly because of the intimidation effect they create and partly because this is in itself a source of satisfaction and an enhanced sense of power. This is particularly true among young men—and one of the most disturbing trends is the increasingly young age at which sicarios are recruited. In July 2011 a 14-year-old sicario who was responsible for four murders (all carried out by throat cutting) received a sentence of 3 years in juvenile detention.[66] It appears that in northern Mexico and increasingly at other locations in the country, so-called drug-related violence has become a way of life with little purpose beyond the empowerment of those who engage in it and no real links to a rational business strategy.

This development is perhaps best understood in terms of anomie, a concept developed originally by Emile Durkheim and subsequently refined by Robert Merton and more recently by Nikos Passas.[67] In spite of differences about the causes of anomie, all agree that it involves a degeneration of rules and norms and the emergence of forms of behavior unconstrained by standard notions of what is acceptable. In effect, anomie involves a behavioral and ethical collapse. For Durkheim, this typically resulted from a crisis in society or some kind of transition in which legal restraints were removed, norms dissolved or disappeared, and inhibitions guiding behavior were discarded. Merton, in contrast, saw anomie as a result of a gap between aspirations and the availability of means to fulfill them. Passas argues very similarly that the lack of opportunities to fulfill expectations typically results in social deviance or criminality. In other words, the decline of behavioral norms and standards feeds into the spread of crime—both organized and disorganized. Indeed, this typically involves a rejection of morality and decency and a readiness to engage in forms of behavior normally regarded as reprehensible.

Charles Bowden's analysis of violence in Juarez fully accords with the notion of anomie, and has elements of both Durkheim's emphasis on a crisis in society and Merton's gap between aspirations and means to achieve them. Both, in a sense, come from the expectations created about and for Ciudad Juarez by NAFTA. Juarez was intended to be a model city, the city of the future where maquiladoras would provide new opportunities for employment. To a degree it did, but earnings were limited. Moreover, jobs eventually moved to China where labor was even cheaper. The economic and social dislocation was increased by the global recession. Indeed, Bowden argues that Juarez was a serious casualty of globalization and of dreams turning sour resulting in what he terms "the collapse of the city—27 percent of the houses have been abandoned, there's 116,000 abandoned houses. At least 100,000 jobs in the factories have disappeared because of the recession. Half of the adolescents in Juarez neither have a job nor attend school. What you're looking at is a kind of disintegration of a society."[68] The gap between expectations and realities became so large that many people in the city migrated from the legal economy to the drug business which was not only important in terms of the smuggling into the United States but also in terms of local markets. Bowden estimates that given the number of retail outlets through the city, the drug business is probably the most important source of income in Juarez.[69]

Although Bowden does not use the term anomic violence, he describes a behavioral morass encompassing politicians and bureaucrats, organized criminals, contract killers, serial killers, domestic violence, as well as violence perpetrated by the military and police. In spite of a murder rate that in 2010 had reached 230 per hundred thousand members of the population, Bowden acknowledged "the killings overwhelm simple explanations."[70]

This argument suggests something more sinister and uncontrollable that goes beyond the competition among illicit businesses. The violence has taken on a dynamic all of its own and become a race towards the bottom in terms of extreme ruthlessness, an almost exuberant brutality, and repulsive forms of ingenuity. The danger is that when such perversity is accepted as the norm then the situation can only deteriorate. As the Mexican artist Pablo Szmulewicz put it, "People are losing the ability to be shocked, and when you lose the capacity for shock, it creates an opening for worse things."[71]

A closely related way of thinking about the violence in Mexico is in epidemiological terms. The violence has become a contagion reproduced and spread by imitation and emulation as well as by endless cycles of reprisal and revenge. In Malcolm Gladwell's terms, the violence has passed the tipping point and become an epidemic that will prove difficult to contain let alone reverse.[72] It is not simply that the way business is done in the drug world has changed; the shift is larger and more profound, going to the heart of the society and the way relations are governed. Civil society in Mexico has been both eroded and corroded by levels and forms of violence that not only make true institutional reform impossible but also create a pervasive fear, and generate deep resentment at the failure of the state to meet its most fundamental requirement—the provision of public or citizen security.

In Gladwell's terms, the law of the few, the stickiness of ideas, and the power of context are critical to the development of social epidemics. All three can be seen at work in Mexico. The major drug traffickers have become almost mythical figures, successful entrepreneurs, who are lauded in narco-ballads and in Mexican cinema. The rise of the narco-saints, Santa Muerte and Jesus Malverde, has also given a veneer of legitimacy to traffickers and sicarios alike, offering a pseudo-religious respectability to the violence that accompanies the drug business.

In Mexico, violence has become simultaneously a perceived means of advancement, a source of income, a statement of identity, and a form of personal power and affirmation. Moreover, it meets at least one of the criteria that Gladwell identifies in relation to stickiness—it is memorable. From this perspective, the incident in 2006 in which La Familia threw severed heads onto the floor of a disco can be understood as the model for much of what has happened since. And all this has taken place, as suggested above, in a context in which expectations have been raised and disappointed, in which there is a large gap between aspirations and the means to fulfill them in the legal economy. From the perspective offered by Gladwell, violence in Mexico has become the perfect storm. Indeed, it is hard to disagree with Bowden's argument that "violence is now woven into the very fabric of the community and has no single cause, no single motive and no on off button."[73] Although Bowden made this comment about Juarez, which remains the epicenter of much of the violence, the description is equally applicable to other states and cities in northern Mexico, although not yet to the country as a whole.

Conclusions and Implications

Unfortunately, there is no end in sight to drug-related violence in Mexico. If, as this analysis suggests, the violence has become both inherently expansive and self-perpetuating, the prospects for halting let alone reversing the trends are dismal. Even if the major drug trafficking organizations were able to come to some agreement on distinct spheres of influence, norms of prudence, and market share, it is unlikely this will be sufficient. If the model of incoherent factions is combined with the idea of anomic and epidemic forms of violence then the trafficking competition—although it still provides the broad framework—is no longer the sole, and perhaps not even the major, driver of violence. Similarly, even if the Calderon government is replaced by a government that adopts a much more permissive or even collusive policy akin to that of the 1990s, this will not be enough to reduce violence that has become a way of life, an end in itself, a defining characteristic of identity and even a source of empowerment. Unfortunately, the Mexico of 2011 is characterized not by terrorism or political violence but rather by a form of existential violence, the leitmotif of which can be summarized as "I kill, therefore, I am." The implications are chilling.

Notes

1. See, for example, "Mexico Drugs War Murders Data Mapped," *Guardian Datablog,* January 14, 2011, http://www.guardian.co.uk/news/datablog/2011/jan/14/mexico-drug-war-murders-map#data.
2. Ibid.
3. See *Iraq Body Count* at www.iraqbodycount.org/.
4. See *Operation Enduring Freedom,* http://icasualties.org/OEF/Index.aspx.
5. Laura King, "U.N.: 2010 Deadliest Year for Afghan Civilians," *Los Angeles Times*, March 10, 2011, http://articles.latimes.com/2011/mar/10/world/la-fg-afghan-civilian-deaths-20110310.
6. These figures are drawn from the CIA, *World Factbook.*
7. This was something emphasized by U.S. Army General (Ret.) Barry McCaffrey: "Mexico Trip Report," http://smallwarsjournal.com/blog/2008/12/general-barry-mccaffrey-mexico/.
8. John P. Sullivan and Adam Elkus, "State of Siege: Mexico's Criminal Insurgency," http://smallwarsjournal.com/blog/journal/docs-temp/84-sullivan.pdf.
9. Jo Tuckman, "Revellers killed in grenade attack on Mexican independence celebrations," *Guardian.co.uk*, September 16, 2008, http://www.guardian.co.uk/world/2008/sep/16/mexico.drugstrade.
10. The bombings were a cover story in the *Saturday Evening Post*, 1963. See J. R. de Szigethy, "Christmas in Murdertown," 1999, http://americanmafia.com/Feature_Articles_3.html.
11. This is closely related to what Roy Godson termed the "political-criminal nexus." See Roy Godson, ed., *Menace to Society: Political-Criminal Collaboration Around the World* (New Brunswick, NJ: Transaction, 2003).
12. On the violence this generated see Gerardo, "Caballeros Templarios execute 23 this weekend in Michoacan," *Borderland Beat*, June 19, 2011, http://www.borderlandbeat.com/2011/06/caballeros-templarios-execute-23-this.html.
13. George Grayson, *La Familia Drug Cartel: Implications for U.S.-Mexican Security*, (Carlisle, PA: Strategic Studies Institute, 2010), 14, http://www.strategicstudiesinstitute.army.mil/pubs/display.cfm?pubID=1033.
14. It should be acknowledged though that the emergence of Los Caballeros Templarios has been rapid and deadly. See Ioan Grillo, "Crusaders of Meth: Mexico's Deadly Knights Templar," *Time World*, June 23, 2011, http://www.time.com/time/world/article/0,8599,2079430,00.html.

15. Graham Allison, "Conceptual Models and the Cuban Missile Crisis," *American Political Science Review* 63, no. 3 (Sep. 1969): 689–718.

16. See, for example, Ed Vulliamy, *Amexica: War Along the Borderline* (New York: Farrar, Straus and Giroux, 2010).

17. Allison (see note 15 above).

18. Malcolm Gladwell, *The Tipping Point* (New York: Little Brown and Company, 2000).

19. Ibid.

20. Vadim Volkov, *Entrepreneurs of Violence: The Use of Force in the Making of Russian Capitalism* (Ithaca, NY: Cornell University Press, 2002).

21. Mexican officials emphasized the point about strategic warehouses in an interview conducted by the author in Mexico City, May 2008.

22. Both Jorge Chabat and Francisco Thoumi have made this point to the author in private communications.

23. Vulliamy (see note 16 above).

24. For a brief but fascinating and provocative discussion of communication and signaling in the Mexican criminal world see Peter Reuter, "Gambetta's Insight: A Review of *Codes of the Underworld*," *Global Crime* 12, no. 2 (May 2011): 146–149.

25. Pamela L. Bunker, Lisa J. Campbell, and Robert J. Bunker, "Torture, Beheadings, and Narcocultos," *Small Wars & Insurgencies* 21, no. 1 (March 2010): 145–178 discuss both the strategic dimensions of beheadings and the relationships to some of the narco-cults.

26. Sebastian Rotella, *Twilight on the Line* (New York: Norton, 1998).

27. For an excellent account of the Sinaloa organization see Malcolm Beith, *The Last Narco* (New York: Penguin, 2010).

28. Ibid.

29. "Mexican Police Find Ammunitions, Detains No One," *EFE* (Internet Version-WWW in English), January 13, 2009, OSC: LAP20090113061003.

30. On the Zetas see Lisa J. Campbell, "Los Zetas: Operational Assessment," *Small Wars & Insurgencies* 21, no. 1 (March 2010): 55–80.

31. Ibid.

32. Samuel Logan, *Los Zetas: Evolution of a Criminal Organization*, ISN Security Watch, Zurich, http://www.isn.ethz.ch/isn/Current-Affairs/Security-Watch/Detail/?id=97554&lng=en.

33. "Mexican Soldiers Find Los Zetas Gang Camp in Tamaulipas," *EFE* (Internet Version-WWW in English), April 16, 2010, OSC: LAP20100416061005.

34. I would like to thank my wife Surratt Williams for several helpful discussions of simultaneous targeting and why it is so difficult.

35. John Burnett, Marisa Peñaloza, and Robert Benincasa, "Mexico Seems To Favor Sinaloa Cartel In Drug War," *National Public Radio*, May 19, 2010, http://www.npr.org/2010/05/19/126906809/mexico-seems-to-favor-sinaloa-cartel-in-drug-war.

36. Richard H. Friman, "Forging the Vacancy Chain: Law Enforcement Efforts and Mobility in Criminal Economies," *Crime, Law and Social Change* 41, no. 1 (February 2004): 53–77.

37. Michael Doyle and Nicholas Sambanis, *Making War and Building Peace* (Princeton, NJ: Princeton University Press, 2006), 50.

38. "La Linea," *Borderland Beat*, October 14, 2009, http://www.borderlandbeat.com/2009/10/la-linea.html.

39. Scott Stewart, "The Buffer Between Mexican Cartels and the U.S. Government," *Stratfor*, August 17, 2011, http://www.stratfor.com/weekly/20110817-buffer-between-mexican-cartels-and-us-government.

40. "Mexican Police Capture Key Juárez Kingpin: Police Say Drug Cartel Enforcer Jose Antonio Acosta Hernandez admits ordering 1,500 killings," *Associated Press*, August 1, 2011, http://www.guardian.co.uk/world/2011/aug/01/mexican-police-capture-juarez-kingpin.

41. Alejandro Paez, quoted in Vulliamy, *Amexica* (see note 16 above), 127.

42. Ibid., 128.

43. Ibid., 129.

44. Ibid., 130.

45. Ibid.

46. Ibid.

47. "Treason Broke Up Beltran Leyva and Sinaloa Cartels," 29 October 2008, http://www.jornada.unam.mx/2008/10/29/index.php?section=politica&article=018n1po, translated in Foreign Military Studies Office, FMSO/JRIC International Borders Security Research Team, Fort Leavenworth, Kansas, Mexico, Central America, and Caribbean Newsbriefs for 29–31, October 2008. For a different emphasis see Beith (note 27 above), 148–149.

48. See the discussion in Beith (note 27 above), 148.

49. "A 7th Mass Grave Found in Durango Reveals a Possible Split Within the Sinaloa Cartel," *Justice in Mexico*, Posted by Alizano on May 27, 2011, http://justiceinmexico.org/2011/05/27/a-7th-mass-grave-found-in-durango-reveals-a-possible-split-within-the-sinaloa-cartel/.

50. Ibid.

51. Ibid.

52. The author is grateful to Alfredo Corchado for this account. See his forthcoming book, *Midnight in Mexico*.

53. Olivia Torres, "Mexico: 13 Dead in Massacre at Ciudad Juarez Party," *The Washington Times*, October 23, 2010, http://www.washingtontimes.com/news/2010/oct/23/mexico-13-dead-massacre-ciudad-juarez-party/.

54. Elizabeth Malkin, "Death Toll in Juárez Attack Rises to 14," *New York Times*, October 24, 2010, http://www.nytimes.com/2010/10/25/world/americas/25mexico.html.

55. Ibid.

56. MSNBC, "Migrants Killed for Refusing to be Assassins, Teen Says: Source: Ecuadorian who Survived says Zetas Gang Offered them $2,000 a Month," www.msnbc.msn.com/id/38867434/ns/world_news-americas/t/migrants-killed-refusing-be-assassins-teen-says/#.Tk2d3us9oig.

57. Dane Schiller, "Cartels Have Taken Cruelty up a Notch, Says One Drug Trafficker: Kidnapping Bus Passengers for Gladiatorlike Fights to the Death," *Houston Chronicle*, June 11, 2011, http://www.chron.com/news/nation-world/article/Mexican-crook-Gangsters-arrange-fights-to-death-1692716.php.

58. See Tony Rogers, "In Mexico, a Killing Zone for Journalists: *El Diario* Editorial Sparks Outcry Over Murders of Reporters by Drug Lords," *About.com*, September 23, 2010, http://journalism.about.com/b/2010/09/23/in-mexico-a-killing-zone-for-journalists.htm; See also Katherine Corcoran, "Mexico Journalists Debate Cartels, Self-Censorship," *Associated Press*, September 23, 2010, http://www.boston.com/news/world/latinamerica/articles/2010/09/23/juarez_editorial_ignites_a_beleaguered_mexico/.

59. Rogers, Ibid.

60. "Gunmen in Mexico Kill Crime Journalist Lopez Velasco," June 21, 2011, http://www.bbc.co.uk/news/world-latin-america-13853748.

61. "Mexico: Missing Journalist Yolanda Ordaz Found Killed," *BBC News*, July 27, 2011, http://www.bbc.co.uk/news/world-latin-america-14305364. For a somewhat more cynical view see Tim Johnson, "Mexican Journalist Killing Raises Questions About Cartel Ties," *McClatchy*, August 13, 2011, http://blogdrugtrafficker.com/2011/08/mexico-journalist-killings-raise-questions-about-cartel-ties/.

62. Cindy Combs, "The Media as a Showcase for Terrorism," in *Teaching Terror: Strategic and Tactical Learning in the Terrorist World,* ed. James Forest (Lanham, MD: Rowman & Littlefield, 2006).

63. Ken Ellingwood, "18 killed in Juarez Clinic for Addicts," *Los Angeles Times*, September 4, 2009, http://www.latimes.com/news/nationworld/world/la-fg-mexico-rehab-attack4-2009sep04,0,5425770.story.

64. Casey Nicholas, "Gunmen Kill 13 at Tijuana Drug-Treatment Center," *Wall Street Journal*, October 25, 2010, http://www.mapinc.org/drugnews/v10/n869/a08.html.

65. Geoffrey Ramsey, "Why Mexico's Drug Gangs Target Rehab Centers," *Christian Science Monitor*, June 11, 2011, http://www.csmonitor.com/World/Americas/Latin-America-Monitor/2011/0609/Why-Mexico-s-drug-gangs-target-rehab-centers.

66. "14-year old U.S Citizen Sentenced to 3 years in Mexican Prison," *Justice in Mexico,* http://justiceinmexico.org/2011/07/30/14-year-old-u-s-citizen-sentenced-to-3-years-in-mexican-prison/.

67. The analysis here draws on the Durkheim and Merton Page at Middlesex University, London, available at www.mdx.ac.uk/WWW/STUDY/yDurMer.htm. See also Nikos

Passas, "Global Anomie, Dysnomie, and Economic Crime: Hidden Consequences of Neoliberalism and Globalization in Russia and Around the World," *Social Justice* 27, no. 2 (2000): 16–44.

68. See "How Juarez Became Murder City," *U.S.-Mexico Immigration News Stories*, http://usmexico.blogspot.com/2010/03/how-juarez-became-murder-city.html.

69. Charles Bowden, *Murder City* (New York: Nation Books, 2010), 45.

70. Bowden (see note 69 above), p. 162.

71. Ken Ellingwood, "Dismembered Bodies, Warped Minds," *Los Angeles Times*, November 8, 2010, http://articles.latimes.com/2010/nov/08/world/la-fg-mexico-depravity-20101109.

72. Gladwell (see note 18 above).

73. Bowden (see note 69 above), p. 105.

Terrorists Next Door? A Comparison of Mexican Drug Cartels and Middle Eastern Terrorist Organizations

SHAWN TERESA FLANIGAN

School of Public Affairs, San Diego State University, San Diego, California, USA

Drawing from interviews, surveys, and other forms of research conducted in Lebanon, Gaza and the West Bank, and Mexico, this article compares Mexican cartels to Hamas and Hezbollah. The similarities between them are striking: these are all by necessity territorially specific organizations tied to relatively defined geographic locations, and have deep and sophisticated relationships with the states within which they operate. However, there are critical differences between Mexican drug cartels and Hamas and Hezbollah as well, the most important (according to an analysis of multiple definitions of terrorism) being the presence of political and ideological motivations. This analysis illustrates the conceptual challenges and classificational ambiguity involved in analyzing terrorism and organized crime.

If you look at the definition of a terrorist, that's what they are. They cut heads off and they're burning people alive.
  —U.S. Congressman Michael McCaul, in reference to Mexican drug cartels[1]

Rebranding the violent activities of Mexican drug cartels[2] as "terrorism" is useful both legally and politically; so useful, in fact, that cartels themselves have labeled rival cartels as terrorists in order to gain popular support.[3] In 2010 Mexican lawmakers approved legal reforms that could classify the violent and extortionist acts of drug trafficking organizations as terrorism,[4] and in 2011 legislation was introduced in the U.S. Congress (HR 1270) to designate six Mexican drug cartels as foreign terrorist organizations. Legally, these changes would allow Mexican judges to assign drug traffickers longer prison sentences, and would allow the United States government to freeze assets, restrict travel, and impose harsher penalties on those providing material support to cartels. Politically, labeling cartel activities as terrorism is a useful strategy employed by both the Mexican government and the Gulf cartel[5] to capitalize on popular anti-terrorist sentiment and weaken the Mexican public's tolerance for the cartels' operations.[6]

Shawn Teresa Flanigan is an associate professor at the School of Public Affairs at San Diego State University.

But how do cartels compare to other organizations the U.S. government has labeled as terrorist organizations? In the case of Mexican drug cartels, is the label merely a rhetorical tool, or is it actually useful as a descriptor? If the terrorist label is meaningful, why would non-ideological groups like drug cartels employ terrorist tactics? This article explores those questions by comparing the activities of Mexican drug cartels to several government definitions of terrorism, and comparing Mexican cartels to the Middle Eastern "terrorist" organizations Hamas and Hezbollah.[7] Mexican drug trafficking organizations are compared to Hamas and Hezbollah for several reasons. First, similar to Hamas and Hezbollah (but unlike more mobile, networked organizations such as al-Qaida), Mexican drug cartels are, by necessity, territorially specific organizations tied to relatively defined geographic locations.[8] While this is not characteristic of most types of organized crime groups,[9] Mexican drug cartels have an interest in controlling specific territory in order to preserve drug trade routes and maintain access to rural, mountainous terrain that provides advantage in evading authorities. Second, both Mexican drug cartels and Hamas and Hezbollah have deep and sophisticated relationships with the states within which they operate. Hamas and Hezbollah both have political wings and hold democratically elected office, in essence becoming part of the state and giving them important influence over the state's activities. In contrast, drug cartels' relationships with the Mexican government are characterized by high degrees of corruption and sometimes violence.[10] However, these tactics give cartels a great deal of influence over the activities of politicians and the bureaucracy. Through these tactics Mexican drug cartels exercise sufficient control over the state that experts warn of state capture,[11] with Sullivan and Elkus going so far as to warn that Mexico is becoming "a criminal-state largely controlled by narco-gangs."[12] While the relationships between Hamas, Hezbollah, Mexican drug cartels, and their respective states certainly fall into quite different categories, this influence and control makes Mexican drug cartels more similar to Hamas and Hezbollah than to truly clandestine terrorist organizations such as al-Qaida.

The readership of *Terrorism and Political Violence* can be assumed to have greater familiarity with politically motivated organizations like Hamas and Hezbollah than with organized crime groups like Mexican drug cartels. Thus, this article will give greater attention to the characteristics of Mexican drug cartels while contrasting them to Hamas and Hezbollah, and exploring if the "terrorism" label is an appropriate descriptor for these organizations' activities. Data for this comparison comes from a variety of sources. The information on Hezbollah in Lebanon is based on existing literature, interviews conducted with members of Hezbollah and other experts in Lebanon in 2005-2006, and content analysis of publications and publicity materials produced by Hezbollah. The information on Hamas is based on the extant literature and data from oral surveys conducted with over 1,000 low to moderate income individuals in Gaza and the West Bank. The information on Mexican drug cartels is based on existing literature, content analysis of Mexican newspaper articles, and expert interviews.

Defining Terrorism, Defining Cartel Violence

Academic, legal, and political definitions of terrorism abound. For the purposes of this examination we will concern ourselves with the ways in which terrorism is defined by a variety of government agencies and international organizations. As we see in Table 1, definitions differ even among government agencies in the same

Table 1. Definitions and descriptions of terrorism by select governments and international organizations

Source	Definition and/or description of terrorism (*emphasis added to key themes of the definition)	Key themes
Arab Convention for the Suppression of Terrorism	Any act or threat of violence, whatever its motives or purposes, that occurs in the advancement of an individual or collective criminal agenda and *seeking to sow panic among people, causing fear* by harming them, or placing their lives, liberty or security in danger, or seeking to cause damage to the environment or to public or private installations or property or to occupying or seizing them, or seeking to jeopardize national resources.	**Goal**: Create atmosphere of fear/terror and intimidation
European Union (Art.1 of the Framework Decision on Combating Terrorism, 2002)	This provides that terrorist offences are certain criminal offences set out in a list comprised largely of serious offences against persons and property which: given their nature or context, may seriously damage a country or an international organization where committed with the aim of: *seriously intimidating a population*; or *unduly compelling a Government or international organization to perform or abstain from performing any act*; or seriously destabilizing or destroying the fundamental political, constitutional, economic or social structures of a country or an international organization.	**Goal**: Create atmosphere of fear/terror and intimidation
Mexican government	The use of toxic substances, chemical or biological weapons, radioactive materials, explosives or firearms, arson, flooding, or any other means of violence against people, assets, or public services, *with the aim of causing alarm, fear*, or *terror* among the population or a sector of it, of attacking national security or *intimidating society*, or of *pressuring the authorities into making a decision.*	**Goal**: Create atmosphere of fear/terror and intimidation **Goal**: Influencing government actions or decisions

(*Continued*)

Table 1. Continued

Source	Definition and/or description of terrorism (*emphasis added to key themes of the definition)	Key themes
United Nations General Assembly (Resolution 49/60, 1994)	Criminal acts intended or calculated to *provoke a state of terror* in the general public, a group of persons or particular persons *for political purposes* are in any circumstance unjustifiable, whatever the considerations of a political, philosophical, ideological, racial, ethnic, religious or any other nature that may be invoked to justify them.	**Goal**: Create atmosphere of fear/terror and intimidation **Motivations**: Political/ideological
United Nations Security Council (Resolution 1566, 2004)	Criminal acts, including *against civilians*, committed with the intent to cause death or serious bodily injury, or taking of hostages, with the *purpose to provoke a state of terror* in the general public or in a group of persons or particular persons, *intimidate a population* or *compel a government or an international organization to do or to abstain from doing any act.*	**Tactic**: Target civilians **Goal**: Create atmosphere of fear/terror and intimidation **Goal**: Influencing government actions or decisions
United States Army (Field Manual No. FM 3-0, Chapter 9, 37 2001)	Calculated use of unlawful violence or threat of unlawful violence *to inculcate fear.* It is intended to *coerce or intimidate governments or societies... [to attain] political, religious, or ideological goals.*	**Goal**: Create atmosphere of fear/terror and intimidation **Motivations**: Political/ideological
United States Department of Defense (Dictionary of Military Terms)	The calculated use of unlawful violence or threat of unlawful violence to *inculcate fear*; intended to *coerce or to intimidate governments or societies* in the pursuit of *goals that are generally political, religious, or ideological.*	**Goal**: Create atmosphere of fear/terror and intimidation **Motivations**: Political/ideological
United States Federal Criminal Code. (Title 18 Section 2331 of	Activities that involve violent... or life-threatening acts... that are a violation of the criminal laws of the United States or of any State and... appear to be intended (i) to *intimidate or coerce a civilian*	**Tactic**: Targeting civilians **Goal**: Create atmosphere of fear/terror and intimidation

(Continued)

Table 1. Continued

Source	Definition and/or description of terrorism (*emphasis added to key themes of the definition)	Key themes
Chapter 113(B))	*population*; (ii) to *influence the policy of a government by intimidation or coercion; or (iii) to affect the conduct of a government* by mass destruction, assassination, or kidnapping; and ... occur primarily within the territorial jurisdiction of the United States ...	**Goal**: Influencing government actions or decisions
United States Federal Bureau of Investigation	The unlawful use of force or violence against persons or property *to intimidate or coerce a Government, the civilian population*, or any segment thereof, in furtherance of *political or social objectives*.	**Tactic**: Targeting civilians **Motivations**: Political/ideological **Goal**: Create atmosphere of fear/terror and intimidation
United States Patriot Act of 2001	Threatening, conspiring or attempting to hijack airplanes, boats, buses or other vehicles; threatening, conspiring or attempting to commit *acts of violence on any "protected" persons, such as government officials*; any crime committed with "the use of any weapon or dangerous device," when the intent of the crime is determined to be the endangerment of public safety or substantial property damage rather than for "mere personal monetary gain."	**Tactic**: Targeting public officials

*Parts of this table are adapted from a list originally complied by Arizona Department of Emergency and Military Affairs.

country. Nonetheless, among the ten definitions and descriptions listed, some similar themes emerge. Common to all but one of the definitions is the perpetrator's goal of creating an atmosphere of fear, intimidation, and terror among the general population or a specific group. Other common themes shared by the definitions are a goal of influencing government actions or decisions, political or ideological motivations, and targeting civilians or public officials as tactics. Each of these themes will be discussed below, examining how the characteristics of Mexican drug cartels align with the themes and comparing cartels' characteristics to those of Hamas and Hezbollah.

Characteristics of Hamas, Hezbollah, and Mexican Drug Cartels

Before examining the ways in which Hamas, Hezbollah, and Mexican drug cartels are similar and whether the activities of Mexican drug cartels resemble terrorism, it is useful to provide some basic background information on each of these organizations.

Brief History and Context

Hamas is an armed Sunni Islamic organization in the Palestinian Territories well known for its ongoing armed struggle against Israel. Hamas has the expressed goal of replacing Israel and the Palestinian Territories with an Islamic Palestinian state.[13] In 2006 Hamas won a majority of seats in the Palestinian Parliament through an open election[14] and since then has gained control of several ministries of the Palestinian Authority. In addition to its military and political role, Hamas is an important provider of public services in the Palestinian Territories, running an array of charities, hospitals, schools, orphanages, and summer camps.[15]

Hezbollah is an armed Shiite Islamic organization in Lebanon that is active as a paramilitary force, a political party, and a health and social service provider. Outside of Lebanon Hezbollah perhaps is best known for its armed resistance against the Israeli occupation of southern Lebanon.[16] In 2000 Israel withdrew from most of the regions it occupied, and since Hezbollah had so thoroughly incorporated military resistance into its identity and mission some scholars predicted that Hezbollah would dissolve as a political party.[17] However, Hezbollah remains a primary actor in the Lebanese political system, continuing to win a number of key seats in parliamentary and municipal elections, and engaging in armed attacks against Israel as recently as 2006.[18] While Hezbollah has never espoused a goal of overthrowing the Lebanese state, its relationships with other political parties and religious sects in Lebanon are often tense. Some members of Lebanese society, including Prime Minister Saad Hariri and the head of the Lebanese Forces Samir Geagea, consider the organization a threat to the country's stability and democracy.[19]

For the purposes of this article, "Mexican drug cartels" refers collectively to the six predominant drug trafficking organizations operating in Mexico: the Arellano Félix Organization, the Beltrán Leyva Organization, the Gulf Cartel, La Familia Michoacán/Knights Templar, Los Zetas, and the Sinaloa Cartel. Though they often will be referred to collectively, it is important to make clear that these cartels are distinct organizations with distinct leadership. The relationships among the cartels are dynamic; organizations face rifts and split from one another (notably, Los Zetas was formerly the protection arm for the Gulf Cartel), or occasionally form temporary alliances when economically or strategically useful. The groups are largely non-ideological[20] and are engaged in the lucrative activity of drug smuggling and drug production. The cartels interact with the Mexican state through bribery, corruption, political relationships, and violence as necessary to ensure business can operate free of the constraints of law enforcement.[21]

Finances, Training, and Weaponry

Albeit for different reasons, all three of these groups of actors engage in violence, and on the whole all three are relatively well armed and well trained militarily. This may not be surprising to hear about groups like Hamas and Hezbollah, which are recognized as having formal military wings. Both Hamas and Hezbollah are said to receive a great deal of funding, weapons, and training from Iran and Syria.[22] According to Cohen and Levitt,[23] Hamas smuggles small arms, explosives, fertilizer, rocket-propelled grenades, and rockets into the Palestinian Territories through Egypt, the amount of which has increased since Hamas began governing the Gaza Strip in 2007. While most rockets used by Hamas are locally produced, an influx of more and better materials has increased the quality of these weapons, and new Iranian-produced rockets with increased range have been used by Hamas in recent years as well.[24] Hamas also receives military training from Iran, Hezbollah, and others. However, in spite of Hamas' fairly well-developed military structure, experts agree that militarily Hamas is far less prepared than the Israeli military in terms of intelligence gathering, weaponry, and training. The conflict between Israel and Hamas in Gaza in late 2008 raised additional doubts about Hamas' combat capabilities.[25]

Like Hamas, Hezbollah also receives significant support from Iran, reportedly up to $200 million per year.[26] This figure is substantially more than the $50 million maximum estimate of funding to Hamas from Iran.[27] By most accounts Hezbollah is the better funded, better equipped, and better trained of the two organizations. In fact, Hezbollah itself provides funds to a number of organizations in Palestine, including Hamas, and Hezbollah and Iranian experts are said to train terrorist organizations throughout the region. Sophisticated weaponry is flown into Syria from Iran, and then transported overland the short distance to Lebanon's Hezbollah-dominated Beka'a Valley.[28] Hezbollah primarily targets its violent activity toward Israel, and the organization touted its 2006 war with Israel as a military victory. While Hezbollah has not yet targeted the Lebanese state with violence, the organization has significant ability to interfere in the Lebanese political process, paralyzing the government in 2006 by withdrawing from the cabinet, erecting a tent city in downtown Beirut, and occupying various ministries.[29]

Like Hamas and Hezbollah, Mexican drug cartels are also quite technologically advanced and well trained, with some experts asserting that these drug trafficking organizations have better weapons and armor than Mexican or U.S. law enforcement.[30] In 2006 drug cartels reportedly smuggled up to $25 billion into Mexico for laundering,[31] and drug sales in the United States bring as much as $39 billion to Mexican cartels each year,[32] giving the cartels resources that are likely enviable even to groups like Hamas and Hezbollah. As part of a multi-billion dollar drug trade, the cartels have access to, as one local expert described, "a bottomless flow of arms and a bottomless flow of money."[33] In addition, many drug cartels have extremely skilled employees. Perhaps most notably, Los Zetas is made up primarily of former Mexican Special Forces soldiers who were lured from the more poorly paid Mexican military to lucrative careers protecting the drug cartels. As Longmire and Longmire note, these individuals "maintain expertise in heavy weaponry, specialized military tactics, sophisticated communications equipment, intelligence collection, and countersurveillance techniques."[34] Supporting this assertion, several Mexican experts interviewed for this research project took special precautions in their communications due to concerns that their phone calls and e-mail might be monitored by cartels.

Motivations: Economic or Ideological?

Common to several of the definitions in Table 1 and to most academic definitions of terrorism is an organization's ideological motivation and goal of political, religious, or social change. The activities of terrorist groups and organized crime may overlap. In some instances organized crime may adopt terrorism as a tactic, as is discussed at length in this article. Similarly, terrorist groups like Hamas and Hezbollah often have some involvement in organized crime.[35] Hamas' primary criminal activities are counterfeiting and money laundering,[36] complemented by counterfeiting merchandise such as software, CDs and DVDs, clothing, and cosmetics. Hamas is also reported to have some involvement in drug trafficking.[37] Hezbollah raises funds through substantial drug production and trafficking, illegal car sales,[38] fraud, selling pirated software, smuggling cigarettes and other goods, and the illegal diamond trade.[39]

When terrorist organizations engage in criminal activity, it usually is fairly apparent that crime is used as a means to reach sociopolitical ends. The goals of militant groups employing terrorism are typically ideological, and their criminal activities are normally conducted with the goal of financing their ideological goals. In contrast, the goals of organized crime groups like drug cartels are primarily economic. As Longmire and Longmire note,

> Mexican DTOs *(drug trafficking organizations)* do not wish to remove the Mexican Government and replace it with one of their own. They are not religious zealots wishing to convert the Mexican people or the rest of the world. They simply want to maximize their profits and keep government and law enforcement out of their business.[40]

While they may have other motivations as well, the ideological motivations of Hamas and Hezbollah are clear. Both are religious organizations that express a strong adherence to Islamic teachings and use their own interpretations of those teachings to mobilize supporters and justify their activities, including violence.[41] Both organizations view themselves as representing a repressed minority group; Hamas the Palestinian people, and Hezbollah the Shiite population in Lebanon which historically has been economically and politically disenfranchised.[42] Both organizations have a shared political goal of liberating territory that they consider to be unfairly occupied by the state of Israel, and both organizations are active in national politics, holding important elected offices.[43]

Mexican drug cartels, on the other hand, do not have clear ideological goals. As Hazen argues, drug cartels take what actions are necessary to ensure they can continue to profit from their illegal activities without interference from law enforcement, but they do not seek political goals or aim to destabilize the Mexican government. As she notes, "They *(Mexican drug cartels)* threaten democracy certainly, yet they demonstrate no interest in causing state failure; that would be bad for business."[44] Mexican drug cartels may target state actors and attempt to influence government decisions, as will be discussed later, but this is done only for the utilitarian purpose of maximizing profits, not for political or ideological purposes.

An exception to this may be La Familia Michoacán, a cartel that disbanded and then reconfigured itself as the Knights Templar in early 2011. La Familia has a religious orientation and also presents itself as a representative and protector of the people of Michoacán. Communications from the cartel suggest that La Familia claims to be a representative voice for citizens in Michoacán, addressing the economic, political, and social grievances of the people, not unlike the efforts of Hamas or Hezbollah to represent and address the needs of Palestinians or the Shiite population. In a newspaper advertisement La Familia posed the question, "Who are we?" answering, "Workers from the Tierra Caliente region in the state of Michoacán, organized by the need to end the oppression, the humiliation to which we have constantly been subjected by people who have always had power."[45] La Familia, who often communicates with the public through newspapers or publicly displayed banners, also has insisted that the organization will disband once the Mexican government demonstrates that it will adequately address the needs of the people of Michoacán.[46] While La Familia is not proposing to enter mainstream elective politics, these statements nonetheless have a political premise that is unlike the motivations of other cartels in Mexico.

La Familia also has a decidedly religious orientation. Members of the cartel reportedly attend church regularly, carry bibles, and distribute bibles in local government offices.[47] La Familia leader Nazario Moreno Gonzalez is said to be a Jehovah's Witness convert who has penned his own book of religious teachings, sometimes referred to as a "bible."[48] One expert describes this book as a "religious self-help tome mixed with old-time social justice sloganeering."[49] Moreno Gonzalez is reportedly highly influenced by John Eldredge, an American evangelist and author of the self-help best-seller *Wild at Heart*, who promotes a highly masculine, "muscular" form of Christianity.[50] The book is reportedly studied, in Spanish translation, at La Familia training camps.[51] The cartel's leaders haze recruits by requiring them to engage in particularly bloody and gruesome acts so they are "prepared to do the Lord's work—that is, safeguarding women, combating competing cartels, and preventing the local sale of drugs,"[52] and leaders justify executions as "orders from the Lord."[53] While it is not clear the degree to which La Familia members or the public adhere to this particular Christian philosophy, La Familia leaders certainly have used religion as a rhetorical strategy to justify some of their most brutal acts.

Targeting and Influencing Government

Hand in hand with political ideology often comes a desire to target the government and influence the government's actions or decisions, and this is a characteristic that emerges in several of the definitions of terrorism in Table 1. How do the activities of Mexican drug cartels compare to those of Hamas and Hezbollah when interacting with states? How and why do organized crime groups engage in "terrorist-like" activities such as targeting the government in the absence of ideological motives?

As has been mentioned previously, Hamas and Hezbollah both have a sophisticated involvement in mainstream politics within their respective states, and thus they are able to influence the actions of the Palestinian Authority and the Lebanese state in democratically legitimate ways. However, these groups are best known outside the region for their use of violence as a tactic to influence government decision making. Hamas has targeted the Israeli government with violence primarily through attacks on the Israeli military and on individuals deemed to be collaborators with the Israeli state,[54] as well as targeting both Israeli and Palestinian civilians. Hamas' goal is to create a Palestinian Islamic state and it targets the Israeli government as a means of coercing the state to make decisions that align with that goal. The exact nature of the actions Hamas would like to pressure Israel to take can vary. While at times the organization's leaders state Hamas will accept nothing less than the full eradication of the state of Israel, at other times Hamas says it will cease violence if Israel adheres to the border designated by the 1948 Armistice Agreement, or the borders designated following the 1967 Six-Day War.

Hezbollah has targeted a number of state actors, foremost the Israeli military. Hezbollah's targeting of Israel is based not only on its desire to pressure Israel to retreat from Lebanese territory, but also to retreat from the Palestinian territories and from Jerusalem.[55] Hezbollah also is reported to target Israeli interests outside Lebanon, such as the Israeli embassy bombing in Argentina in 1992. Additionally, Hezbollah targeted the French and U.S. military in Lebanon in the early 1980s as well as U.S. Embassy staff, achieving their objective of coercing the French and U.S. governments to withdraw troops from the region during the Lebanese Civil War.

In contrast to Hamas and Hezbollah, who target states in pursuit of distinct political and ideological objectives, Mexican drug cartels target the state with the goal of engaging in their economic activities unhampered by government intervention. Mexican cartels direct much more violence toward one another than they do toward the state,[56] and they most often shape the behavior of the state through substantial corruption that grants them control of the bureaucracy.[57] However, drug cartels also direct violence toward the Mexican state, particularly by way of targeting public officials. Drug cartels engage in assassinations of law enforcement and local and federal government officials; according to Longmire and Longmire, "As many as one or two dozen assassinations occur throughout Mexico in any given week."[58] Between 2004 and 2010 twenty-seven mayors were killed by drug cartels, and in 2010 thirteen candidates for governorships were killed by organized crime, presumably due to these officials' refusal to allow cartels to operate without obstruction.[59] According to Hazen, this may be a strategy on the part of cartel leaders to reduce officials' readiness to take posts in violent areas, thereby causing posts to go unfilled or to be filled by individuals more willing to accommodate the cartels for the sake of survival.[60] Cartel members have also engaged in car bombings aimed at local and federal police, and have killed U.S. Consulate staff along the U.S.-Mexico border. While not explicitly political in nature, these attacks have the goal of influencing the state by intimidating Mexico's government into suspending its efforts to defeat the cartels. The cartels' efforts against the state are substantial enough that media outlets, academic experts, and U.S. Secretary of State Hillary Clinton have referred to the cartels as an "insurgency," and warn of an impending "failed state" in Mexico.[61] Others such as Hazen insist that cartels pose a real threat to democratic accountability within the state, but assert that predictions of an insurgency or failed state are exaggerated.[62]

Using Violence and Generating Fear: Tactics, Targets, and Goals

The most common theme in the definitions and descriptions of terrorism shown in Table 1 is an organization's intention of creating an atmosphere of fear, terror, and/or intimidation through its acts. Many are familiar with the idea that terrorism is theater; as Cohen notes, "Terrorism is a spectacle produced for viewers, many of whom live apart from the violent staged events."[63] Given this, it is not surprising that terrorist groups like Hamas and Hezbollah successfully create an atmosphere of fear in the societies they target with violence. The tactic of targeting civilians, also found as a theme in Table 1, can be particularly useful for generating an atmosphere of terror. Both Hamas and Hezbollah launch rockets into communities in Israel and at times hit civilians, though the organizations often claim this as accidental. The risk of a wayward rocket hitting one's home or workplace is a powerful producer of fear and serves as an effective means of gaining attention to one's political cause. Hamas and less frequently Hezbollah also have engaged in suicide bombing, targeting state installations or civilians at large, such as in buses or public markets. The use of suicide terrorism is particularly effective as a tactic for instilling public fear.[64] Grisly and unexpected events such as suicide attacks, car bombings, and the like draw attention that not only creates fear, but attracts media attention and helps gain support for one's cause. As Bloom[65] notes, violence—specifically suicide attacks—may resonate with individual members of an organization and has been shown to increase popular support for organizations that use the tactic. In this context one may witness an increase in violence as groups compete for power and popular support. Support for one's cause may come not only from those sympathetic to an organization's political goals, but indirectly from the citizen targets of violence who may pressure the state to give way to the perpetrators in order to regain security.

These violent strategies are logical for ideologically motivated groups, but why would organized crime groups like Mexican drug cartels engage in similar behavior? By many experts' accounts, they should not, or at least not with much frequency. Hazen notes that while organized crime groups do have the capacity to use violence, "violence is not their primary tool of the trade,"[66] because less violence is typically better for business and violence is costly, reducing profitability. A recent Stratfor report asserts that organized crime groups that use terrorist-style tactics risk losing the public support essential for maintaining the extensive network of policemen, bankers, politicians, businessmen, and judges necessary to provide them protection.[67]

Yet we have seen in Mexico in recent years gruesome acts of violence that have certainly created an atmosphere of fear and terror in the country, so much so that in winter 2010 the Mexican government warned Mexicans in the U.S. to travel home for the Christmas holiday only in groups and during daylight hours.[68] While in the past cartel violence typically involved the quick execution of rivals in a remote location, the violent activities of cartels have become increasingly grisly and public. Some experts suggest that much of these new forms of violence originated with the Zetas, with rival cartels then pressured to engage in similar activities.[69] With violent acts seeming to be quickly matched by rival cartels, Mexico may provide another context for the application of Bloom's strategic competition thesis, with rival cartels outbidding one another with increasingly gruesome acts.[70]

Cartels have begun using road blockades, car bombs, and improvised explosive devices. Groups like La Familia Michoacán first gained national repute when members dumped five severed human heads onto the dance floor of a night club.[71] Further decapitations have taken place around the country, becoming a preferred method of intimidation among prominent cartels.[72] Burned and tortured bodies are left in public with message from the cartels; banners and bodies are hung from bridges; internet videos have been posted of torture and killings.[73] These acts, ghastly in nature and showcased in public locations like nightclubs, bridges, or the internet, are clearly performed for an audience. The result is a palpable sense of fear among the Mexican population, particularly in geographic areas where the death toll is high.[74]

The intent of such shocking murders is to frighten rival cartels, the government, and the public. Violence may be targeted toward competitors or used internally to maintain discipline. Much like in the case of Hamas or Hezbollah, violence may be used to discourage the government's current actions, in this case, Mexico's drug war. Organized crime rarely targets non-associated individuals, and as such, until recently there has been little evidence of indiscriminate killing of civilians by

Mexican drug cartels. However, some experts believe those numbers have begun to escalate.[75] In that case the intent of violence, much like the targeting of civilians in the Middle East, may be to diminish public support for the government's efforts against the cartels in order to return to a period of calm. There is ample evidence that public sentiment aligns with this intent, with tens of thousands of people protesting in Mexico City in May 2011 asking President Calderon to withdraw from the battle with cartels.[76] While there is a lack of systematic reliable data on casualties that would allow one to assess changes in the number of civilian targets,[77] particularly disturbing are recent accounts of mass graves discovered in northern Mexico in early 2011. As of April 2011 at least 177 bodies of bus passengers had been found in two dozen hidden graves near the town of San Fernando in the border state of Tamaulipas; a number had been raped or burned alive. Cartel gunmen are believed responsible.[78] While the hidden graves suggest that these murders were not intended to send a public message, it provides a disconcerting example of civilian targeting by Mexican drug cartels.

Conclusion

How do Mexican cartels compare to other organizations the U.S. government has labeled as terrorist organizations, such as Hamas and Hezbollah? Is the label merely a political and legal tool, or does it have greater meaning? Looking at Table 2, we see that based on several themes from government definitions of terrorism, the key difference between Mexican drug cartels and Hamas and Hezbollah is the presence of political and ideological motivations. Hamas and Hezbollah are motivated ideologically by both politics and religion, and see themselves as representatives of oppressed groups. Mexican drug cartels are businesses whose motives, much like those of large corporations, are defending markets, expanding market share, and ultimately, maximizing profit.[79]

How important is Mexican drug cartels' lack of ideological motivation? A number of academics[80] and some of the government agencies listed in Table 1 would say this difference is at the crux of what makes a terrorist organization different from any other armed group. However, more than half of the definitions in Table 1 did

Table 2. Goals, motivations, and tactics of Hamas, Hezbollah, and Mexican drug cartels Compared to definitions and descriptions of terrorism

Key themes from definitions of terrorism	Hamas	Hezbollah	Mexican drug cartels
Goal: Create atmosphere of fear/ terror and intimidation	Yes	Yes	Yes
Goal: Influencing government actions or decisions	Yes	Yes	Yes
Motivations: Political/ideological	Yes	Yes	No (exception *may* be La Familia Michoacán)
Tactic: Target civilians	Yes	Yes	Yes
Tactic: Targeting public officials	Yes	Yes	Yes

not include ideology as an essential component, and some would argue that the semantic debate matters very little for citizens on the ground in communities experiencing violence. Longmire and Longmire assert,

> Mexican drug traffickers are more than criminals. They are terrorists. And that's not hyperbole. The tactics, strategy, organization, and even (to a limited extent) the goals of the Mexican drug cartels are all perfectly consistent with those of recognized terrorist organizations.[81]

This analysis illustrates the conceptual challenges and classificational ambiguity involved in analyzing terrorism and organized crime. There is a great deal of commonality among the activities of both types of groups. Criminal activity justified by ideological intent nonetheless remains a crime; illegal activity aimed at profit maximization may necessitate violence that targets government and strikes fear in the hearts of citizens. Arguably all terrorist groups employing violence are engaged in some form of criminal activity, and this article demonstrates that, although perhaps less often, criminal organizations may choose to use terrorism as a tactic in their pursuit of profit. To the extent that the activities of these two types of entities overlap, perhaps one key element in determining which label to apply is a matter of proportion. Is an organization engaged in 90% terrorist activity and 10% criminal activity? Or vice versa? As groups' activities and tactics shift, as in the case of Mexican drug cartels, does their label shift as well? If so, where is the tipping point at which an organized crime groups becomes a terrorist organization? Ultimately, perhaps the most useful technique for labeling violent groups is the practical strategy already in use by some law enforcement, legal prosecutors, and security policy makers: applying the label that under current conditions provides the most powerful tools for curtailing an organizations' activity.[82]

Notes

1. Satara Williams, "Congressman McCaul Discusses Strategies to Combat Drug Cartels," *The Sun*, April 6, 2011, http://www.houstonsun.com.2011/04/.

2. It is worth noting that some experts and government agencies prefer the term "drug trafficking organizations" to "drug cartel" because "cartel" often refers to price-setting groups, and it is not clear that Mexican drug cartels are involved in this practice; Colleen W. Cook, *CRS Report for Congress: Mexico's Drug Cartels* (Washington, DC: Congressional Research Service, 2008). However, because the term "drug cartel" still dominates, that is the term that will be used in this article.

3. Stratfor, *Mexico: Rebranding the Cartel Wars*, http://www.stratfor.com/analysis/20101223-mexico-rebranding-cartel-wars.

4. Ibid.

5. In the case of the Gulf Cartel, the goal was to use anti-terrorist rhetoric to weaken support for rival cartel La Familia Michoacán. In September 2008 a grenade attack in the capital of Michoacán, ostensibly by the cartel La Familia Michoacán, was one of the first instances of indiscriminate killing of civilians in Mexico's drug war. Shortly thereafter the Gulf cartel posted banners in several cities condemning the attack and offering a $5 million reward for the capture of those involved. Banners called the attack an act of terrorism, and accused La Familia of "fundamentalist Islamic practices"; STRATFOR, *Mexico Security Memo*, http://www.stratfor.com/node/125267/analysis/20081013_mexico_security_memo_oct_13_2008).

6. STRATFOR (see note 3 above).

7. Labeling groups as terrorist organizations is by nature contentious, political, and subjective. For discussions of this, see Michael V. Bhatia, "Fighting Words: Naming Terrorists,

Bandits, Rebels and Other Violent Actors," *Third World Quarterly* 26, no. 1 (2005): 5–22; and Leonard Weinberg, Ami Pedahzur, and Sivan Hirsch-Hoefler, "The Challenges of Conceptualizing Terrorism," *Terrorism and Political Violence* 17 (2005): 1–18. Different individuals, populations, and governments disagree about whether they consider Hamas and Hezbollah to be terrorist organizations, and some governments differentiate between these organizations' military, political, and charitable arms; see Shawn Flanigan and Mounah Abdel-Samad, "Hezbollah's Social Jihad: Nonprofits as Resistance Organizations," *Middle East Policy* 16, no. 2 (2009): 122–137. I refrain from taking a normative stance on the activities of these two groups, and use the term "terrorist" here in reference to the U.S. Department of State's identification of Hamas and Hezbollah as Foreign Terrorist Organizations (see http://www.state.gov/s/ct/rls/other/des/123085.htm).

8. It should be noted that Hezbollah is reported to operate outside Lebanon, in locations as far flung as Argentina and Thailand. However, Hezbollah's espoused goals are based on territorial claims—liberating southern Lebanon from Israeli occupation—and as such, much of the organization's activities are geographically based. Even when Hezbollah is reported to operate outside Lebanon, it does so, typically, with the goal of attacking Israeli interests.

9. Jennifer M. Hazen, "Drug Cartels and their Fiefdoms: What Challenge to the Mexican State?", Paper presented at the annual convention of the International Studies Association, Montreal, Canada, March 17, 2011.

10. Ibid.

11. Ibid.; Local experts, interviews with author 2010–2011.

12. John P. Sullivan and Adam Elkus, "State of Siege: Mexico's Criminal Insurgency," *Small Wars Journal* (2009): 1–12, p. 1.

13. Hamas, *The Charter of Allah: The Platform of the Islamic Resistance Movement* (Hamas, 1988).

14. This election was deemed fair and legitimate by independent observers, which proved problematic because the U.S. had worked hard to convince the Israeli government to allow Hamas members to stand for election.

15. Matthew Levitt, *Hamas: Politics, Charity and Terrorism in the Service of Jihad* (New Haven, CT: Yale University Press, 2006).

16. Shawn Flanigan and Mounah Abdel-Samad, "Hezbollah's Social Jihad: Nonprofits as Resistance Organizations," *Middle East Policy* 16, no. 2 (2009): 122–137.

17. Howard Vincent Meehan, *Terrorism, Diasporas, and Permissive Threat Environments: A Study of Hezbollah's Fundraising Operations in Paraguay and Ecuador* (Monterey, CA: Naval Postgraduate School, 2004).

18. Flanigan and Abdel-Samad (see note 16 above).

19. "Geagea: Hezbollah's Arms Hinder Solutions," *The Daily Star*, May 13, 2011, http://www.dailystar.com.lb/News/Politics/2011/May-13/Geagea-Hezbollahs-arms-hinder-solutions.ashx#axzz1mNh4clmr.

20. There is some evidence that La Familia Michoacán, reconfigured as Knights Templar in early 2011, has some ideological orientation as will be discussed later in the article. It is unclear as of yet whether the newly configured Knights Templar shares this ideological orientation.

21. Hazen (see note 9 above).

22. Rachel Ehrenfeld, *Funding Evil: How Terrorism Is Financed—and How to Stop It* (Chicago: Bonus Books, 2005).

23. Yoram Cohen and Matthew Levitt, *PolicyWatch #1484. Hamas Arms Smuggling: Egypt's Challenge* (Washington, DC: The Washington Institute for Near East Policy, 2009).

24. Ibid.

25. Yoram Cohen and Jeffrey White, *Policy Focus #97. Hamas in Combat: The Military Performance of the Palestinian Islamic Resistance Movement* (Washington, DC: The Washington Institute for Near East Policy, 2009).

26. United States Secretary of Defense, *Unclassified Report on Military Power of Iran* (Washington, DC: Department of Defense, 2010).

27. Matthew Levitt, *Iranian State Sponsorship of Terror: Threatening U.S. Security, Global Stability, and Regional Peace. Testimony before the House Committee on International Relations, Subcommittee on the Middle East and Central Asia, and the Subcommittee on International Terrorism and Nonproliferation* (Washington, DC: House Committee on International

Relations Subcommittee on the Middle East and Central Asia and Subcommittee on International Terrorism and Nonproliferation, 2005).

28. Ibid.

29. Magnus Norell, *Policy Focus #98 A Victory for Islamism? The Second Lebanon War and Its Repercussions* (Washington, DC: The Washington Institute for Near East Policy, 2009).

30. Sylvia M. Longmire and John P. Longmire IV, "Redefining Terrorism: Why Mexican Drug Trafficking is More than Just Organized Crime," *Journal of Strategic Security* 1, no. 1 (2008): 35–52.

31. Colleen W. Cook, *CRS Report for Congress: Mexico's Drug Cartels* (Washington, DC: Congressional Research Service, 2008).

32. Peter O'Dowd, "Are U.S. Drug Users to Blame for Mexican Border Violence?," *Marketplace*, Wednesday, June 15, 2011, http://www.marketplace.org/topics/life/are-us-drug-users-blame-mexican-border-violence.

33. Local expert, interviews with author 2011.

34. Longmire and Longmire (see note 30 above), 41.

35. Stratfor (see note 3 above); Also, see many of the articles in this Special Issue of Terrorism and Political Violence, particularly those by Victor Asal et al., James Forest, and John Parachini.

36. Aaron Mannes, Amy Sliva, V.S. Subrahmanian, Jonathan Wilkenfeld, *Stochastic Opponent Modeling Agents: A Case Study with Hamas*, http://www.cs.umd.edu/~asliva/papers/SOMAHamas-icccd08.pdf; Erhenfeld (see note 22 above); Levitt (see note 15 above).

37. Levitt (see note 15 above).

38. Stratfor (see note 3 above).

39. Matthew Levitt, *Hezbollah: Financing Terror through Criminal Enterprise* (Washington, DC: Senate Committee on Homeland Security and Governmental Affairs, 2005).

40. Longmire and Longmire (see note 30 above), 47.

41. Ahmed Nizar Hamzeh, *In the Path of Hizbullah* (Syracuse, NY: Syracuse University Press, 2004); Levitt (see note 15 above); Amal Saad-Ghorayeb, *Hizbu'llah: Politics and Religion* (London: Pluto Press, 2002).

42. Flanigan and Abdel-Samad (see note 16 above); Shawn Flanigan. "Nonprofit Service Provision by Insurgent Organizations—The Cases of Hizballah and the Tamil Tigers," *Studies in Conflict and Terrorism* 31 (2008): 499–519.

43. Hamas (see note 13 above); Hamzeh (see note 41 above); Levitt (see note 15 above); Saad-Ghorayeb (see note 41 above).

44. Hazen (see note 9 above), 3.

45. William Finnegan, "Silver or Lead," *The New Yorker*, May 31, 2010, 38–51.

46. Local expert, interviews with author 2011.

47. George Grayson, *La Familia Drug Cartel: Implications for U.S.–Mexican Security* (Carlisle, PA: Strategic Studies Institute, 2010).

48. Local expert, interviews with author 2011; ibid.

49. Ibid.

50. Ibid., Finnegan (see note 45 above), Grayson (see note 47 above).

51. Finnegan (see note 45 above).

52. Grayson (see note 47 above), 35.

53. Ibid., 37.

54. Jeroen Gunning, *Hamas in Politics: Democracy, Religion, Violence* (New York: Columbia University Press, 2008).

55. Saad-Ghorayeb (see note 41 above).

56. According to Hazen (see note 9 above), approximately 90% of Mexican drug cartel-related killings involve the cartels themselves, with an estimated 7% of victims being police or military.

57. Sullivan and Elkus (see note 12 above).

58. Longmire and Longmire (see note 30 above), 42.

59. Hazen (see note 9 above).

60. Ibid.

61. Local expert, interviews with author 2011; Longmire and Longmire (see note 30 above); Sullivan and Elkus (see note 12 above).

62. Hazen (see note 9 above).

63. Tyler Cowen, "Terrorism as Theater: Analysis and Policy Implications," *Public Choice 128* (2006): 233–244, p. 233.

64. Mia Bloom, *Dying to Kill: The Allure of Suicide Terrorism* (New York: Columbia University Press, 2005).

65. Mia Bloom, "Palestinian Suicide Bombing: Public Support, Market Share, and Outbidding," *Political Science Quarterly* 119, no. 1 (2004): 61–88.

66. Hazen (see note 9 above), p. 7.

67. Stratfor (see note 3 above).

68. Daniel Hernandez, "Mexican Expats Warned About Holiday Travel Home," *Los Angeles Times,* November 24, 2010, http://articles.latimes.com/2010/nov/24/world/la-fg-mexico-convoys-20101124.

69. Local experts, interviews with author 2010–2011.

70. Bloom (see note 65 above).

71. Local expert, interviews with author 2011; Grayson (see note 47 above).

72. Stratfor (see note 3 above).

73. Longmire and Longmire (see note 30 above); Hazen (see note 9 above); Ibid.

74. Local experts, interviews with author 2010–2011.

75. Hazen (see note 9 above).

76. Ken Ellingwood, "In Mexico City, Crowds Protest Drug Violence," *Los Angeles Times,* May 8, 2011, http://articles.latimes.com/2011/may/08/world/la-fg-mexican-violence-protest-20110509.

77. Hazen (see note 9 above).

78. Tracy Wilkinson, "Police, Bus Companies Failed to Act as Graves Filled in Tamaulipas," *Los Angeles Times*, April 25, 2011, http://articles.latimes.com/2011/apr/25/world/la-fg-mexico-mass-graves-20110425.

79. For the purposes of this discussion we will disregard the possible ideological and religious motives of La Familia Michoacán/Knights Templar, which are atypical of the major Mexican drug cartels. Also, it is important to consider that the cartels' desire to consolidate power and secure geographic territory is not unlike the goals of many ethnonationalist terror organizations, which Hezbollah and Hamas are sometimes labeled.

80. Brigette Nacos, *Terrorism and Counterterrorism: Understanding Threats and Responses in the Post-9/11 World* (New York: Penguin, 2006).

81. Longmire and Longmire (see note 30 above), p. 37.

82. As previously mentioned, public officials in both Mexico and in the United States have made efforts to apply anti-terrorism law to drug cartels in order to assign drug traffickers longer prison sentences, impose harsher penalties upon those providing material support to cartels, and allow government to freeze assets and restrict travel of those involved in drug trafficking.

Terrorist and Non-Terrorist Criminal Attacks by Radical Environmental and Animal Rights Groups in the United States, 1970–2007

JENNIFER VARRIALE CARSON

Department of Criminal Justice, University of Central Missouri, Warrensburg, Missouri, USA

GARY LAFREE AND LAURA DUGAN

Department of Criminology and Criminal Justice, University of Maryland, College Park, Maryland, USA

Despite concerns about the growing threat posed by domestic radical environmental and animal rights groups to the United States, there has been little systematic quantitative evidence depicting the characteristics of their attacks over time. In this paper we analyze data on 1,069 criminal incidents perpetrated by environmental and animal rights extremists from 1970 to 2007. Based on the Global Terrorism Database's definition of terrorism, we classified 17 percent of these incidents as terrorist. To supplement the analysis, we also conducted interviews with a non-random sample of twenty-five activists who self-identified as part of the environmental or animal rights movements. We find that overall, the attacks staged by radical environmental and animal rights groups thus far have been overwhelmingly aimed at causing property damage rather than injuring or killing humans. Further, results from our interviews suggest that activists appear to weigh carefully the costs and benefits of illegal protest. Despite the fact that attacks by environmental and animal rights groups have thus far been almost universally nonviolent, concerns linger that this situation might change in the future.

Jennifer Varriale Carson is affiliated with the Department of Criminal Justice, University of Central Missouri. Gary LaFree is the director of the START Center, and is affiliated with the Department of Criminology and Criminal Justice, University of Maryland. Laura Dugan is affiliated with the Department of Criminology and Criminal Justice, University of Maryland.

Support for this research was provided by the Science and Technology division of the Department of Homeland Security through the National Consortium for the Study of Terrorism and Responses to Terrorism (START), grant number N00140510629. Any opinions, findings, conclusions or recommendations in this document are those of the authors and do not necessarily reflect the views of the Department of Homeland Security. We want to thank Hillary McNeel, Alexandra Prokopets, Katrina Rudyj, and Kyle Saud for database support.

Despite substantial popular and policy interest in radical environmental and animal rights groups in the United States, few researchers have systematically examined the frequency and severity of attacks by these groups. This is surprising given the claims that members of such groups pose an important domestic terrorist threat to the security of the United States. For instance, John Lewis, the Deputy Assistant Director of the Federal Bureau of Investigation (FBI) in 2005, stated that "one of today's most serious domestic terrorism threats come from special interest extremist movements such as the Animal Liberation Front, the Earth Liberation Front, and Stop Huntingdon Animal Cruelty campaign."[1] Similarly, FBI Director Robert Mueller has more recently noted that, "Animal rights extremism and eco-terrorism continue to pose a threat."[2]

In a survey conducted by Simone, Freilich, and Chermak in 2008, approximately 75% of U.S. state police agencies reported that radical environmental and animal rights groups exist in their state and pose a major security threat, second only to that of Islamic jihadists.[3] Further, in 2009 animal rights activist Daniel Andreas (who is suspected of two nonlethal bombings) was added to the FBI's Most Wanted Terrorists List.[4] Also in 2009, James Lee—who held hostages at the corporate headquarters of the Discovery Channel in Silver Spring, Maryland before being killed by the police—was described by some news outlets as an environmental militant.[5] Given the substantial interest generated by these events and the potential risk environmental and animal rights extremists pose to the security of the U.S., our main purpose in this paper is to analyze newly collected data to determine the extent and severity of the attacks that are attributed to these groups.

Scholars have also addressed the threat of radical environmental and animal rights groups, although much of this attention has focused on the appropriateness of terminology, particularly in regards to the use of the term "eco-terrorism."[6] Critics like Steven Vanderheiden and Randall Amster have argued that classifying these cases as terrorism is misleading because supporters of environmental and animal rights extremists do not seek to injure or kill humans.[7] Similarly, Donald Liddick argues that it is incorrect to characterize incidents perpetrated by environmental and animal rights groups as terrorism because the vast majority involve minor property damage and do not target people.[8] Vanderheiden prefers the term "ecotage," which he defines as "the economic sabotage of inanimate objects thought to be complicit in environmental destruction," and contends that conflating these acts with terrorism ignores an important moral distinction.[9] By contrast, Gary Perlstein claims that by not considering members of these groups as terrorists, we are erroneously treating them as pranksters and underestimating the true threat that they pose.[10]

Our understanding of the criminal activities perpetrated by environmental and animal rights extremists has thus far been limited because valid empirical data simply have not existed. Yet, the persistent claims of serious threat associated with these groups by federal law enforcement and certain researchers make it especially important that we empirically assess presumed hazards and how they might have evolved over time. John Wigle notes that collecting data on the characteristics surrounding incidents perpetrated by radical eco-groups is an important step to develop more effective policing measures and recommends that the effort should be "directed at gathering discrete date, time, and location characteristics of any data collected."[11]

In accordance with these suggestions, we have assembled an Eco-Incidents Database (EID) that includes criminal incidents perpetrated by members of radical environmental and animal rights groups in the United States from 1970 to 2007. We include *illegal activity in the United States from 1970 through 2007 that was principally motivated to protest the destruction or degradation of the environment, the mistreatment of animals, or both.* The EID was first constructed by selecting the relevant terrorist cases from the Global Terrorism Database (GTD), which defines terrorism as "the threatened or actual use of illegal force and violence to attain a political, economic, religious or social goal through fear, coercion or intimidation."[12] We then searched the open source literature for other sources of incidents for relevant non-terrorist criminal incidents, eventually supplementing the GTD with incidents from ten other open source databases on animal rights and environmental extremism. In all, we collected data on 1,069 criminal and terrorist incidents committed by individuals or members of radical eco-groups from the years 1970 through 2007. We describe the characteristics of these incidents and examine trends in the characteristics of attacks over time.

We complement the analysis of these data with a set of open-ended interviews with a nonrandom sample of animal rights and environmental activists in order to get a sense of how noncriminal members of the movement weighed the costs and benefits of engaging in illegal activities to support their activism. We are especially interested in the attitudes of these activists to threatened sanctions and to their evaluations of the costs and benefits of illegal activity in support of environmental and animal rights causes.

Environmental and Animal Rights Philosophies

Many ecological and animal rights activists adhere to the ideas of Arne Naess, a Norwegian philosopher, who referred to a strong support for protecting the natural environment as "deep ecology." The primary tenet of this philosophy is biocentrism, or the belief that everything in nature is of equal value. Consequently, biocentrism promotes the protection of not just living things, but also inanimate objects like rocks and rivers. Perhaps the most alarming aspect of deep ecology is what Sean Eagan refers to as restoration ecology, or the idea that we should roll back civilization and return to an earlier state that is wilder and more primitive.[13] The implied threat in such a philosophy is that the world might be a better place with a few billion less people.

Nonetheless, very few interpret the canons of deep ecology in this apocalyptic way. In fact, Naess himself was a follower of Gandhian principles that promoted nonviolent resistance. Overall, the philosophies of deep ecology and biocentrism directly promote a peaceful coexistence with nature and indirectly support legitimate avenues to obtain these goals. In practice, there is a divide in the environmental and animal rights movements between groups that promote such legitimate avenues (e.g., Greenpeace) and those that opt for more criminal, sometimes violent strategies (e.g., Stop Huntingdon Animal Cruelty). The movement known as "green anarchy" is typical of the more radical wing.

Green anarchy opposes modern industrialized development and practices, and contends that society was better off before the advent of industry and farming.[14] Often linked to the green anarchy philosophy is an anti-capitalism sentiment that justifies more radical strategies, including the destruction of property. The Anti-Defamation League cites a letter published in the newsletter *Green Anarchy*, that reads, "When someone picks up a bomb instead of a pen, is when my spirits really soar."[15] As Gary Ackerman notes, this broader focus encourages green anarchists to act outside the legal system and discourages adherents from compromising on fundamental beliefs and goals.[16]

However, Taylor cautions that green anarchy should be considered a distinct ideology from what groups like Animal Liberation Front (ALF) and the Earth Liberation Front (ELF) subscribe to as the former focuses more on the battle against industrial civilization; thus, there are clear intellectual boundaries between the environmental, animal rights, and anarchist ideologies.[17] In response, Ackerman argues, "there are several indicators of relational bridges between these movements across which fragments of ideology, tactics, and occasionally cooperation can flow...so while these groups may not constitute a single entity, they are at the very least close cousins."[18] These complex characteristics are well represented by three of the most important and best known extremist environmental and animal rights groups: ALF, ELF, and Stop Huntingdon Animal Cruelty (SHAC).

ALF, ELF, and SHAC

Eagan argues that there are three main elements that all environmental and animal rights groups share: an uncompromising position, status as a grass roots organization (without any clear chain of command or any pay/benefits), and resources directed toward direct action rather than aimed at lobbying and nonviolent protest.[19] ALF, ELF, and SHAC all share these characteristics. While all three originated in Great Britain, the nature of their origins differs. ALF splintered from the less radical Hunt Saboteurs Association (HSA) in 1976. ELF was established in 1992 by former Earth First! members. Both organizations were created in response to a more militant movement embracing criminal strategies. SHAC was formed in 1998 after a documentary aired about the research organization Huntingdon Life Sciences (HLS), demonstrating the mistreatment of animals under its supervision.

ALF's primary objective is "to effectively allocate resources (time and money) to end the 'property status' of nonhuman animals" (Animal Liberation Front, under "ALF Mission Statement").[20] ALF is influenced by a number of theorists, most notably Peter Singer and his work advocating for the equality of animals.[21] ALF encourages direct action in order to accomplish this mission, primarily through rescuing animals and/or damaging the property of individuals and companies whom they perceive to be animal exploiters.

ELF, which has very similar ideals to ALF, also promotes the destruction of the assets of those who, in the judgment of ELF members, threaten the environment.[22] However, as Ackerman notes, radical environmentalists like ELF are more broadly focused on the entire ecosystem, while animal rights extremists are concerned more narrowly with sentient beings.[23] ELF publicizes acts of environmental destruction through various tactics. Perhaps most influential to the development and strategies of ELF is Edward Abbey, whose 1985 book on "monkeywrenching"[24] has become a symbolic guidebook to environmental and animal rights extremists through its description of four individuals who sabotaged a number of sites in the southwestern United States. The primary difference between Earth First! and ELF is that the latter focuses more than the former on direct action.

Although created in Great Britain around 1999, SHAC only became criminally active in the U.S. in 2001 and scaled up its efforts after Huntingdon Life Sciences (HLS) moved its headquarters to New Jersey in 2002. SHAC has targeted businesses or organizations that support HLS, including Stephens Incorporated, one of their main financial backers. After a series of protests including some posted on a website titled "StephensKills," the financial organization sold its shares of HLS. The protests, along with two bombings of HLS facilities in California, were perceived by many SHAC members as major victories. SHAC has continued to use extremely aggressive tactics including death threats and harassment directed toward people connected to Huntingdon Life Sciences and its business partners.[25] However, the U.S. contingent of this group will likely be limited by the recent conviction of six of its prominent members.[26]

All three of these organizations lack a true hierarchical structure, operating as individuals or clusters of individuals who work separately, without one central leader.[27] This "leaderless resistance" or "lone wolf" strategy allows members of these groups to maintain a certain amount of anonymity, enhancing their chances of avoiding detection; this has become a clear and deliberate tactic for this movement. Ackerman argues that their cell-like structure explains why relatively few members have been arrested and convicted.[28] Further, perpetrators who operate through autonomous cells are less constrained by geographic boundaries and are very difficult to infiltrate and subvert. This structure allows activists to become members of the movement simply by carrying out uncoordinated illegal actions on the movement's behalf. Moreover, this lack of a hierarchical organization provides little opportunity for a central administration to reduce the impact of more extreme cell members.

Background to the Current Study

Overall, there has been little empirical work that systematically documents the illegal activities of environmental and animal rights extremists. Despite the energetic academic debate on how to conceptualize these acts and the important qualitative case studies detailing a primarily nonviolent movement,[29] little effort thus far has been made to quantify the assumptions upon which many of these opinions are based. An important exception is a joint report published in 1993 by the Departments of Justice and Agriculture that descriptively assesses the criminal activities of groups that targeted animal enterprises from 1977 to June 30, 1993.[30] This report, while limited in scope, drew important conclusions, such as, "the high incidence of minor vandalism suggests that most extremist animal rights-related acts continue to be small scale and fairly haphazard"[31] and a more cautionary statement concluding that, "extremists associated with the animal rights cause demonstrated an increased willingness to engage in more militant and costly activities."[32] The authors cite a total of 313 incidents committed primarily by ALF-affiliated entities, with a peak of activity in 1987.

Another empirical assessment of this type of criminal activity was made in a 2008 report by the Department of Homeland Security, which expands the scope from that of the 1993 report to cover acts motivated by both environmental and animal rights ideologies from 1981 to 2005.[33] The authors note that "ecoterrorists have perpetrated more illegal acts commonly associated with terrorism on U.S. soil than any other known group"[34] and that "the economic cost of these acts exceeds $100 million dollars and is likely to grow in the future."[35] The report documents the majority of attacks as vandalism (45 percent) and cites a peak in activity causing more than 10,000 dollars of damage at the end of their collection effort (2003–2005).

While these research contributions are vital to accurately assess the threat of the environmental and animal rights extremist movement, each has limitations that raise concern about the strength of their conclusions. Both reports are vague on their sources, which makes it difficult to ascertain the reliability of the data. The 1993 report cites interviews with targeted companies and with law enforcement, while the 2008 report lists its sources as communiqués, media reports, and law enforcement, without offering more specificity. Further, both reports are limited in their scope; the 1993 report only includes acts against animal enterprises, while the 2008 report only focuses on incidents after 1981. Our main goal in this project is to respond to these limitations by presenting an empirical database that includes both terrorist and non-terrorist criminal acts by radical and environmental organizations and individuals in the United States since 1970. As noted, we include any illegal activity in the U.S. from 1970 through 2007 that was principally motivated to protest the destruction or degradation of the environment, the mistreatment of animals, or both.

Data and Methods

We began this analysis by compiling a comprehensive set of data that documents incidents by radical environmental and animal rights groups. Sources used to compile the Eco-Incidents Database (EID) are shown in Table 1. Construction of the EID began by extracting relevant cases from two primary sources: (a) the Foundation for Biomedical Research for criminal cases and (b) the Global Terrorism Database (GTD) for all terrorism cases. Below we describe these sources in detail and explain the process that was used to extract and assess incidents for inclusion. As a guide, we sought to include all illegal activity whose main motivation was related to the environment, animal rights, or both concerns, occurring in the United States between 1970 and 2007. We used the GTD definition to determine whether individual cases should also be classified as terrorist attacks.[36]

Table 1. Eco-incidents database

Source	Years	Number of U.S. incidents
Foundation for Biomedical Research	1981–2007	474
Global Terrorism Database	1970–2007	187
National Alliance for Animals	1983–2007	479
Fur Commission	1980–2007	271
Arnold (1997)	1958–1996	215
Department of Homeland Security Report (2008)	1984–2007	156
Hewitt (2005)	1984–2004	119
Leader and Probst (2003)	1996–2001	100
Southern Poverty Law Center	1984–2002	97
Seattle Post-Intelligencer (2001)	1996–2001	49
Anti-Defamation League	2004–2007	38
Department of Agriculture/Department of Justice Report (1993)	1984–1992	21

Foundation for Biomedical Research Chronology

As shown in Table 1, we included nearly 500 cases from the Foundation for Biomedical Research (FBR). The FBR has collected information on terrorist and criminal activities conducted by members of radical eco-groups in the United States since 1981. The data are publicly available on the FBR website[37] and are compiled primarily through U.S. media sources, which the foundation checks regularly for incidents perpetrated in the name of environmental or animal rights groups. The FBR data also includes information from group communiqués. We verified all incidents from the FBR using open sources and recoded the cases to comply with GTD coding. In order to avoid duplicate cases, we compared the major characteristics of each case (especially date, location, and perpetrator) with those in the GTD and removed cases found in both.

Global Terrorism Database

The Global Terrorism Database (GTD) is currently the most comprehensive unclassified open-source database that includes both domestic and international terrorist attacks. As noted above, terrorism in the GTD is defined as "the threatened or actual use of illegal force and violence to attain a political, economic, religious or social goal through fear, coercion or intimidation."[38] The GTD records information on over 80,000 domestic and international incidents for the years 1970 to 2007. We identified potential cases from the GTD by first including cases attributed to relevant groups, such as ELF and ALF, and then searching comments and summary fields in the database for key terms (e.g., animal, ecology, earth, and environment) for those attacks not attached to a group (about 23 percent). These procedures resulted in 187 relevant GTD attacks from 1970 to 2007.

Supplemental Sources

After we assembled a set of incidents from the FBR and the GTD, the most comprehensive and reliable data sources available on this phenomenon, we next examined the ten additional data sets listed in Table 1. Each supplemental source has a somewhat different purpose and format for their data, but were all used to fill in any possible gaps from the first two sources. The National Animal Interest Alliance[39] and the Fur Commission[40] post chronologies on their websites. The former organization promotes animal welfare as opposed to animal rights, with a focus on the legal protection of animals. The Fur Commission is intrinsically more biased, serving as an important lobby for mink farms. Ron Arnold's 1997 book includes over 200 additional events and comes from a perspective aimed at preventing the attacks of radical environmental and animal rights groups.[41] Given the biases of these and other sources, we were careful to check for secondary sources, but acknowledge that not all cases were available in the news media.[42] However, it is safe to say that most of the cases missing from our database are likely to be relatively minor criminal offenses. Table 1 shows the total number of cases added to the EID from each source.

The 2008 Department of Homeland Security Report listed 156 cases.[43] Christopher Hewitt's 2003 book, an important academic contribution to chronicling acts of terrorism and political violence, documents 119 eco-related events.[44] Data were also extrapolated from Leader and Probst's 2005 article[45] and from the Southern Poverty Law Center, a nonprofit organization primarily focused on civil rights education and activism. The *Seattle Post-Intelligencer* chronology is from an article published in 2001.[46] Finally, the Anti-Defamation League,[47] a nonprofit organization also concerned with racism and anti-Semitism in particular, and the 1993 Department of Agriculture/Department of Justice report[48] contributed a handful of incidents. In the end, we checked over 2,200 incidents from twelve sources for inclusion in the EID resulting in 1,069 unique incidents after removing duplicates (based on fields like date, perpetrator, and incident summary).

Interview Data

In order to get a sense of how environmental and animal rights activists felt about criminal attacks made on behalf of their movements, we also conducted twenty-five interviews in a large northeastern city. Our only criterion for selection was that interviewees had participated in some type of environmental or animal rights motivated activism (e.g., lobbying, demonstrations, and protests). The activists were initially recruited from meet-up.com (an online resource utilized by environmental and animal activist groups, among others) and through related organizational websites. From there, a snowball sample was used to recruit additional activists. We asked the first set of informants to recommend other informants and continued this process with new recruits until the final set of interviews was obtained (determined once saturation of responses occurred). Finding an initial informant was difficult as many activists were concerned that by describing their participation even in legal environmental and animal rights activity they would be vulnerable to adverse consequences.[49] Despite this, 92 percent of those who replied to our initial requests for interviews followed through by completing them.

We followed Andrea Fontana and James Frey's (1994) suggestions for gaining access and trust by using language that projects a sense of understanding through presentation (e.g., dressing causally, knowing the vernacular of the movement) and by establishing rapport.[50] However, the extremist fringe of the environmental and animal rights movement remains a difficult group in which to gain entry. Consequently, we acknowledge that the conclusions drawn from this nonrandom sample cannot be generalized either to the movement as a whole or to its more extreme elements. Nevertheless, 8 of the 25 participants we interviewed (32 percent) admitted to having a criminal record associated with their participation in movement activities. Most of these offenses were relatively minor misdemeanors such as trespassing, although one participant was arrested for larceny.

In general, while the sample was fairly balanced across movements and by gender, it was predominately young (mostly between the ages of 18–25, but as old as 65), highly educated (nearly all respondents were in college or held a bachelor's degree), and white. About 60 percent of the sample was affiliated with mainstream environmental or animal rights organizations,[51] while the others participated in activities, but were not formally attached to a specific group. Without information on the demographics of the movements as a whole, we are unable to draw conclusions about the nature of the selection bias within this sample.

We conducted face-to-face semi-structured interviews that encouraged discussion. The introductory questions were based on Donald Liddick's questionnaire[52] (see Appendix 1 for the introductory questions). The remaining questions were designed to be general enough to encourage discussion, leaving room for follow-up or clarifying questions. All interviews were taped and transcribed for analysis.

Results

Figure 1 shows total attacks by environmental and animal rights groups in the United States from 1970 to 2007. We see that during the 1970s, incidents were relatively rare; they began to increase in the early 1980s, reaching a peak of 39 incidents in 1989. After a slight decline in 1989, incidents began to increase again in the early 1990s, reaching over 50 incidents for the first time in 1997, over 90 in 2000, and finally peaking in 2001 with 159 events. Thus, from 1991 to 2001, total incidents increased by 90 percent. After the peak in 2001, the number of incidents witnessed an aggregate drop of 79 percent through 2007.

In general, the results suggest an exponential increase in incidents from 1970 to 2001 and substantial declines thereafter. However, we should hasten to add that our coverage of events in the 1970s was likely not as extensive as it was after 1980. Of the twelve databases used to construct the EID, only two (GTD and Arnold's) included events prior to 1980. While we tried to identify missing cases from this period, it is undoubtedly the case that some of these incidents, particularly those that were less serious, were not recorded in the archives and databases we consulted. However, we expect that the cases that we missed from this time period are relatively minor compared to those representing the 1970s in the EID.

Thus, even with missing cases, these data suggest that the alarm raised by federal and state law enforcement may have been over-stated. Only one incident out of more than 1,000 resulted in a death. On February 8, 1990, Dr. Hyram Kitchen, the Dean of the Veterinary School of the University of Tennessee, was shot and killed in his driveway. While nobody has claimed responsibility, one month before this incident animal rights groups made several threats to kill one veterinary dean per month for 12 months. The homicide drew nationwide publicity as police issued an alert to all university officials after the attack. Despite the apparent link between the action described in the threats and the murder, without clear evidence federal law enforcement are reluctant to conclude that a radical animal rights group was responsible for the murder.

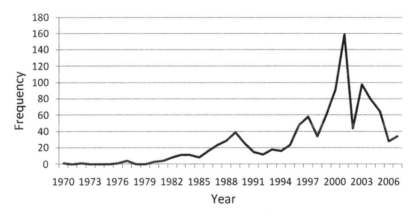

Figure 1. Total incidents perpetrated by radical environmental and animal rights groups, 1970–2007.

While these groups rarely kill, they also seek to avoid injury to people in other ways. Thus, not only are fatalities rare but so too are events by environmental and animal right extremists that cause any injury. In total, only ten incidents resulted in any injury, and nine of those resulted in only one person injured. The most noteworthy of these incidents occurred on May 8, 1987, when George Alexander, a logger, was severely injured by a tree-spike. In fact, this event was the impetus for the tree-spiking clause added to the Anti-Drug Abuse Act of 1988. Judy Bari, who went on to be a prominent leader of Earth First!, noted in the *Albion Monitor* that, "When George Alexander was nearly decapitated working a shift at the Cloverdale mill, I was just getting interested in Earth First! and it kind of backed me off, because of this tree-spiking thing."[53] Bari was later behind a larger nonviolent movement that publicly denounced tree-spiking as a tactic through a partnership with loggers.

Despite this tendency to avoid harm, about 17 percent of the events in the EID are considered to be terrorism based on the GTD's definition. The key distinction between non-terrorist criminal incidents and terrorist attacks is that the latter include violence against property that leads to permanent damage. Thus, the terrorist attacks in the EID included everything from the destruction of power lines to the setting of an animal-testing facility on fire. Most of the events classified as terrorism in the EID took the form of a facility or infrastructure attacks (78 percent), where the target was primarily businesses (69 percent). This description of the terrorist attacks in the EID demonstrates why radical eco-groups are rarely associated with traditional conceptualizations of violence. Members of these groups in the United States principally turn to tactics that damage the physical structure of targeted businesses rather than harming the people working for such businesses.

As Tables 2 and 3 demonstrate, neither attack type nor target type varies considerably by ideology, especially in regards to the preferred method of facility attack against a business. Types of these incidents include the release of two dolphins from the University of Hawaii in 1977 and a fire that was set to the veterinary medicine research building at the University of California-Davis in 1987. However, the majority of armed assaults (63 percent) are environmentally-motivated incidents.

Table 2. Movement type by attack type

	Animal $n = 600$	Environment $n = 391$	Both $n = 28$	Unknown $n = 49$	Total $n = 1069$
Assassination	3.00	0.00	0.00	0.00	3.00
	0.50	0.00	0.00	0.00	0.28
Armed assault	15.00	28.00	0.00	1.00	44.00
	2.50	7.16	0.00	2.00	4.12
Bombing/explosion	29.00	18.00	0.00	8.00	55.00
	4.83	4.16	0.00	16.00	5.14
Facility attack	531.00	337.00	26.00	39.00	933.00
	88.50	86.19	92.86	78.00	87.28
Unarmed assault	19.00	7.00	2.00	2.00	30.00
	3.17	1.79	7.14	4.00	2.81
Unknown	3.00	1.00	0.00	0.00	4.00
	0.50	0.26	0.00	0.00	0.37

Table 3. Target type by movement type

	Animal $n = 600$	Environment $n = 391$	Both $n = 28$	Unknown $n = 50$	Total $n = 1069$
Business	431.00	308.00	16.00	22.00	777.00
	71.83	78.77	57.14	44.00	72.68
Government	19.00	23.00	6.00	6.00	54.00
	3.17	5.88	21.43	12.00	5.05
Police	0.00	2.00	0.00	1.00	3.00
	0.00	0.51	0.00	2.00	0.28
Airport/airlines	0.00	1.00	0.00	0.00	1.00
	0.00	0.26	0.00	0.00	0.09
Diplomatic	1.00	1.00	0.00	0.00	2.00
	0.17	0.26	0.00	0.00	0.19
Educational institution	78.00	15.00	2.00	6.00	101.00
	13.00	3.84	7.14	12.00	9.45
Food/water supply	3.00	4.00	0.00	0.00	7.00
	0.50	1.02	0.00	0.00	0.65
Media	0.00	1.00	0.00	0.00	1.00
	0.00	0.26	0.00	0.00	0.09
Maritime	1.00	1.00	0.00	0.00	2.00
	0.17	0.26	0.00	0.00	0.19
NGO	3.00	0.00	0.00	0.00	3.00
	0.50	0.00	0.00	0.00	0.28
Private citizens	43.00	20.00	1.00	8.00	72.00
	7.17	5.12	3.57	16.00	6.74
Telecommunication	1.00	1.00	0.00	0.00	2.00
	0.17	0.26	0.00	0.00	0.19
Transportation	0.00	1.00	0.00	0.00	1.00
	0.00	0.26	0.00	0.00	0.09
Utilities	1.00	10.00	1.00	2.00	14.00
	0.17	2.56	3.57	4.00	1.31
Unknown	1.00	0.00	0.00	0.00	1.00
	0.17	0.00	0.00	0.00	0.09
Other	18.00	3.00	2.00	5.00	28.00
	13.00	0.77	7.14	10.00	2.62

Unarmed assaults are typically the work of radical animal rights groups, as are the bulk of educational institution attacks.

In Figure 2, we present the trend in total incidents partitioned by non-terrorist criminal incidents and terrorist attacks, demonstrating that the two trends are clearly related ($r = 0.85$, $p = .00$). However, criminal events are much more common than terrorist attacks, occurring more than three times as often. Figure 2 shows that criminal events increased throughout the 1980s, peaking at 32 events in 1989. They then rapidly increase in the mid to late 1990s, reaching a series peak of 128 events in 2001, and then fall off dramatically. The majority of these types of incidents take the form of small acts of vandalism or animal releases.

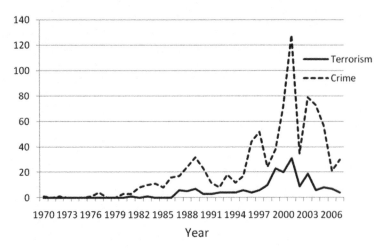

Figure 2. Terrorist attacks and non-terrorist crime perpetrated by radical environmental and animal rights groups, 1970–2007.

According to Figure 2, environmental and animal rights terrorist attacks increased throughout the 1980s and 1990s, reaching a series peak of 31 attacks in 2001. Some key examples of attacks in that year were the torching of 11 homes under construction in the Phoenix area and the arson of offices belonging to a tree research project, causing an estimated 5.4 million dollars in damages. Following the peak in 2001, environmental and animal rights terrorist attacks drop and then peak again in 2003, with an overall dramatic decrease to only 4 attacks in 2007.

In Figure 3, we track total environmental and animal rights cases (both terrorist and criminal) that targeted specific people; a minority of cases (about 19 percent of total attacks). Included here are events where the offenders glued the locks and smashed the windows of a researcher in Utah, damaged an Oregon primate research-er's car, and threatened to bomb a UCLA researcher's home. Beginning in the mid-1990s, the frequency of radical environmental and animal rights attacks that targeted people increased steadily before reaching a high point in 2005. It then fell

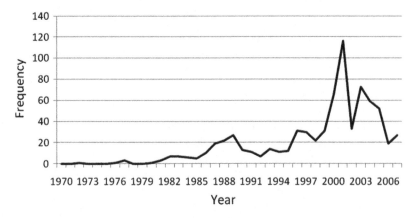

Figure 3. Incidents perpetrated by radical environmental and animal rights groups that target people, 1970–2007.

Table 4. Whether people are targeted by crime type

	Non-terrorist crime $n=882$	Terrorism $n=187$	Total $n=1069$
Person targeted	176.00	27.00	203.00
	19.95	14.44	18.99
Other target type	706.00	160.00	866.00
	80.05	85.56	81.01

off by about 58 percent to the end of the series in 2007. These results suggest that over time, a larger proportion of radical eco-cases are targeting people. In fact, during the 2005 peak, almost half of the incidents targeted people as opposed to 8.6 percent during the 1997 peak.

Table 4 shows incidents that target people disaggregated by crime type. Interestingly, most of the incidents, regardless of crime type, target something other than a specific person. Criminal incidents are slightly more likely to target people than terrorist incidents (19.9 percent versus 14.4 percent, $p=.00$). Examples of criminal events that target specific people include the stealing and misuse of credit cards, the spray painting of slogans, and even the throwing of tofu pies in the faces of various targets that groups felt were responsible for either the destruction of the environment or the harming of animals. However, there have also been more serious terrorist attacks targeting people, including the 1988 thwarted bombing originally intended for U.S. Surgical's President, Leon Hirsch.

In Table 5, we compare the type of movement to whether persons were targeted in the attacks. In general, a minority of attacks specifically target people (18.9 percent). However, compared to environmental extremists, radical animal rights groups are more than five times more likely to target people (26.3 percent versus 5.4 percent, $p=.00$). These types of events include threatening and throwing rocks at an animal researcher in Massachusetts, harassing McDonald's customers and employees in Virginia, and burning an effigy of a University of California professor outside his home.

In Figure 4 we show trends for all incidents perpetrated by radical environmental and animal rights groups that involve property damage, a variable determined by whether any physical destruction resulted from the incident. In general, the property damage trends look similar to the overall trends described above. We see general

Table 5. Whether people are targeted by movement type

	Animal $n=600$	Environment $n=391$	Both $n=28$	Unknown $n=50$	Total $n=1069$
Person targeted	158.00	21.00	3.00	21.00	203.00
	26.33	5.37	10.71	42.00	18.99
Other target type	442.00	370.00	25.00	29.00	866.00
	73.67	94.63	89.29	58.00	81.01

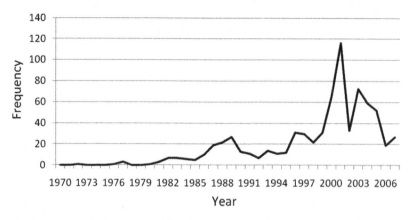

Figure 4. Incidents perpetrated by radical environmental and animal rights groups that involve property damage, 1970–2007.

increases throughout the 1980s, with a steep rise peaking at 116 incidents in 2001 and decreasing thereafter.

In Table 6 we show the percentage of cases involving property damage for the terrorist and non-terrorist cases, demonstrating that a majority of both types resulted in damage (79.1 versus 67 percent respectively). Not surprising given our definition of terrorism, compared to criminal incidents, these attacks more often involve damage. More than 69 percent of events in the EID involved some sort of damage, although the extent of this damage is not reliably recorded. Only 23 percent of the incidents involving damage listed a specific monetary amount. Of the incidents where a damage amount was given, the average loss was $814,993 with a total of over $194 million. The EID incident associated with the most damage is the ELF arson of a condominium complex in San Diego, resulting in an estimated loss of $50 million. Events like this one may explain why so much attention has been paid to these groups by federal and local law enforcement; that is, while these extremists appear not to be a major violent threat, in some cases they have been responsible for major property damage. Most often, incidents that did not involve damage but were considered terrorism were attacks that targeted people, like the aforementioned killing of Dean Kitchen.

In Table 7 we show total property damage by type of movement. The majority (62.5 percent) of animal rights events caused damage. Nevertheless, a greater percentage of environmentally-motivated incidents involved damage—nearly 80 percent. Notable animal rights-related damage incidents include the 1.5 million destruction of a National Food Corporation's egg farm in Virginia and the break-in

Table 6. Property damage by crime type

	Non-terrorist crime $n = 882$	Terrorism $n = 187$	Total $n = 1069$
Damage	591.00	148.00	739.00
	67.01	79.14	69.13
No damage	291.00	39.00	330.00
	32.99	20.86	30.87

Table 7. Property damage by movement type

	Animal n = 600	Environment n = 391	Both n = 28	Unknown n = 50	Total n = 1069
Damage	379.00	311.00	20.00	29.00	739.00
	63.17	79.54	71.43	58.00	69.13
No damage	221.00	80.00	8.00	21.00	330.00
	36.83	20.46	28.57	42.00	30.87

and stealing of several animals from two research labs at the University of Minnesota causing an estimated 2 million dollars in damage. However, the most significant of damage incidents is that of the aforementioned environmentally-motivated attack on a San Diego condominium complex.

In Figure 5 we contrast trends for environmental and animal rights incidents. The overall patterns are related, as indicated by the correlation between the two ($r = 0.66$; $p = .00$). Trends for environmental and animal rights incidents followed each other fairly closely until the mid-1990s. Total environmental cases rose steeply in 1997, reaching a series peak of 102 incidents in 2001. Driving this peak are several incidents that involve significant destruction to construction sites like the smashing of several windows of a PNC bank in Louisville, Kentucky resulting in an estimated $800,000 in damages. Animal rights incidents remain at relatively high levels from 1996 through 2005 and then fall off steeply in 2006. Popular tactics during this time period range from releasing animals to setting fire to various targets, including one attack that completely destroyed a McDonald's restaurant in Utah.

In Table 8 we show the types of weapons used in these crimes by whether they were designated as terrorist or non-terrorist. In general, there was relatively little evidence of weapons use in these cases; only around 22 percent of the cases are associated with a weapon. The majority of terrorist attacks involved an incendiary (26.7 percent). However, the other popular weapon of choice was the sabotaging of equipment (for example, the pouring of sugar in a gas tank of a bulldozer), which

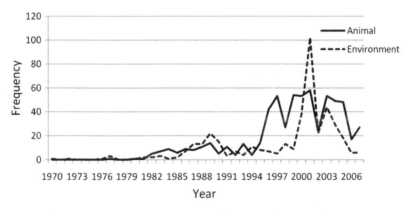

Figure 5. Incidents perpetrated by radical environmental and animal rights groups by ideology, 1997–2007.

Table 8. Weapon type by crime type

	Non-terrorist crime $n = 882$	Terrorism $n = 187$	Total $n = 1069$
Biological/chemical	10.00	3.00	13.00
	1.13	1.60	1.22
Firearms	4.00	0.00	4.00
	0.45	0.00	0.37
Explosives/bombs/dynamite	17.00	13.00	30.00
	1.93	6.95	2.81
Fake weapons	7.00	2.00	9.00
	0.79	1.07	0.84
Incendiary	23.00	50.00	73.00
	2.61	26.74	6.83
Melee	4.00	14.00	18.00
	0.45	7.49	1.68
Sabotage equipment	60.00	6.00	66.00
	6.80	3.21	6.17
Other	14.00	0.00	14.00
	1.59	0.00	1.31
Unknown	4.00	4.00	8.00
	0.40	2.14	0.70
No weapon	739.00	95.00	834.00
	83.79	50.80	78.02

constituted 6.8 percent of non-terrorist criminal incidents. Thirteen attacks involved the use of a biological or chemical weapon. The most serious of these incidents, and the ones most often classified by the GTD as terrorist, involved the pouring of various acids (including muriatic and sulfuric) on researcher's equipment.

In Table 9 we show weapon type by movement. Overall, radical animal rights groups are less likely to use weapons than their environmental counterparts (82.8 percent versus 72.1 percent of incidents respectively did not involve a weapon). When weapons are used, radical environmental groups seem to differentially prefer the sabotaging of equipment (15.3 percent of their incidents), while their animal rights counterparts favor incendiaries (5.8 percent of their events). A weapon unique to radical environmental groups, the use of tree-spikes, was primarily utilized after the Alexander incident, despite the aforementioned renunciation by Bari and others.

Discussion

Perhaps the single most striking conclusion from our descriptive analysis of the EID is that thus far, environmental and animal rights terrorist attacks and crimes in the United States have been aimed overwhelmingly at property damage rather than causing injury or death to humans. Over time, the total number of terrorist and criminal incidents perpetrated by environmental and animal rights groups has

Table 9. Weapon type by movement type

	Animal $n = 600$	Environment $n = 391$	Both $n = 28$	Unknown $n = 50$	Total $n = 1069$
Biological/chemical	10.00	2.00	0.00	1.00	13.00
	1.67	0.51	0.00	2.00	1.22
Firearms	3.00	1.00	0.00	0.00	4.00
	0.50	0.26	0.00	0.00	0.37
Explosives/bombs/dynamite	17.00	8.00	0.00	5.00	30.00
	2.83	2.05	0.00	10.00	2.81
Fake weapons	6.00	1.00	0.00	2.00	9.00
	1.00	0.26	0.00	4.00	0.84
Incendiary	35.00	29.00	2.00	7.00	73.00
	5.83	7.42	7.14	14.00	6.83
Melee	16.00	2.00	0.00	0.00	18.00
	2.67	0.51	0.00	0.00	1.68
Sabotage equipment	4.00	60.00	0.00	2.00	66.00
	0.67	15.35	0.00	4.00	6.17
Other	10.00	3.00	1.00	0.00	14.00
	1.67	0.77	3.57	0.00	1.31
Unknown	2.00	3.00	0.00	3.00	8.00
	0.33	0.77	0.00	0.06	0.75
No weapon	497.00	282.00	25.00	30.00	834.00
	82.83	72.12	89.29	60.00	78.02

increased substantially, especially since the late 1970s. However, the steady decrease in total and disaggregated incidents from various peaks in the early part of this century, save those that target people, suggests that attack levels have been declining in recent years.

Despite the argument that there is considerable overlap between radical environmental and animal rights groups,[54] our data suggest important differences in the characteristics of the attacks attributed to these two groups. Incidents perpetrated in the name of animal rights are more likely to target people. While environmental extremists are marginally more likely to use a weapon, in general their choices (e.g., sabotaging equipment) have less potential for lethality, but are more likely to cause property damage than the weapons choices of animal rights groups. However, as with the aggregate trends, events motivated by both ideologies have recently decreased.

In order to gain some understanding about what has motivated these aggregate patterns and to see whether activists were sensitive to considerations regarding traditional sanctions, we questioned activists about their motivations. When asked whether they would participate in illegal behavior, many respondents expressed concern about the law, and several activists said that they would refrain from illegal actions. In the case of many of our subjects, being arrested was a cost that outweighed any benefits that could possibly be achieved from illegal conduct (e.g., an ecosystem is not developed [benefit] because someone pours sugar in the gas tank of a bulldozer [illegal act], but is arrested [cost]). When asked about federal legislation like the Animal Enterprise Terrorism Act of 2006, two participants responded:

> I value my freedom too much. I am concerned about legal sanctions. (Participant 008)

> I'm sure that's affected me in a lot of ways. I'm not sure that piece of legislation, but laws. (Participant 013)

In fact, certain activists talked about avoiding those who would risk incarceration to get a point across:

> If someone is radical we like to distance ourselves from that. (Organization withheld) members wear going to jail as a badge of honor. But none of us want to go to jail. (Participant 001)

Many participants also explained that legal sanctions could adversely affect their future. In other words, they were deterred beyond the immediate consequence of getting arrested or going to jail. Perceived future costs include the effect of having a criminal record on future opportunities and in their verbal accounts, those costs outweighed any benefits to illegal activity:

> It just never has been an option for me (getting arrested). It would produce an inability for me to get a job . . . affect things further down the line. I don't like fur, but I'm never going to chain myself to a fur companies' door. (Participant 001)

> [Acts of vandalism] would probably be on your record and I would be in trouble with my parents. You might not be able to get certain types of jobs if they saw that you were arrested. (Participant 003)

> I just don't want to protest and risk arrest, because that may mean risking medical school. I have to take my future into consideration. (Participant 006)

> The only reason I would really be scared of an action against me would be that it might prevent me from things later in life like applying to a job (Participant 011).

The activists in our sample often said that there were other legitimate avenues to achieving their goals and that illegal activity was often unnecessary. Several respondents noted that the benefits of noncriminal activity outweighed its criminal counterpart in many situations—even those situations that seemed hopeless or at times, insensitive to legal dissent:

> Lobbying makes an impression and our leaders realize that issues might not affect us now, but in the future. In law we can counter. Ultimately, the voice and education of the youth can change minds. (Participant 006)

Sometimes it [lobbying, petitioning] feels ineffective, but we have to do it. It will help make things better now. It is successful when you talk to people in a respectful, knowledgeable way and present them with what you know and feel about over an issue. (Participant 008)

I do not believe in bombing everybody. I do not believe in going out and doing all of these really radical, violent things. We get little bits and pieces of what we want [from lobbying]; it is the most effective [activity] that I participate in. (Participant 012)

Interestingly, some activists also said that they would not do anything illegal themselves, but in a way, admired those that did:

Sometimes I think that what they [radical animal rights groups] are doing is sort of good; they throw paint on ships and do other things to try to get the whales to go away. As long as they aren't doing anything to harm or [anything] super illegal then I guess they are okay. (Participant 003)

And to me, I almost commend the activists because they're standing up for what they believe in, even though it's criminal. Maybe that goes against what I said earlier, but they are standing up for what they believe in. (Participant 015)

In summary, it appears that legal sanctions are an important consideration for the environmental and animal rights activists in this sample when they decide whether to engage in illegal activity. Both sanctions from such laws and the expected penalties associated with them (especially regarding future employment) were costs that outweighed any benefits of criminal activity. In fact, many activists anticipated that sanctions would affect their future in a negative way and consequently were deterred. Participants also spoke to the benefits that could be achieved from noncriminal actions; for example, lobbying was often cited as an effective way to get problems solved.

Many activists also verbalized similar themes to those that are described in previous research publications[55] regarding the role that especially brutal incidents played in the decline of related terrorism—specifically, the idea that a major criminal act, and especially a major terrorist act, could delegitimize the movement and be counterproductive to its goals. Being associated with highly destructive or violent acts was perceived as a cost that far outweighed any benefit achieved from illegal conduct:

I remember when I started organizing this, a lot of students were like "We should camp out there, we should build a tree house, we should get a lot of people, we should raise hell." And we had to step back and be like I don't think that is going to work. I think that is going to embarrass us and we could actually be penalized for that and I think we would take the risk of looking stupid and not looking strategic, not like we thought this out. (Participant 004)

> Violence is too extreme; it really does threaten any hope to have a trustful relationship and to come to a common ground on something. (Participant 005)

> Threatening someone is not going to make them more conscious. It is going to make it appear like you are crazy. (Participant 006)

> We are not going to work against the cause; it is not strategic. (Participant 007)

> I feel like it (force) discredits the movement as a whole. I believe that in order to be effective there has to be education and diplomacy. (Participant 009)

> I haven't really gotten much of a feel of how environmental terrorism has really helped the cause. It just seems like they have been hurting the cause by garnering negative media attention to the movement. (Participant 011)

Interestingly, attacks motivated by other ideologies like the Oklahoma City bombing or September 11th did not have an influence on our sample's viewpoint toward terrorism as a tactic. However, this may have been a measurement error due the age composition of the sample (many participants were between the ages of 18-25 and therefore did not have great recollection of these events). The older participants acknowledged the effect of these events on their perception of terrorism, but not on their individual-level decision-making:

> Sure, it (September 11, 2001) changed how aware I was of terrorism, but not what I thought about it. (Participant 021)

> It didn't make me think about terrorism differently. Just about what we're doing as a country to bring such acts on. (Participant 023)

As a whole, our sample put the legitimacy of the environmental and animal rights movement above the short-term benefits any criminal action could accomplish. Many participants felt that it was more important to accomplish goals through legal avenues, rather than criminal ones, as the latter would only hurt their objective in the long run by making them appear to be crazy, dangerous, or both.

Almost every activist in our sample described an internal moral compass as important to guiding their decision-making, although these beliefs were wholly unrelated to any tie-in to deep ecology or biocentrism.[56] In fact, personal assessments of whether the act was morally wrong was as important, and sometimes more important, than possible legal sanctions. In other words, moral inhibitions[57] seemed to be very important in respondents' calculations of the costs and benefits in participating in criminal acts associated with environmental or animal rights causes:

> I guess I'm saying that it's the fact that it (illegal activity) goes against my values...that's the big thing. (Participant 002)

> It is morally wrong to exert excessive force or harm to make a point. You have to try to make others understand, but leave and move on when you meet people who don't get it (Participant 006).

> There is a moral boundary that I... that tells me what is going too far and what is not going too far. I'm just pre-destined to participate in behavior that is legal and morally right. (Participant 011)

Several participants also described illegal behavior, especially forceful and violent behavior, as being hypocritical when juxtaposed to their overall message of valuing human life:

> Ninety-nine point nine percent of people in the groups are pacifists or hippies... or are into the metaphysical, mind-body-spirit thing... and have jobs where they are working for something they believe in. (Participant 001)

> Animal rights is such a fundamentally nonviolent movement or it should be... the thing is, it is all based on 'you don't need to be violent towards other creatures' and if you don't need to be, then it's wrong as far as I am concerned. So using violence... using violence is just... inconsistent. (Participant 002)

> I would never get violent. I would never push someone. I don't want to hurt anyone in the process. Like hateful letters are hurtful. You have to practice what you preach. (Participant 004)

> We believe in principles of nonviolence; in nonviolent direct action. We follow the teachings of Martin Luther King. We can prevent something from happening. We also follow Quaker principles of bearing witness and passive resistance. You have to be there in the zone of exposure and insist on being involved. (Participant 007)

> I believe in nonviolent action. We should be peaceful and be guided by our ethics. (Participant 008)

As a whole, the environmental and animal rights activists in our nonrandom sample seemed to be guided in part by concerns about the moral implications of criminal behavior. To some participants, these inhibitions were more important than possible legal consequences, while others had difficulty ranking one above the other and argued for the importance of both in decision-making.

Conclusions

Researchers and policy makers have long been challenged by data limitations in studies of radical environmental and animal rights groups. We contribute to the research in this area by providing information and analysis from a systematic data-base on both terrorist and non-terrorist criminal activities of these organizations over time. We also interviewed a nonrandom convenience sample of individuals that self-identified as part of the environmental or animal rights movements. Our research suggests that while the amount of illegal activity attributed to these movements in the United States has increased dramatically since the 1970s, the overwhelming majority of this activity has been nonviolent. On the other hand, incidents with property damage have increased substantially since the 1970s and have declined less than other types of criminal acts since the peak years at the beginning of the twenty-first century. It is quite possible that the recent rise in youth protests may even exacerbate these trends. Taken together, members of radical environmental and animal rights groups have so far been overwhelmingly more of a threat to property than to persons.

Although our interviews were with a nonrandom sample of activists, they support the contention that many members of these movements consider traditional sanctions, and especially the possible ramifications of these sanctions, in their movement-related decision-making. Respondents also emphasized the importance of gaining benefits from legal activities, such as lobbying. In addition, many participants referred to the role that illegal conduct—and especially terrorist conduct—may have on decreasing the legitimacy of the environmental and/or animal rights movement. It would seem that overall, support for the radical fringe that advocates the targeting of people and/or violent tactics is limited based on this concern for legitimacy, which is consistent with our empirical findings. The concept of moral inhibitions was also a common theme in our respondents; most participants argued that illegal activity was morally wrong to them. Thus, criminal and especially terrorist activity was often perceived as an immoral alternative. In some cases, respondents told us that their moral evaluations of illegal acts were more important than the potential legal consequences, but many responses indicated themes consistent with both conceptualizations. This again may add to the explanation behind our empirical findings, where property damage is typical of incidents perpetrated by radical eco-groups and violence is atypical.

We should emphasize important limitations of the current study. Despite our best efforts, it is likely that the EID is missing many of the less serious incidents (like the spray-painting of a wall with the letters "ALF" or a mink release). In addition, some parts of the data were taken from certain organizations that may have specialized biases. The Foundation for Biomedical Research, the entity where the most incidents were extracted from, had a major role in the passing of the Animal Enterprise Terrorism Act of 2006. Also, our qualitative sample was limited by access issues and was not randomly generated, perhaps leading to bias in our conclusions regarding rationality in decision-making. Nonetheless, and despite these limitations, we believe that we have created the most objective set of data on this phenomenon currently available.

Future research would benefit from a focus on the role of countermeasures in combating this activity. For instance, it may be that local law enforcement might be the best line of defense against terrorism; it would be valuable to examine the impact of local measures taken against members of radical environmental and animal rights groups. For instance, has additional security at a company like Huntingdon Life Sciences deterred attacks? Or, how effective have local police departments been at catching members of radical eco-groups before an attack because of pre-incident behaviors like the purchasing of bomb-making equipment? Thus far attacks staged by radical environmental and animal rights groups have resulted in very few deaths or injuries. The unanswered question is whether this almost universally nonviolent movement will remain so in the future.

Notes

1. John E. Lewis, "Congressional Testimony before Senate Committee on Environment and Public Works," May 18, 2005, http://www2.fbi.gov/congress/congress05/lewis051805.htm (Paragraph 2).

2. Robert S. Mueller, "Statement before the Senate Select Committee on Intelligence," January 11, 2007, http://www.fbi.gov/news/testimony/global-threats-to-the-u.s.-and-the-fbis-response. (See the section, "The Threat Posed by Domestic Terrorist Groups").

3. Joseph Simone, Joshua Freilich, and Steven Chermak, *Surveying State Police Agencies about Domestic Terrorism and Far-Right Extremists*, [Research Brief] (College Park, MD: National Consortium for the Study of Terrorism and Responses to Terrorism, 2008).

4. Terry Frieden, "Animal Rights Activist on 'FBI's Most Wanted Terrorist List,'" April 21, 2009, http://articles.cnn.com/2009-04-21/justice/fbi.domestic.terror.suspect_1_animal-rights-activist-daniel-andreas-san-diego-bombing?_s=PM:CRIME.

5. Lauren Effron and Russell Goldman, "Environmental Militant Killed by Police at Discovery Channel Headquarters," *ABC News,* September 1, 2010, http://abcnews.go.com/US/gunman-enters-discovery-channel-headquarters-employees-evacuated/story?id=11535128.

6. As defined by the FBI, eco-terrorism is "the use or threatened use of violence of a criminal nature against innocent victims or property by an environmentally orientated sub national group for environmental-political reasons, aimed at an audience beyond the target, and often of a symbolic nature" (Jarboe 2002, para 6). James F. Jarboe, "The Threat of Eco-Terrorism," February 12, 2002, http://www.fbi.gov/news/testimony/the-threat-of-eco-terrorism.

7. Steven Vanderheiden, "Eco-terrorism or Justified Resistance? Radical Environmentalism and the 'War on Terror,'" *Politics and Society* 33, no. 3 (2005): 425–447; and Randall Amster, "Perspectives on Ecoterrorism: Catalysts, Conflations, and Casualties," *Contemporary Justice Review* 9, no. 3 (2006): 287–301.

8. Donald Liddick, *Ecoterrorism: Radical Environmental and Animal Liberation Movements* (Westport, CT: Praeger, 2006).

9. Vanderheiden, p. 432 (see note 7 above).

10. Gary Perlstein, "Comments on Ackerman," *Terrorism and Political Violence* 15, no. 4 (2003): 171–172.

11. John Wigle, "A Systematic Approach to Precursor Behaviors," *Criminology and Public Policy* 8, no. 3 (August 2009): 612.

12. Gary LaFree and Laura Dugan, "Introducing the Global Terrorism Database," *Terrorism and Political Violence* 19, no. 2 (2007): 184.

13. Sean Eagan, "From Spikes to Bombs: The Rise of Ecoterrorism," *Studies in Conflict and Terrorism* 19 (1996): 1–18.

14. Anti-Defamation League, "Ecoterrorism: Extremism in the Animal Rights and Environmentalist Movements," http://www.adl.org/learn/ext_us/Ecoterrorism.asp?LEARN_Cat=Extremism&LEARN_SubCat=Extremism_in_America&xpicked=4&item=eco#intro.

15. Ibid.

16. Gary Ackerman, "Beyond Arson? A Threat Assessment of the Earth Liberation Front," *Terrorism and Political Violence* 15, no. 4 (2003): 143–170.

17. Bron Taylor, "Threat Assessments and Radical Environmentalism," *Terrorism and Political Violence* 15, no. 4 (2003): 173–182.

18. Ackerman, p. 188 (see note 16 above).

19. Eagan (see note 13 above).

20. Animal Liberation Front, "ALF Mission Statement," http://www.animalliberationfront.com/ALFront/mission_statement.htm.

21. Anti-Defamation League (see note 14 above).

22. Liddick (see note 8 above).

23. Ackerman (see note 16 above).

24. Edward Abbey, *The Monkeywrench Gang* (Salt Lake City, UT: Dream Garden Press, 1985).

25. Anti-Defamation League (see note 14 above).

26. CBS News, "Animal Rights Group Convicted in N.J.," *CBS News,* February 11, 2009, http://www.cbsnews.com/stories/2006/03/02/national/main1364346.shtml.

27. A prominent exception is the "Family," an organized group of ALF and ELF members responsible for the largest federal case involving these groups.

28. Ackerman (see note 16 above).

29. For example, Ackerman (see note 16 above) and Taylor (see note 17 above).

30. U.S. Department of Justice and U.S. Department of Agriculture, "Report to Congress on the Extent of Domestic and International Terrorism in Animal Enterprises," *The Physiologist* 36, no. 6 (1993): 251.

31. Ibid., p. 256.

32. Ibid., p. 256.

33. U.S. Department of Homeland Security, "Ecoterrorism: Environmental and Animal Rights Militants in the United States," May 17, 2008, http://humanewatch.org/images/uploads/2008_DHS_ecoterrorism_threat_assessment.pdf: 1-40.

34. Ibid., p. 1.

35. Ibid., p. 1.

36. LaFree and Dugan (see note 12 above) for more regarding criterion for inclusion in the GTD.

37. See http://www.fbresearch.org/ for information on data.

38. LaFree and Dugan (see note 12 above), p. 184.

39. See http://www.naiaonline.org/.

40. See http://www.furcommission.com/.

41. Ron Arnold, *The Violent Agenda to Save Nature: The World of the Unabomber* (New York: Free Enterprise Press, 1997).

42. We attempted to independently verify all non-terrorist criminal incidents through another open source. We were able to locate 56 percent of the cases in secondary unbiased media sources. An additional 30 cases had two sources, but neither could be considered an unbiased media source. In general, we were much more likely to find secondary sources to verify incidents involving substantial property damage than minor or no damage. In cases where we identified contradictory information from secondary news sources (e.g., different damage amount), we adopted information from the most recent source.

43. U.S. Department of Homeland Security (see note 33 above).

44. Christopher Hewitt, *Political Violence and Terrorism in Modern America: A Chronology* (Westport, CT: Praeger Security International, 2005).

45. Stefan Leader and Peter Probst, "The Earth Liberation Front and Environmental Terrorism," *Terrorism and Political Violence* 15, vol. 4 (2003): 37–58.

46. Scott Sunde and Paul Shukovsky, "Elusive Radicals Escalate Attacks in Nature's Name," June 17, 2001, http://www.seattlepi.com/default/article/Elusive-radicals-escalate-attacks-in-nature-s-name-1057490.php.

47. See http://www.adl.org.

48. U.S. Department of Justice and U.S. Department of Agriculture (see note 30 above).

49. For example, one participant told us that their activities primarily involved handing out vegan literature, yet the FBI had been to their house twice for questioning.

50. Andrea Fontana and James Frey, "Interviewing: The Art of Science," in *The Handbook of Qualitative Research,* ed. Norman Denzin and Yvonna Lincoln (Thousand Oaks, CA: Sage, 1994), 361–376.

51. These withheld due to confidentiality reasons.

52. Liddick (see note 8 above).

53. Judi Bari, "The Attempted Murder of Judi Bari," accessed at http://www.albionmonitor.com/bari/jbint-14.html. (See Paragraph 4).

54. Gary Ackerman (see note 16 above).

55. See, for example, Joseph Wheatley and Clark McCauley, "Losing Your Audience: Desistance from Terrorism in Egypt after Luxor," *Dynamics of Asymmetric Conflict* 1, no. 3 (2008): 250–268.

56. The majority of participants discussed themes consistent with deep ecology, but were unfamiliar with this ideology when asked to identify it by name.

57. For greater detail on the concept of moral inhibitions, see Raymond Paternoster and Sally Simpson, "Sanction Threats and Appeals to Morality: Testing a Rational Choice Model of Corporate Crime," *Law and Society Review* 30, no. 3 (1996): 549–583.

Appendix 1. Consent Form Interview Questions

The procedures involve a one-hour interview. The following pre-selected questions will be asked:

1. How did you first get involved in the movement?
2. What kinds of activities do you participate in?
3. Do you ascribe to any particular environmental philosophy? Deep ecology? Biocentrism?
4. Do you believe that the damage that has been done to the environment is irreversible?
5. Do you think that lobbying is an effective strategy for solving problems? What about civil disobedience or nonviolent criminal acts? What, if any, benefits are there to these strategies?
6. Are you familiar with the Anti-Drug Abuse Act of 1988 that criminalized tree-spiking? Has this influenced your behavior in any way? Do laws or potential legal sanctions affect your behavior in any way?
7. What about the PATRIOT act and the redefinition of terrorism it suggested? How about the Animal Enterprise Protection Act of 1992 and the more recent Animal Enterprise Terrorism Act of 2006?
8. Did the Oklahoma City bombing and/or September 11th change your views on terrorism and/or the use of criminal activity as a tactic? Is terrorism a useful tactic?
9. Is harming a human ever justified? Threatening harm? Is violence a possible strategy in obtaining an environmental or animal rights goal?
10. Do you feel that with the release of Al Gore's documentary and the emergence of a more mainstream green movement that there is more hope today than before? Will this have a spillover effect with animal rights?

Fluctuations Between Crime and Terror: The Case of Abu Sayyaf's Kidnapping Activities

McKENZIE O'BRIEN

Matthew B. Ridgway Center for International Security Studies,
Graduate School of Public and International Affairs, University of
Pittsburgh, Pittsburgh, Pennsylvania, USA

The Abu Sayyaf Group (ASG) in the Philippines is often labeled a terrorist organization, yet there are periods when the group has engaged in far more criminal activity than terrorism. Specifically, this article describes phases in which organized criminal activity far exceeds any terrorist activities before returning to a more predominant focus on terrorism. This study explores reasons for these temporal fluctuations in criminal versus terrorist activity from 1991 thru August 2011, identifying four categories of explanatory factors: leadership, structure, membership and grievances, and linkages to other actors. The study concludes by highlighting some implications for policy, research, and the future of ASG.

In an international arena where financial institutions and *hawala* systems are coming under more scrutiny for their parts in threat finance, terrorist groups are increasingly turning to criminal activity to fund themselves. Kidnapping is a prominent example of criminal fundraising activity by a terrorist group—and, indeed, by various other types of actors as well. Rebel groups from numerous regions have engaged in, or have begun to engage in kidnapping, whether it is the FARC in Colombia, the Taliban in Afghanistan, the Haqqani network in the Afghanistan-Pakistan border region, criminal groups in Mexico, or the Abu Sayyaf Group in the Philippines.

As a terrorist group with a couple decades of experience, Abu Sayyaf provides an important window into how terrorism and criminal activity intersect. It is the intent of this article to highlight this intersection and provide new areas of focus and new frameworks for analyzing the crime-terror relationship of Abu Sayyaf that could possibly be extended to other violent non-state entities as well. To accomplish this objective, the article will first provide a history of the Abu Sayyaf Group (ASG).

McKenzie O'Brien is affiliated with the Matthew B. Ridgway Center for International Security Studies, part of the Graduate School of Public and International Affairs, University of Pittsburgh.

The author wishes to express special thanks to James Forest, for his help and patience during the editing process, and to Phil Williams, for his support on this research project.

The article will then look at the ASG's capacities in both terrorism and kidnapping, and the historical fluctuation that has existed between the group's two activities, before going on to offer four "frames" that attempt to analyze those fluctuations. The article concludes by offering some implications for policy, research, and the future of ASG.

While originally founded to achieve political objectives, the ASG has since its inception developed a proclivity for kidnapping-for-ransom (KFR). That is to say, Abu Sayyaf kidnaps mostly for financial reasons, as opposed to political reasons (such as demands for government and policy changes, or for the release of other terrorists in custody). So why has the ASG developed such a penchant for kidnapping-for-ransom? There are plenty of other lucrative activities that terrorists have turned to, including drug trafficking. Simply put, kidnapping is an easy, lucrative, and—relative to other forms of illicit activity—potentially a safer, more assured method of fundraising. The overwhelming majority of kidnappings in the Philippines go unreported, as is the case globally, with approximately only ten percent of kidnappings worldwide reported to authorities.[1] Most often, the families of the kidnapped themselves are threatened with harm should they not comply with demands or report the incident. Additionally, it is often deemed both easier and safer to simply give in to the ransom demands if possible, rather than risk the lives of both the kidnapped and his or her family by turning to authorities, who have sometimes been the cause of hostage deaths in dangerous rescue attempts.

Kidnapping offers a useful analytical lens for exploring the intersections of crime and terrorism because it so centrally defines Abu Sayyaf. Despite the ASG's small size (the latest credible estimates put the group at 400-600 armed combatants[2]), it is uniquely effective at not only executing kidnappings, but in profiting from them as well. Indeed, the group has become so effective at kidnappings, and its reputation for success and profit has become so well known, that ASG has spawned "little Abus"—small groups engaging solely in kidnapping-for-ransom. From 1991—the year that the ASG was officially founded—through August 2011, Abu Sayyaf was responsible for 137 documentable kidnappings, and many more that were not reported.[3] In a 16-year period (from 1992–2008), the ASG is believed to have raised over $35 million from kidnapping activities.[4]

The Abu Sayyaf Group in the Philippines is often labeled a terrorist organization, yet throughout its history, the group has had noticeable periods of heightened criminal activity, phases in which organized criminal activity far exceeded, or indeed completely replaced, any terrorist activities. These fluctuations are particularly noticeable when examining the group's kidnapping activities (See Figure 1).

Beginning in 1998, ASG kidnappings began to steadily climb, moving from only one documentable kidnapping in 1997 to 20 documentable kidnapping incidents at the group's first peak in 2000. At this point, kidnappings again tapered off, falling to only one again in 2005 before once more climbing and peaking for a second time at 20 in 2009 and 19 in 2010.[5] This study attempts to illustrate why and how these fluctuations occur, in order to shed light on facets of ASG that warrant further study and may improve the effectiveness of the Philippine military and law enforcement in countering and mitigating the Abu Sayyaf threat.

In plotting ASG kidnappings from the period of 1991 through August 2011 and analyzing the status of the group during kidnapping peaks and troughs, four factors have emerged as potential contributors to the group's oscillations: leadership, structure, membership and grievances, and linkages to other actors. It would appear that,

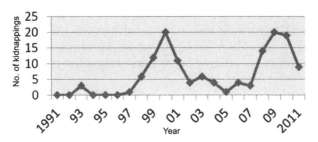

Figure 1. Abu Sayyaf kidnapping incidents, January 1991–August 2011.
Note: Data from author's own research, although the University of Maryland's National Consortium for the Study of Terrorism and Responses to Terrorism (START) provided a starting point. (Color figure available online.)

in the case of Abu Sayyaf—and perhaps other terrorist groups in a phase of "increased criminality"—the extensive turn to kidnappings and crime indicates a departure from the radical ideological foundations. This could be a result of disillusionment with the ideology or an attraction to the power and profit that comes from crime—or, most likely, a combination of the two. When there is a transformation of a terrorist group such as this, with movement away from ideology and toward criminality, there similarly emerges a different set of vulnerabilities. By recognizing this, and working to further research and exploit these different vulnerabilities when they appear, we can find ways to combat terrorist groups more effectively.

Background

The foundation of Abu Sayyaf is actually, as Rommel Banlaoi notes, somewhat "nebulous."[6] While some sources place the group's formation in the early 1990s, when the ASG engaged in a combined bombing and assassination, it actually was founded in the 1980s, when Abdurajak Janjalani formed al-Harakatul al-Islamiyyah (AHAI), or the "Islamic Movement," as an Islamic proselytizing movement. Janjalani had an adept grasp of the Islamic religion, particularly the radical Wahhabi Islamic theology, and saw a necessity in spreading this view throughout the Muslim population in the Philippines, in the spirit of the 400-year-old Muslim resistance—or "*Bangsamoro* struggle"—in the Philippines, which is key to understanding the roots of terrorism in the Philippines. The Bangsamoro problem, as Soliman M. Santos and Octavio Dinampo define it, is:

> ...the historical and systematic marginalization and minoritization of the Islamized ethno-linguistic groups, collectively called *Moros*, in their own homeland in the Mindanao islands, first by colonial powers Spain from the 16th to the 19th Century, then the U.S. during the first half of the 20th Century, and more recently by successor Philippine governments dominated by an elite with a Christian-Western orientation since formal independence in 1946. This marked full-fledged Filipino nation-statehood but ironically Philippine independence also sealed the loss of Moro independence because *Moroland* was incorporated (*Moro* nationalists would say annexed) into Philippine territory.[7]

This long-standing historical plight, coupled with a set of current and legitimate political and economic grievances, is the fertile environment that produced and sustains Abu Sayyaf. Banlaoi writes that:

> The situation that gives rise to the ASG is marred by poverty, lack of services, inadequate infrastructure and lack of opportunity. This situation is aggravated by the fact that the Philippine state has a poor record in the ASG heartland of Mindanao. The *Moro*, which account for only 5% of the total Philippine population, suffers the lowest poverty and highest mortality rates, the least developed economy and minimal institutional government support.[8]

Janjalani's views and lectures were popularly received in the areas that were traditionally part of the Moro homeland, the "Zamboanga-Basilan-Sulu-Tawi Tawi (Zambasulta) region"[9]—areas that remain significant to ASG operations today. This movement eventually turned into what is now known as the Abu Sayyaf Group (literally "Father of the Sword") in 1991 with the mission to create an independent and free state for the Muslims in the southern Philippines. And, indeed, the ASG is very much a "homegrown" movement: Janjalani outlined the ASG's ultimate goal as "establishing a pure Islamic government through a necessary war to seek *kaadilan* (justice) for the Muslims in Mindanao and Sulu."[10] With the exception of a heavy emphasis on Islam, the other key terms addressed in Janjalani's ideological statement—including *kaadilan, bangsa* (nation), *hulah* (homeland), and *agama* (religion)—are all Moro National Liberation Front (MNLF) terms.[11] In other words, the ideological foundation of ASG, while Islamic, is also purely Philippine and not significantly connected to Middle Eastern and Central Asian veins of radical Islamist ideologies. Janjalani, as well as several of Abu Sayyaf's early core, were once members of the MNLF who grew disenchanted with that group's choice to engage the Philippine government in a peace process. The Abu Sayyaf movement was never intended to be a transnational one, and in the political realm, it has essentially held to that. In terms of its criminal activity, however, the group may be more akin to a transnational organized criminal group, as it has crossed borders to conduct maritime kidnapping raids in Malaysia on more than one occasion.

Areas of Operation, Links, and Funding

Abu Sayyaf operates mainly in the southern half of the Philippines, with bases in Mindanao, as well as in Basilan, Sulu, and Tawi-Tawi Provinces in the Sulu Archipelago. However, it is important to note that the group has operationally expanded into metro Manila as well, albeit on a much smaller scale. ASG's main links are with the Moro Islamic Liberation Front (MILF), another Philippine Islamist separatist group, and the Indonesian-based terrorist group Jemaah Islamiya (JI), although the ASG does also cooperate with smaller, mostly criminal groups in the region as well.[12] Abu Sayyaf's relationship with JI is tactical and strategic; they collaborate on bombing operations, but more importantly to ASG, JI provides advanced explosives training. ASG's relationship with MILF is more complex. There is no formal agreement on cooperation between the two. Rather, cooperation has often been based on individual MILF commands' personal relationships to ASG leadership, particularly the 106th, 108th, and 109th Base Commands.[13] The MILF leaders of these particular base commands are more radical members who have generally been less amenable to negotiation with the Philippine government, something in which the MILF leadership has been engaged for several years. MILF generally prefers to use the ASG as a proxy, as this gives a degree of plausible deniability in any type of action that may violate or adversely impact the peace process.

Abu Sayyaf has often been linked by the media and others to al-Qaeda. A December 2004 statement from the United Nations Security Council, for instance, identified ASG founder Janjalani as being "associated with al-Qaeda."[14] This comes from at least two notions: first, that Janjalani fought in Afghanistan against the Soviets, and second, that ASG has received funding from al-Qaeda and other transnational entities such as JI. Regarding the first, according to Southeast Asia terrorism expert Zachary Abuza, Janjalani received training in the late 1980s and early 1990s at a training camp near Khost, Afghanistan, and "fought the Soviets for several years."[15] Further, his younger brother Khadaffy Janjalani was trained at an al Qaeda camp near Mazar e-Sharif in the early 1990s, where he led a group of 20 Moros in fighting alongside the Afghan mujahideen.[16] Philippine National Police (PNP) intelligence documents suggest another link with al-Qaeda as well, through a relationship with Ramzi Yousef, the mastermind of the 1993 World Trade Center bombing. Yousef, who was teaching bomb making at the Khost camp, traveled with Janjalani to the Philippines from December 1991 to May 1992 at Osama bin Laden's request, where he trained ASG members in bomb making in their camp on Basilan Island.[17] Overall, these experiences and contacts helped Janjalani portray himself as a courageous mujahideen, successfully cultivating an image that attracted local recruits to ASG.

Regarding the second, Abu Sayyaf was at one time supported financially by al-Qaeda and Osama bin Laden himself, after Janjalani traveled to Pakistan in 1988 to study the Islamic Revolution and reportedly personally met bin Laden.[18] The actual extent of al-Qaeda funding of Abu Sayyaf cannot be determined from open source information, but it appears to have been considerable. Bin Laden's brother-in-law, Mohammad Jamal Khalifa, helped to organize a network of Islamic charities in the Philippines through which al-Qaeda could support the Abu Sayyaf group. Thus the Islamic International Relief Organization (IIRO) expanded into the Philippines, providing millions of Philippine Pesos in assistance in the region.[19] Of this funding, however, a defector from ASG noted that "only 10 to 30 percent of the foreign funding [went] to the legitimate relief and livelihood projects and the rest [went] to terrorist operations."[20] Al-Qaeda funding was cut off in the 1990s, when international and Philippine authorities became aware of Ramzi Yousef's cell and several of his terrorist plots, most notably the "Bojinka" plot to assassinate the pope and simultaneously take down eleven airliners over the Pacific.[21]

After this significant source of funding was removed, Abu Sayyaf had to find other avenues of fundraising. Despite the fact that the ASG is an extremely small group, sustaining it can still be expensive—even if members are living with bare necessities. The ASG is constantly on the move, with cells rarely staying long in one location in order to avoid the Armed Forces of the Philippines (AFP). Consequently, the group must frequently buy provisions, as well as replace anything lost in each move. Furthermore, families of ASG members, the leadership in particular, are also often dependent on the group's funds for survival. As a result, in order to sustain itself, the group has increasingly turned to criminal activity, engaging in kidnappings, extortion, and the provision of security for illicit marijuana cultivation and trafficking. However, the overwhelming majority of ASG funding, perhaps more than 90%, according to Philippine police terrorism expert Rodolfo Mendoza, comes from its kidnapping-for-ransom activities. In a 2008 forum on terrorist financing, Mendoza explained that the ASG had "amassed an estimated P1.4 billion pesos [US$34 million] from its criminal activities from 1992 to 2007."[22] In 2008, according to a report by the Associated Press, "the ASG raised more than 70 million pesos [US $1.5 million] through ransoms."[23] The lesson learned by the ASG after more than a decade is that it can make a great deal of money for group members and their families through kidnapping activities.

ASG as Terrorists

Abu Sayyaf is most well-known as a terrorist group, one of 49 groups on the U.S. State Department's List of Designated Foreign Terrorist Organizations (FTOs), where it was placed in 2005 after a stretch of heightened terrorist activity. The ideologically-motivated violence that ASG has carried out since its inception has typically come in the form of small-scale to moderate bombings, although some assassinations and raids have also been executed. The ASG initially appeared to focus primarily on Christian and government targets, when the group was tightly woven ideologically under founder Abdurajak Janjalani. In 1991, the ASG carried out a grenade attack in Zamboanga City, killing two American evangelists, and bombed the Christian missionary ship *M/V Doulos*. In 1992, the group was responsible for the assassination of Italian priest Father Salavatorre Carzedda in Zamboanga and the bombing of a building (also in Zamboanga) that housed workers aboard a missionary ship. In 1993, the ASG carried out three separate kidnappings of religious figures, and bombed a cathedral in Davao in December. Attacks in 1994 and 1995 resulted in numerous fatalities: bombings in Zamboanga killed 71 people and an attack on Ipil killed 53, wounded 48, and destroyed 17 commercial buildings.[24] These early attacks, while also producing a degree of fear and a lethal reputation for the ASG, also had the effect of demonstrating to more radical and powerful terrorist groups like JI that Abu Sayyaf was a serious player in the world of radical Islam.

As the group's skills expanded, thanks in large part to links to (and training from) JI, the ASG target list has since also expanded to include cities and private Philippine persons and businesses. A bombing on March 4, 2003 at the main terminal of the Davao International Airport killed twenty and injured more than 150. On February 27, 2004, the ASG executed its most lethal attack, bombing the *SuperFerry 14* in Manila Harbor, killing 116 and wounding many others. Finally, simultaneous bombings on Valentine's Day 2005 in Manila, General Santos, and Davao cities killed eight and wounded approximately 150. Compared to their attacks in the early 1990s, these attacks were much more indiscriminate; people and infrastructure of all persuasions were affected, not just those of Christian faith or of the Philippine state. And while the ASG's earlier attacks produced for the group some benefits—namely in reputation and partnership with JI—these latter attacks seemed to have produced real detriments for ASG, bringing upon the group heightened attention from the Philippine state, as well as from powerful foreign actors like the United States, and a greater degree of fear among the Philippine population, who became far less willing to aid and support the ASG (intentionally or tacitly).

Abu Sayyaf remains active and quite capable of executing criminal activities and small-scale bombings. As Rommel Banlaoi notes, it is a "resilient" threat because of its deep "reservoir" of new recruits.[25] Despite its small size, the group asserts a strong degree of control in its base territories. While the group could count upon fresh recruitments of ideologically-driven students and members while the charismatic Abdurajak Janjalani led the ASG, since his death (and that of his younger brother Khadaffy, also a strong ideologue in his later years), the group has been less able to recruit a strongly ideological following as they have moved from leadership utilizing precisely targeted terrorist attacks to leadership engaging in indiscriminate bombings and kidnappings. This is not to say the group finds it impossible to recruit; despite several leadership decapitations and arrests of members, the ASG continues to thrive as a threat entity in the Philippines largely because of its ability to replenish its ranks. The ASG, when not motivating and recruiting along religious lines, attracts new members through financial reward. Indeed, according to Banlaoi, and discussed further in the "Membership Frame" below, the current "majority of ASG members are not motivated by the promise of an Islamic state or the virtue of jihad, but by the allure of money and power that comes from the barrel of a gun."[26]

ASG as Profiteering Kidnappers

Kidnapping and hostage-taking for criminal reasons (i.e., for profit) have become alarmingly common in the terrorist world.[27] It is one of the easiest and most lucrative ways for the group to raise money. ASG engages in rather smaller-scale and inexpensive bombing attacks, some of which cannot be ruled out as extortion bombings.[28] So, while the group could be "stockpiling" funds from kidnapping schemes in order to engage in future, more frequent, and more powerful terrorist attacks, it appears that these kidnapping operations are a means of livelihood for ASG members and their families.

Abu Sayyaf's first kidnappings were carried out in 1993, when in separate incidents the group took hostage two Spanish nuns, a Spanish priest, an American missionary,[29] a businesswoman, and (reportedly) a businessman's son.[30] The success of these initial kidnappings (in terms of generating ransoms) was crucial to ASG's development later into a capable kidnapping outfit. The kidnappings were seen as significant from within the group's highest echelon; indeed, it is telling that Khadaffy Janjalani highlights the group's kidnapping ventures in his own history of the ASG, written during his time as *amir* (leader).[31] In its earliest, most formative years, the ASG had already experienced firsthand that it could make money and gain attention through kidnapping. It is difficult to imagine that Abu Sayyaf leaders would have continued to engage in increasingly larger, more complex, and more frequent kidnapping-for-ransom activities had these earliest ones not ended so successfully for the group.

Abu Sayyaf has not been particularly selective in its choice of kidnapping targets: foreigners (i.e., non-Filipinos), Christian religious figures, business people, journalists, and ordinary civilians, including children, have all been targeted. However, there does appear to be a greater emphasis on locals, who are kidnapped at a rate far higher than foreigners,[32] and on local businesspeople, particularly successful Chinese-Filipino businesspeople. This would seem to indicate that the ASG prefers kidnap targets for whom they can easily and successfully extract ransom payments. While foreigners, particularly those from wealthy Western countries, have the potential to bring in higher ransom payments,[33] locals can be ransomed more quickly and with less attention. Among the most high-profile ASG kidnappings have been:

- The April 23, 2000 abduction of 21 people from the Sipadan resort of Malaysia;
- The May 27, 2001 abduction of 20 people, including the American missionary couple Martin and Gracia Burnham, from the Dos Palmas resort in Palawan, Malaysia. Gracia Burnham was eventually freed, but her husband, Martin Burnham was killed by AFP forces in a rescue attempt. Naturalized American citizen Guillermo Sobero was beheaded as an "Independence Day gift" to then-President of the Philippines Gloria Macapagal-Arroyo, perhaps to hasten ransom payments for the remaining hostages.
- The July 7, 2008 abduction of well-known Filipina journalist Ces Drilon, her two cameramen, and Filipino professor Octavio Dinampo; and
- The January 15, 2009 abduction of three workers of the International Committee of the Red Cross (ICRC). Since this kidnapping, the ICRC has refused to send workers back to the Philippines, choosing instead to financially support its now only locally-staffed Philippine office.

Again, it is important to keep in mind that while these high-profile kidnappings indeed gain the ASG notoriety and bolster the group's funds, local kidnappings are the norm and constitute the main revenue base for Abu Sayyaf.

Explaining Temporal Fluctuations Between Terrorism and Kidnapping

When comparing the two primary areas of ASG activity (terrorism and kidnapping), we see some interesting patterns evolve, which can be graphically represented. For example, Figure 2 illustrates how during periods of heightened kidnapping activity, incidents of terrorism take a "back seat," while during other years terrorist activity seems to instead drive the ASG.

An important question to examine here is what accounts for these fluctuations in kidnapping activities over time. A related issue to explore is whether KFR, as engaged in by ASG, is a tactic meant to generate funds to support an ideological strategy, or if the profits derived from KFR has become the strategy itself. This study identifies four frames of analysis which yield insights about the potential contributors to the fluctuations of ASG kidnapping activity: (a) leadership; (b) structure; (c) membership and grievances; and (d) linkages with other actors.

Leadership Frame

During periods of heightened kidnapping activity, ASG leadership appears to be characterized by one of two patterns—either the leadership is decimated or in disarray (a sort of "leadership vacuum") or the leaders act more like "bandits" than ideologues. These patterns can be seen most clearly in a chronological review of ASG's evolution.

Foundation period. Abu Sayyaf was, under its founder and first *amir* (leader), very much an organization focused on waging jihad in pursuing its goal of an independent Muslim state in the southern Philippines. Through the mid-1990s, the group executed several acts of pure terrorism, many of which targeted Christian people or symbols. Moreover, until 1998, the group engaged in very few kidnappings. The

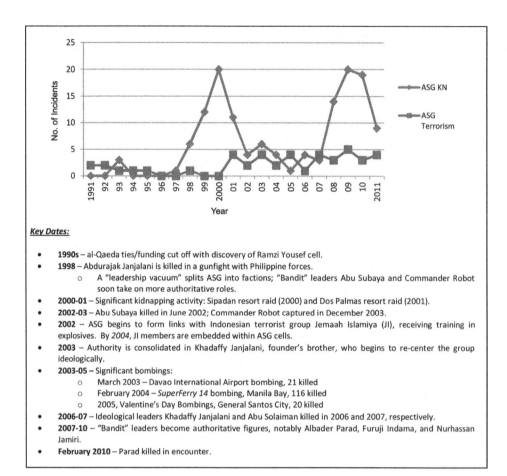

Key Dates:

- **1990s** – al-Qaeda ties/funding cut off with discovery of Ramzi Yousef cell.
- **1998** – Abdurajak Janjalani is killed in a gunfight with Philippine forces.
  - A "leadership vacuum" splits ASG into factions; "Bandit" leaders Abu Subaya and Commander Robot soon take on more authoritative roles.
- **2000-01** – Significant kidnapping activity: Sipadan resort raid (2000) and Dos Palmas resort raid (2001).
- **2002-03** – Abu Subaya killed in June 2002; Commander Robot captured in December 2003.
- **2002** – ASG begins to form links with Indonesian terrorist group Jemaah Islamiya (JI), receiving training in explosives. By *2004*, JI members are embedded within ASG cells.
- **2003** – Authority is consolidated in Khadaffy Janjalani, founder's brother, who begins to re-center the group ideologically.
- **2003-05** – Significant bombings:
  - March 2003 – Davao International Airport bombing, 21 killed
  - February 2004 – *SuperFerry 14* bombing, Manila Bay, 116 killed
  - 2005, Valentine's Day Bombings, General Santos City, 20 killed
- **2006-07** – Ideological leaders Khadaffy Janjalani and Abu Solaiman killed in 2006 and 2007, respectively.
- **2007-10** – "Bandit" leaders become authoritative figures, notably Albader Parad, Furuji Indama, and Nurhassan Jamiri.
- **February 2010** – Parad killed in encounter.

Figure 2. Abu Sayyaf kidnapping vs. terrorism incidents, January 1991–August 2011. *Note*: Data from author's own research, although the University of Maryland's National Consortium for the Study of Terrorism and Responses to Terrorism (START) provided a starting point. (Color figure available online.)

"tipping point" in 1998 was the death of founder Abdurajak Janjalani in a gunfight with Philippine police. At this point, a power struggle ensued and the ASG split into factions.

Degeneration.[34] The two members who eventually seemed to gain some degree of higher authority within the group, Aldam Tilao (aka Abu Subaya) and Ghalib Andang (aka Commander Robot), were popularly known in the Philippines as "bandits." That is to say, their focus lay more on financial gain rather than on ideology. Thus began a rise in kidnapping activity, as these new ASG leaders pursued criminal activity that brought wealth to the group and established it as a particularly effective kidnapping unit. It was under these leaders that Abu Sayyaf engaged in several of its high-profile kidnappings, including the 2000 Sipadan resort incident and the 2001 Dos Palmas resort incident described earlier. In each of these attacks, the ASG abducted more than twenty people of various nationalities, and collected millions of dollars in revenue via ransom payments.

Regeneration.[35] In 2002, Abdurajak Janjalani's brother, Khadaffy, began to centralize power and reaffirm the group's ideological commitment. Aiding him was the death of Abu Subaya, who was killed in a joint U.S.-Filipino ambush in June 2002, and the capture of Commander Robot in December 2003. With the elimination of two "bandit leaders" and a re-centering of the group around ideology under Khadaffy, the kidnapping activity declined noticeably. Moreover, as Abuza has pointed out, during this period most ASG kidnappings resulted in executions, particularly beheadings, rather than ransoms.[36] He notes that while Khadaffy had been involved in kidnapping incidents in the past, "PNP [Philippine National Police] debriefs of six ASG members who were captured in October 2002 present a very clear picture that Khadaffy Janjalani was focused primarily on waging jihad through an urban bombing campaign. He directed his underlings to reconnoiter targets and acquire bomb making skills and ingredients, and organized training by Middle Eastern operatives."[37]

Relapse. Khadaffy's death in August 2006—along with that of another key ideological leader, Jainal Antel Sali, Jr. (aka Abu Solaiman)—at the hands of Philippine forces in Oplan Ultimatium led to another leadership vacuum within ASG. As with the first leadership vacuum following Abdurajak's death, those rising to authority were notorious within ASG and Philippine communities as "bandits," notably: Albader Parad, Furuji Indama, Nurhassan Jamiri, Puwi Ambali, and Sulaiman Pattah. For a second time, ASG kidnappings dramatically spiked as the group once again oriented itself toward criminal activity. This period saw two very high-profile kidnappings: the June 2008 abduction of well-known Filipina journalist, Ces Drilon, her two cameramen, and Filipino professor Octavio Dinampo, who has published research on ASG; and the January 2009 abduction of three workers of the International Committee of the Red Cross (ICRC). It must be noted that in February 2010, Albader Parad—one of the most authoritative ASG leaders, with significant involvement in numerous kidnappings—was killed in an encounter with Philippine forces in Sulu. While it appears that ASG leaders Puruji Indama and Nur Hassan Jamiri were able to successfully maintain the group's high level kidnapping operations through 2010, it remains to be seen if this can and will be continued into 2012.

Structural Frame

According to a Small Arms Survey report, decision-making in ASG takes place at the island group level, especially in Basilan and Sulu. It has been "described as 'a lean, loose, decentralized, highly motivated organization' . . . operating in loosely coupled groups, which gather around particular leaders."[38] ASG members in Basilan are reportedly more hierarchical and centralized than their counterparts in Sulu, which is formed of community or kin groups that form alliances for specific purposes.[39] A first-hand account of this decentralized nature is provided by Gracia Burnham, one of ASG's kidnapping victims, who describes in her memoir an organization with numerous acting leaders, constantly shifting units almost always on the move, and a membership base with variegated personal views and motivations. For over a year, the ASG, structured in this way, was able to keep several Dos Palmas hostages from rescue while awaiting ransom payments.[40]

The loose-knit, decentralized structure of ASG also helps explain temporal fluctuations in the prominence of criminal activities, including kidnapping-for-ransom. This kind of structure exacerbates the issues noted above in the leadership frame, because during periods when there is no strong central leader enforcing ideological adherence, individual ASG cells have gravitated more toward criminal activity. In a decentralized network like ASG, cells must rely on their own funding mechanisms (mainly from engaging in various criminal activities) and entrepreneurship. Of course, motive remains key behind any group's operational decision-making, but what is increasingly becoming the norm is "terrorist organizations stealing whole chapters out of the criminal playbook—trafficking in narcotics, counterfeit goods, illegal aliens—and in the process converting their terrorist cells into criminal gangs."[41] For Abu Sayyaf, kidnapping-for-ransom is a criminal activity that is well-suited for the group's small, decentralized, shifting, and "always on the move" structure. In the absence of a strong, ideologically-driven leader to unify the cells toward a common strategic objective, we can expect to see increases in criminal activity attributed to the various ASG cells.

Membership Frame

In periods of heightened kidnapping activity, ASG's membership appears to be rather young and less ideological. The criminal activities attract members, particularly young members intent on "cashing in" on the group's criminal successes. Indeed, according to one report, "in Basilan, about 15–30 percent of children and minors in the communities influenced by the ASG have become active members,"[42] resulting in what Robin Bowman describes as a "core of 200 to 500 of mostly Muslim young adults between the ages of 16 and 35."[43] And as Banlaoi notes, "With money in their pockets resulting from several ransom payments, the ASG [is] able to accommodate younger recruits not interested in ideology, but in guns and money,"[44] something which only strengthens the group's predisposition, propensity, and capacity to engage in criminal activity. Beyond instances of individuals joining ASG as a means of personal revenue in an economy that offers few decent legitimate alternatives, there are also reports of families sending their sons to join Abu Sayyaf as a way to collect money or goods for the family. According to one account, "Muslim parents in impoverished villages of BASULTA [Basilan, Sulu, Tawi-Tawi provinces—the main areas of operation for ASG] even volunteered their sons to join the ASG in exchange for a monthly supply of rice and financial support to the family of around $200. Some fathers even reportedly traded their sons for guns."[45] Abu Sayyaf has even become an "identity entrepreneur," offering individuals a place of belonging and refuge. One study recently noted "cases where recruits joined the ASG as a status symbol against ordinary gangs in their communities. Some entered the ASG as a result of 'pot' (marijuana) sessions with members."[46] Finally, there are reports, albeit few, of women within the ASG ranks or by some means connected to the group (e.g., by blood or marriage) aiding the group's kidnapping activities. For instance, the sister of slain ASG leader Abu Subaya, Sitra Tilao, was the "major component in sustaining the bandit group's kidnapping operations."[47]

In addition to a youthful membership, size also matters. Larger groups—be they terrorist or criminal—require more funds to survive, let alone arm themselves and operate. Kidnappings bring in easy and fast cash to address this. Additionally, larger groups, particularly decentralized groups, have the greater potential to factionalize into multiple interests and loyalties beyond that of the overall group. ASG has been larger in years past, with up to 3,000 fighters after the Sipadan hostage crisis in 2000, when it had hefty ransom proceeds to distribute."[48] Indeed, following the Sipadan kidnapping, the ASG reportedly offered $1,100 to new recruits, a "sum a Muslim fisherman with a family can only dream of earning legitimately."[49] While it remains somewhat unclear if these membership observations are causes or effects of a group turn to kidnapping, it is still worth noting that such dynamics work to facilitate and perpetuate KFR activity.

It is also important to keep in mind that while there is at times a steady stream of recruits, the ASG also faces frequent desertions. Recruits, young and older alike, leave the group to return to life as noncombatants, often after collecting the recruitment bonus or their share of kidnap revenue. In this sense, kidnappings are not only a means to sustain the ASG, but also to perpetuate it. During periods of little kidnapping activity, intervals when terrorist activity comes to the fore of ASG operations, the group appears to be even smaller in size and more tightly-knit—an elite unit that is better equipped to execute bombings and other terrorist activity rather than engage in kidnappings. In contrast, ASG's *modus operandi* in kidnapping operations includes continually moving hostages between different ASG units and throughout ASG territory, which requires a somewhat larger organization.

External Linkages Frame

In periods of heightened kidnapping activity, the ASG appears to have more prominent links with other criminal actors in the Philippines, especially when those leading the group are bandits rather than ideologues. According to Banlaoi:

> ASG leaders have also mastered the skills of conniving with ordinary criminal groups in their operational areas to mount kidnapping and other criminal activities. The ASG has recognized field commanders who are known bandits in the community. ASG commander Alpader Parad, who was killed in February 2010, was a known kidnapper rather than an ideological leader in Sulu. Other field commanders of the ASG are also leaders of notorious criminal gangs in BASULTA who are engaged in piracy, arms smuggling, drugs trafficking and counterfeiting of goods.[50]

These criminal links only serve to further the ASG's tendency, whether as an entire group or as individual bandit-led cells, toward criminal activity. In 2000, during a kidnapping peak, the ASG was reported to have dealings with Chinese criminal networks, including drug traffickers bringing in methamphetamine (known as "shabu" in the Philippines) from China and arms traffickers supplying the ASG with some of its arms and ammunition.[51] In 2001, the group linked up with remaining members of the Martilyo robbery gang in metro Manila.[52] In 2008, as the ASG was entering another period of heightened kidnapping activity, the Philippine government's Dangerous Drug Board (DDB) reported that the ASG was involved with (and receiving some funding from) drug lords and marijuana plantations in Mindanao.[53] The DDB also reported that the ASG had "connections with foreign drug lords operating in Mindanao to provide protection for their drug laboratories and plantations located in ASG strongholds."[54] While the ASG likely maintains connections with criminal entities regardless of ASG focus (terrorist or kidnapping-for-profit), it appears that the group's criminal connections are expanded and/or emphasized when there is a focus on kidnapping.

Also during kidnapping peaks, there appear to exist weakened or severed ties to transnational terrorist or militant organizations, most notably Jemaah Islamiya. This gives the ASG members not only less exposure to extremist ideology, but also less explosives training. For instance, during the late 1990s, not long after al-Qaeda funding had been cut off, the ASG first began to engage extensively in kidnapping-for-ransom activities. This criminal behavior continued until the group refocused on terrorism and connected with JI. Indeed, before 2004, when Khadaffy had concretely re-centered the group ideologically, Abuza notes that the "ASG had few contacts with other militant groups in the region and in the country. That began to change in 2003, when Indonesian and Malaysian militants sought ASG assistance"[55] in moving around the Philippines. Under bandit leaders, such as Abu Subaya or the late Parad, for instance, the ASG's links tend to emphasize other criminal entities operating in the Philippines rather than any entities of an extremist ideology, as in 2004 under Khadaffy, when, according to Zachary Abuza, JI members were embedded with ASG units.[56]

Some interesting parallels can be seen in the evolution of the ASG-JI relationship and the fluctuations in ASG's kidnapping activities. For example, two senior JI operatives—Umar Patek and Joko Pitoyo (better known as Dulmatin)—spent time with ASG from 2005 through at least 2008, a period which coincides with Khadaffy Janjalani's re-emphasis on ideology and a drastic reduction in incidents of kidnapping-for-profit. During this time, the two JI leaders were not only helping fund the ASG, but were also providing explosives training and helping to organize bombings. Moreover, Patek purportedly brought his own ideological leadership to the ASG,[57] and directed Abdullah Sunata, a JI leader in Indonesia, "to solicit funds for terror attacks in the Philippines and recruit suicide bombers in Indonesia to be sent to central Mindanao."[58] It was not until 2008, at or near the end of Patek's and Dulmatin's stay with ASG, that kidnappings increased again for the Philippine group. Patek recognized this might happen: according to Zachary Abuza, a letter he wrote "warned his colleagues in Indonesia that the ASG might revert to kidnappings if they could not get funds from external supporters—something that the ASG has eschewed since 2002–2003."[59] Similar to membership observations, it must be noted that it is unclear whether the external linkages are a cause or an effect of heightened kidnapping activity, but the ASG-JI connections in particular would suggest ASG linkages could at the least be a way to determine which strategy (i.e., terrorism or criminal activity) dominates ASG at a particular time.

Implications for Policy, Research, and the Future of ASG

Abu Sayyaf provides an interesting example of how crime and terrorism intersect, and there are many other frames of analysis through which we can explore these linkages. Armed groups of all kinds engage in criminal activities in order to obtain funds for survival and operations. Even while still receiving funding from al-Qaeda, the ASG was engaging in various kinds of criminal activity to increase revenue. What is most interesting about Abu Sayyaf, however, is that the group also illustrates how continued criminal activity may actually transform a group from one type of entity into another—in this case from a terrorist group, with strong ideological objectives, into a criminal group, where the pursuit of profit may have eclipsed ideology as the main objective. Kidnapping, for Abu Sayyaf, indeed appears to have become more a livelihood than any type of lever with which to achieve political objectives or receive concessions from the Philippine state. However, the killing in February 2010 of Albadar Parad—one of the group's leaders most active in kidnapping—could have an effect on the group's kidnapping activities unless another leader of a similarly criminal orientation replaces him. Indeed, kidnappings in 2011 have fallen compared to 2009–2010.

Interestingly, the ASG's eventual decline could actually be linked to its transformations—and thus, its decline could possibly be hastened by pushing trans-formation further. Audrey Cronin has identified seven key factors in how terrorist groups decline or end—one of them being a "transition out of terrorism: toward criminality or toward full insurgency."[60] Abu Sayyaf certainly appears to be within a type of transition from terrorism to criminality, a change which Cronin defines as "a shift away from a primary emphasis on collecting resources as a means of pursu-ing political ends toward acquiring material goods and profit that become ends in themselves."[61] From this perspective, continued kidnapping activity—particularly a longer duration of kidnapping (the peaks have generally lasted only a few years)—could bring about the end of Abu Sayyaf as a terrorist group, launching instead its birth as a completely criminal entity. A more extensive focus on kidnap-ping could mean less support from external terrorist groups. But more importantly, where ASG members are often labeled in Tagalog a "bandit" rather than a "terror-ist," an increased and protracted proclivity toward criminal behavior (especially kidnapping) could reduce what little support the group might have among the Philippine population, from which comes the majority of kidnapping victims.

Banlaoi aptly describes Abu Sayyaf as a "symbol of the complexities of armed violence in the southern Philippines that interact with issues of banditry, terrorism, rebellion, separatism, clan conflict, ethnic conflict and warlordism."[62] A similar char-acterization could apply to many terrorist groups around the world. The case of Abu Sayyaf demonstrates how understanding a group's fluctuations in criminal versus ter-rorist activity is useful for generating adaptive policies and strategies. Notably, when ASG is perceived throughout the Philippines as nothing more than an armed kidnap-ping gang, this creates new opportunities to gather intelligence from a population less tolerant of their purely criminal behavior. This, in turn, illustrates the importance among all terrorist groups of maintaining some kind of ideological legitimacy, or at least in providing services to the community, and the challenges such terrorist groups face by an overt over-emphasis on criminal activities. Periods of heightened criminal activity make it more difficult for a group like ASG to portray itself as moti-vated by a "greater good"—thus, law enforcement and security agencies can benefit from noting this and capitalizing on a group's ideological vulnerabilities, weakening its resilience to a point where, eventually, the group can no longer survive.

Notes

1. Frank Zuccarello, "Kidnapping for Ransom: A Fateful International Growth Industry," *Insurance Journal*, June 20, 2011, http://www.insurancejournal.com/magazines/features/2011/06/20/202864.htm. This is also according to statistics from insurance compa-nies, such as BWD Group, which provide Kidnapping and Ransom (K&R) Insurance to clients with an international presence.

2. Estimates taken from Soliman M. Santos, Jr., Paz Verdades M. Santos, et al., *Primed and Purposeful: Armed Groups and Human Security Efforts in the Philippines* (Geneva, Switzerland: Small Arms Survey and South-South Network for Non-State Armed Group Engagement, 2010), 368; and the United States Department of State, www.state.gov.

3. This number comes from the author's own research. "Documentable" kidnappings are those for which the following information can be detailed from multiple sources: name or identifiable description of kidnapping victim; date of kidnapping; location of kidnapping; verification that ASG was the perpetrating entity; and verification or strong belief that financial motivation was the ultimate objective of the kidnapping (as opposed to ASG kidnappings that might be for personal or more ideological reasons, such as those ending in forced marriage and conversion to Islam or kidnappings to make a political point, which usually end with the beheading of the kidnap victim). The author acknowledges that distinguishing the actual motive(s) of each kidnapping can be murky in practice, but has taken care to use for this article only those kidnappings in which ransom was indeed paid out to the ASG or financial motivations were cited or highly suspected by Philippine sources.

4. Associated Press, "Abu Sayyaf's New Generation Threatens Philippines," *The Philippine Star*, 23 February 2009, http://www.philstar.com/Article.aspx?articleId=442769&publicationSubCategoryId=63. See the end of the "Background" section for further detail on ASG profits amassed from kidnapping-for-ransom activities.

5. These peaks are further explained and represented graphically below.

6. Rommel C. Banlaoi, *Al-Harakatul al Islamiyyah: Essays on the Abu Sayyaf Group* (Quezon City: Philippine Institute for Political Violence and Terrorism Research—PIPVTR, 2008), 12.

7. Soliman M. Santos, Jr., *Evolution of the Armed Conflict on the Moro Front* (Quezon City, Philippines: Human Development Network Foundation, Inc., 2005), 1.

8. Banlaoi (see note 6 above), 21.

9. Soliman M. Santos, Jr. and Octavio A. Dinampo, "Abu Sayyaf Reloaded: Rebels, Agents, Bandits, Terrorists," in *Primed and Purposeful* (see note 2 above), 118.

10. Ibid., 117–118.

11. Ibid., 117–118.

12. This includes, for instance, the Pentagon Gang and Abu Sofia.

13. MILF has only seventeen Base Commands, and it appears that these are simply designated names.

14. Security Council Committee pursuant to resolutions 1267 (1999) and 1989 (2011) concerning Al-Qaida and associated individuals and entities. Online at: http://www.un.org/sc/committees/1267/NSQI18004E.shtml.

15. Zachary Abuza, *Balik-Terrorism: The Return of the Abu Sayyaf* (Carlisle, PA: Army War College, Strategic Studies Institute, September 2005), 2.

16. Abuza (see note 15 above), 13.

17. Abuza (see note 15 above), 3.

18. Abuza (see note 15 above), 2.

19. Abuza (see note 15 above), 6.

20. Quoted in Ibid., 6.

21. For a full account of this plot, see Rohan Gunaratna, "The Trajectory from Oplan Bojinka to 9/11," in *Teaching Terror,* ed. James Forest (Lanham, MD: Rowman & Littlefield, 2006), 171–188.

22. Joel Guinto, "Abu Sayyaf Reduced to 'Plain Bandits'—Armed Forces Chief," *Makati City Inquirer.net*, 26 June 2008, http://newsinfo.inquirer.net/breakingnews/nation/view/20080626-144893/Abu-Sayyaf-reduced-to-plain-bandits–Armed-Forces-chief. The P1.4 billion exchanges to roughly $34 million (USD).

23. Associated Press, "Abu Sayyaf's New Generation Threatens Philippines," *The Philippine Star*, 23 February 2009.

24. These early attacks are described from a chart in Zachary Abuza's *Balik Terrorism: The Return of the Abu Sayyaf* (see note 15 above), 5.

25. Rommel C. Banlaoi, "The Sources of the Abu Sayyaf's Resilience in the Southern Philippines," *CTC Sentinel* 3, no. 5 (2010):19.

26. Ibid.

27. See the article by James Forest in this issue of *Terrorism and Political Violence.*

28. There are allegations, although few, that the *SuperFerry 14* bombing was an "extortion bombing," carried out when the SuperFerry management either failed or refused to pay ASG extortion demands.

29. Abuza (see note 15 above), 5.

30. Quoted in Banlaoi (see note 6 above), 11. These come from Khadaffy Janjalani's own written words.

31. For instance, Khadaffy begins with the group's formation, but immediately follows that with a description of the second kidnapping: "1993 was the year when al-Harakatul Islamiyyah was born. . . . Also in 1993, the group of Ustadz Abdur-Razzaq Janjalani launched their second kidnapping operation. They held the son of one of the prominent businessman in Basilan and again was successfully ransomed." Quoted in Banlaoi (see note 6 above), 11. Khadaffy Janjalani is also quoted on kidnappings on page 67.

32. AKE Group, *Quarterly Kidnap Report: Q4 2010*, 7. This report holds that about one foreigner is kidnapped per month in the Philippines, while an estimated sixteen locals are kidnapped every month.

33. Ibid., 7. The average ransom settlement for a foreigner is listed as $250,000 - $3 million (and up to $5 million), while the average ransom demand for a local is $2,000 - $50,000.

34. This term stems from Zachary Abuza's research. See, in particular, *Balik Terrorism: The Return of the Abu Sayyaf* (note 15 above) and "The Philippines Chips Away at the Abu Sayyaf Group's Strength," *CTC Sentinel* 3, no. 4 (April 2010): 11.

35. This term stems from Zachary Abuza's research; see above note.

36. See both of Abuza's works as referenced in this article. Abuza notes that all kidnappings during 2004–2007 resulted in executions, rather than ransoms, but there does appear to be at least one incident, in October 2006, in which some ransom money was believed to have been paid.

37. Abuza (see note 15 above), 13.

38. "Al-Harakatul Al-Islamiyya, aka Abu Sayyaf Group (ASG)," *Primed and Purposeful: Armed Groups and Human Security Efforts in the Philippines* (Geneva: Small Arms Survey, 2010), 368–369.

39. Ibid.

40. Gracia Burnham, *In the Presence of My Enemies* (Carol Stream, IL: Tyndale House Publishers, 2003). For those unfamiliar, Gracia was a hostage of the Abu Sayyaf for more than a year after her abduction at the Malyasian resort in Dos Palmas on 27 May 2001.

41. Ibid.

42. "Al-Harakatul Al-Islamiyya, aka Abu Sayyaf Group (ASG)" (see note 38 above), 374–375.

43. Robin L. Bowman, "Moro Insurgents and the Peace Process in the Philippines," *Countering Terrorism and Insurgency in the 21st Century: International Perspectives, Volume 3: Lessons from the Fight Against Terrorism* (Westport, CT: Praeger Security International, 2007), 485–507; 493.

44. Banlaoi (see note 25 above).

45. Ibid.

46. Ibid.

47. Aurea Calica, "Arrest of Abu Sabaya's Sister To Sustain Drive vs Abu Sayyaf," *The Philippine Star*, 5 September 2004, http://www.philstar.com/Article.aspx?articleId=263637.

48. "Al-Harakatul Al-Islamiyya, aka Abu Sayyaf Group (ASG)" (see note 38 above), 368.

49. Richard Lloyd Parry, "Abu Sayyaf at Heart of Islamic War After $17 m Hostage Deal; Enriched by Libya's Multi-Million Dollar Pay-Off, the World's Most Ruthless Terrorists now pay $1,000 a Head for new Recruits," *London Independent*, 29 August 2000, http://www.independent.co.uk/news/world/middle-east/abu-sayyaf-at-heart-of-islamic-war-after-17m-hostage-deal-711564.html.

50. Banlaoi (see note 25 above).

51. Rose Tamayo, Joy Cantos, and Llilia Tolentino, " 'High-Powered' Firearms Flood Abu Sayyaf Camp," *Pilipino Star Ngayon*, 23 August 2000, FBIS Document ID SEP20000831000062. See also Glenn E. Curtis et al., *Transnational Activities of Chinese Crime Organizations* (Washington, DC: Library of Congress, Federal Research Division, 2003), 44.

52. Jeannette Andrade, "Police: Abu Terror Cell Now in Metro," *The Manila Times*, 12 October 2001 (accessed via World News Connection).

53. Alex Ching, "Abu Sayyaf Now Also Relying on Drug Lords," Manila *Remate*, 26 March 2008 (accessed via World News Connection).

54. Ibid.

55. Zachary Abuza, "The Philippines Chips Away at the Abu Sayyaf Group's Strength," *CTC Sentinel* 3, no. 4 (2010): 11.

56. Ibid.

57. Jacob Zenn, "Makati City Bombing Brings Abu Sayyaf Terrorism to Manila," *Terrorism Monitor* 9, no. 6 (2011), http://www.jamestown.org/single/?no_cache=1&tx_ttnews%5Btt_news%5D=37483.

58. Zachary Abuza, "Umar Patek: Indonesia's Most Wanted," *Terrorism Monitor* 1, no. 4 (2010), http://www.apgml.org/frameworks/docs/7/Abuza%202010_April_Umar%20Patek_Indonesia%E2%80%99s%20Most%20Wanted%20.pdf.

59. Ibid.

60. Audrey Kurth Cronin, "How al-Qaida Ends: The Decline and Demise of Terrorist Groups," *International Security* 31, no. 1 (Summer 2006): 7–48.

61. Ibid., 31.

62. Banlaoi (see note 25 above).

Exploring the Intersections of Technology, Crime, and Terror

School of Criminal Justice, Michigan State University, East Lansing, Michigan, USA

The Internet and computer-mediated communications (CMCs) have drastically changed the way that individuals communicate and share information across the globe. Over the last two decades, financial institutions, private industry, and governments have come to rely on technology in order to access sensitive data and manage critical infrastructure, such as electrical power grids. As a consequence, the threat posed by cybercriminals has increased dramatically and afforded significant opportunities for terrorist groups and extremist organizations to further their objectives. The complex and intersecting nature of both crime and terror make it difficult to clearly separate these issues, particularly in virtual environments, due to the anonymous nature of CMCs and challenges to actor attribution. Thus, this study examines the various definitions for physical and cyberterror and the ways that these activities intersect with cybercrime. In addition, the ways that terrorists and extremist groups use the Internet and CMCs to recruit individuals, spread misinformation, and gather intelligence on various targets are discussed. Finally, the uses of computer hacking tools and malware are explored as a way to better understand the relationship between cybercrime and terror.

The emergence of the Internet and computer-mediated communications over the last three decades has revolutionized the ways that individuals share information and conduct business across the globe. As a result, there are now myriad opportunities for criminality and deviance in online environments, and to utilize technology as a means to facilitate off-line crime. Computer technologies have also spurred the development of cybercrimes, where technology plays a central role in the facilitation of the offense.[1] Criminal and deviant groups can now use computer-mediated communication (CMCs) technologies like forums and newsgroups to share information across great distances.[2] Furthermore, computer hackers have identified ways to exploit virtually all forms of computer software and hardware in order to obtain access to secured resources and steal information.[3]

Extremist and terror groups have also embraced technological innovations across the globe in order to gain advantage over their adversaries. In fact, the Internet and CMCs enable groups to engage in asymmetric attacks that far exceed their

Thomas J. Holt is an associate professor in the School of Criminal Justice at Michigan State University.

existing attack capabilities by leveraging rapid and decentralized communications systems.[4] Computers, cell phones, and technological equipment can be obtained at minimal cost and used with a high degree of anonymity. Additionally, blogs and video sharing sites can be used to deliver propaganda messages in support of an extremist group's position.[5] Such a campaign allows the group to control the delivery and management of their message to interested parties, while at the same time demoralizing and confounding their adversaries. Even more disconcerting is the fact that the Internet can be used as an attack vector to harm the underlying infrastructure that drives modern nation-states. Telecommunications, electrical grids, financial institutions, and governments depend on technology that can be harmed with greater secrecy and fewer resources than might otherwise be required in a traditional physical attack.[6]

The dynamic global online environment, coupled with constant changes in technology and offending techniques, make it exceedingly difficult to understand the nature and scope of extremist groups operating today. Thus, this study will consider the issues inherent in defining and separating cyberterror from physical terror and cybercrimes. Second, the ways that extremist and terror groups use existing technology to gather and disseminate information and recruit new members will be explored, followed by a discussion on the application of hacking techniques in support of extremist ideologies. Finally, the future of cyberterror and the challenges these activities pose for government policymakers, security organizations, and law enforcement agencies will be discussed. In turn, this study will provide a foundation for future research on the problem of cyberterror and its links to the broader community of cybercriminals.

Understanding Cybercrime, Cyberterror, and Physical Terror

In order to understand the phenomenon of cyberterror, it is first critical to understand its relationship to cybercrime and terrorism in general. There are multiple definitions and substantive debate over the nature of both cybercrime and terror, making it difficult to immediately distinguish these acts. In fact, scholars initially debated whether cybercrime should be conceived of as a traditional offense enabled by new tools and devices,[7] or a truly novel form of offending that has no previous parallel.[8] Both perspectives are supported by ample research data—most any existing form of crime can be assisted by technology in some way, while new categories of offenses have emerged that could not otherwise exist without computers, such as malicious software and computer hacking.[9]

As a consequence, there is no single accepted definition of cybercrime, though many argue that it involves criminal behaviors that incorporate cyberspace or computer technology in some fashion.[10] To help clarify what constitutes a cybercrime, David Wall developed one of the most comprehensive frameworks with four specific categories of offending: cyber-trespass; cyber-deception/theft; cyber-porn/obscenity; and cyber-violence.[11] Cyber-trespass concerns the crossing of invisible, yet salient boundaries of ownership online. Computer hackers typically engage in cyber-trespass due to their frequent participation in attacks against computer systems and networks that they do not own.[12] Breaches of computer networks and system boundaries are quite costly, and estimates suggest that U.S. businesses lose millions of dollars annually due to attempts to gain unauthorized access.[13]

The second and related category within this typology is cyber-deception and theft. Computer intrusions and hacking techniques can be used to steal sensitive information from various targets, including intellectual property, state secrets, and money. For instance, businesses reported average losses of $500,000 in 2008 due to financial fraud incidents,[14] while individual consumers lost an average of $575 to various types of fraud in 2009.[15] Similarly, music and media piracy through computer outlets have caused billions of dollars in losses through lost revenue and jobs.[16] As a consequence, the Internet presents a clear opportunity for theft from literally millions of targets across the globe.

The remaining categories within this typology are related in that they may not necessarily violate laws within a given nation. The third category includes cyber-porn and obscenity, reflecting the availability of sexually expressive or explicit materials across the World Wide Web. The final category, cyber-violence, represents the distribution of injurious, hurtful, or dangerous materials online. This category references two forms of violence, the first of which includes behaviors that cause emotional harm to individuals through online environments. For example, individuals have begun to use the Internet as a means to send threatening or harassing messages to others via e-mail, instant messaging services, or social networking sites like Facebook.[17] The second form of violence involves the distribution of materials online that can be used to cause harm in the real or virtual world. The Internet enables individuals to spread bomb-making manuals, guides on guerrilla warfare strategies, and information to facilitate hacking and fraud in a distributed fashion.[18] The publication of such information may not pose a substantive risk to any single individual or group, though the availability of this information can be misused in the wrong hands. Additionally, free speech laws in the United States and elsewhere may actually protect radical positions or ideological documents. In fact, anecdotal evidence indicates that Muslim extremists are increasingly using website hosting services in the United States because of the protections afforded to individual civil liberties.[19]

The wide range of acts that may be viewed as cybercrimes pose a significant challenge to any definition of cyberterror, since many extremist groups may engage in the same activities as non-ideological criminals. This problem is compounded by the fact that most nations treat acts of terror as criminal offenses.[20] There are, however, substantive differences between crime and terror based on motive and the scope of harm caused. For instance, criminal acts often target single individuals and may be motivated by economic or other objectives, while terrorist attacks are often driven by a political motive and are designed to not only hurt or kill innocents but to also strike fear into the larger population.[21]

In order to better understand the complexities of cyberterror, it is first necessary to understand physical terror. There is generally little consensus across governments as to what constitutes an act of physical terror, due to variations in cultural norms, political and religious ideologies, and political relationships.[22] Schmid and Jongman examined over 100 definitions for terror across the world and found few common characteristics across these terms.[23] The most prevalent elements include: the use of violence, political motivations, fear, threats, and psychological effects and reactions.[24] Similarly, Hoffman compared terrorist behavior to criminals and other irregular war-fighters to consider what constitutes terror.[25] He identified terrorism as the "deliberate creation and exploitation of fear through violence or the threat of violence in the pursuit of political change" in order to intimidate and generate fear in the psyche of the population targeted and obtain leverage and power to cause political change.[26] This definition argues that acts of terror are performed by subnational groups or non-state entities regardless of the ideological or political motives of the actors. Thus, though there is no single definition for terror, a common framework can be developed to identify these acts.

The lack of consistency is also present in definitions for "cyberterror," a term which emerged in the mid-1990s as the World Wide Web became an integral component of business and citizen communications.[27] The challenge in defining cyberterror lies in differentiating these acts from cybercrimes. For example, the interconnectivity afforded by the Internet enables attackers to target military systems containing sensitive information, financial service systems that engender commerce, and power grids, switching stations, and other critical infrastructure necessary to maintain basic services.[28] At the same time, these resources can be targeted by hackers, identity thieves, foreign nationals, or other criminal entities with differing motives and ideologies. One way researchers have separated these incidents is through the use of the term "hacktivism," recognizing the use of hacking techniques to promote an activist agenda or express an opinion.[29] Politically-driven groups employ hacking techniques to engage in more serious strikes against governments and political organizations. These attacks may violate the law though not necessarily produce fear or concern among the general population.[30]

As a result, hacktivism is similar to certain forms of real world protest actions, such as vandalism and destruction of private property in furtherance of a political agenda.[31] For instance, a group utilizing hacking techniques to disrupt or otherwise hinder the ability of government agencies to communicate may serve the same function as members of the Earth Liberation Front lashing themselves to trees or buildings in an attempt to reduce the operability of a logging company.[32] These actions may be illegal, though they may not be designed to spur fear in the target or a broader populace. As a result, hacktivism provides a means to identify criminal acts of protest involving hacking techniques which may have some analogue to off-line political action.[33] The use of this term does not, however, help to refine our understanding of cybercrimes generally since it only adds to the jargon of investigators and researchers.

In order to further separate cyberterror from hacktivism and physical terror, some argue that an act of cyberterror must be motivated by a political or ideological agenda and seek to produce fear, coerce, or otherwise intimidate a government or its people.[34] Some have also argued that cyberterror incidents must result in a loss of life or physical harm in the real world, since the concept of physical harm plays a key role in the operationalization of traditional terror incidents.[35] For instance, Pollitt defined cyberterror as "the premeditated, politically motivated attack against information, computer systems, and data which result in violence against noncombatant targets by subnational groups."[36]

Physical violence may not, however, be necessary in online environments due to the increasing dependence on the Internet as both a conduit for service and a medium for expression. For instance, a virtual attack against financial institutions or power systems that produces a loss of service could hinder the ability of a population to engage in commerce or communicate with others. In fact, posts from Islamist extremist websites have noted the value of attacking financial services online, stating that disrupting these resources "for a few days or even for a few hours . . . will cause millions of dollars worth of damage."[37] The economic harm produced by a cyberattack, coupled with fear over the likelihood that it may occur again, could be equal to a physical attack. To that end, some definitions of cyberterror recognize the disruptive effect of virtual attacks against information or infrastructure. Foltz suggested that cyberterrorism involved "an attack or threat of an attack, politically motivated, intended to: interfere with the political, social, or economic functioning of a group organization or country."[38] A similar definition was used by Stambaugh and colleagues, defining cyberterror as a "premeditated, politically motivated attack against information systems, computer programs and data... to disrupt the political, social, or physical infrastructure of the target."[39] As a result, physical harm may be less pertinent relative to the production of fear in defining an incident as an act of cyberterror.

At the same time, terror and extremist groups have not engaged in attacks that conform to these existing definitions of cyberterror, particularly those that incorporate physical harm or the production of fear. For instance, terror groups' use of forums and CMCs to communicate and provide targeting information would largely be excluded from other definitions of cyberterror that emphasize violence or physical harm only. Instead extremist groups utilize the Internet in ways that more closely resemble the characteristics of cybercrimes including the dissemination of information to incite violence and harm. In order to capture this variation, Foltz's definition also recognizes acts which "induce either physical violence or the unjust use of power."[40] A recent definition provided by Britz also includes the "dissemination of information, facilitation of communication, or, attack against physical targets, digital information, computer systems, and/or computer programs... or any utilization of digital communication or information which facilitates such actions directly or indirectly."[41] Thus, while there is no single agreed upon definition for cyberterror, it is clear that this term must encapsulate a greater range of behavior than physical terror due to the dichotomous nature of cyberspace as a vehicle for communications as well as a medium for attacks. More expansive definitions, such as those provided by Britz and Foltz, provide a much more comprehensive framework for exploring the ways that extremist groups utilize technology in support of their various agendas.

Cyberspace as a Medium for Communication and Image Management

Over the last two decades, extremist and terror groups have used the Internet for recruitment, fundraising, and the dissemination and acquisition of attack information. The Internet has also provided criminals and terrorists with new capabilities for clandestine communications between operatives, including through free e-mail accounts, message drop boxes, encrypted messaging, steganography, and other tools. Most all nations have some form of Internet connectivity, thus extremist groups can communicate their messages to the world with ease, and often tailored to specific audiences. Multimedia creation software like Adobe Photoshop enables individuals to develop videos, photos, and stylized text in an easy-to-read and professional manner. These tools can also be acquired with minimal economic investment through pirated software channels.[42] In addition, cell phone cameras and web cams allow individuals to create training videos and share these resources with others through video sharing sites at no cost.[43]

The most significant benefit of the Internet lies in the fact that extremist groups can directly control the way that their message is delivered to the general public. Blogs and social networking sites enable individuals to post and re-post text, videos, and web links so that they spread rapidly across the globe. In turn, a group can influence how they are portrayed in both underground and popular media, rather than waiting for mainstream press to handle the story.[44] Further, extremist groups can directly refute claims made by law enforcement, governments, and the media as part of their overall effort to control their public perception. As James Forest and other terrorism scholars have noted, controlling perceptions is central to what terrorists hope to accomplish.[45] Additionally, these online materials can contribute to the radicalization process by repeatedly exposing individuals to messages that may elicit rage and frustration over oppression or injustices.[46]

There are multiple examples of extremist group utilization of technology for recruitment and message distribution. Web forums like Stormfront.org are extremely popular among the neo-Nazi movement as a means to debate issues publicly and promote their agenda.[47] The forums on this site have over 100,000 members and thousands of new posts made daily. In addition, the Stormfront website maintains pages on a number of social networking sites like Facebook as a means to help recruit and connect members.[48] Hate groups are even creating their own social networking sites, such as "New Saxon," which is a "Social Networking site for people of European descent" produced by the neo-Nazi group the National Socialist Movement.[49] This site enables members to create profiles, blog, post pictures, videos, and even send cards to other members. In turn, this helps to provide a mechanism to connect those in the movement with others despite any geographic boundaries.

The jihad movement has also begun to produce highly stylized websites, videos, and magazines to promote their message as a lifestyle rather than as a marginalized position. In fact, a message posted on the website www.azzam.com stated that "the more Web sites, the better it is for us. We must make the Internet our tool."[50] These pages are often written in multiple languages to communicate their messages across multiple groups, and focus on justifications for resisting foreign occupation or Western ideals rather than on the use of violence. For example, anti-American extremist groups utilized the images of prisoner mistreatment by U.S. soldiers in Abu Ghraib to demonstrate a lack of respect for Islamic value systems.[51] In addition, Al Qaeda operatives have begun to use the Internet as a means to communicate with established media outlets. For example, Al Qaeda agents posted a video ending with a statement welcoming questions from the media that could be posted and answered via web forums online.[52] Thus, they would be able to directly control their responses through the use of new media, rather than traditional dealings with media outlets.

The web also enables the distribution of multi-media resources that help to promote specific agendas. For example, the white supremacist group, the National Alliance, operates a record label called Resistance Records which sells over 1,000 CDs, as well as magazines, books, and clothing via their website.[53] The various items sold enable the spread of hate messages through popular media, introducing individuals to these messages in a way that speaks directly to generational interests. In addition, they have created sophisticated computer games aimed at attracting teenagers to their movement. For instance, the game *Ethnic Cleansing* is a first-person shooting game centered around players killing blacks, Jews, and Hispanics as they run through urban ghettos and subway environments.[54] Other terrorist groups have created video games, like Hizbollah's *Special Force*, that have become wildly popular among supporters and potential new recruits.[55]

Extremist groups can also utilize the Internet as a critical resource for the dissemination of attack information. For example, the jihadi movement has developed various videos and documents on bomb making, developing improvised explosive devices, and conducting suicide bombing operations.[56] Eco-terrorist groups have also provided resources online to enable individuals to engage in attacks on their behalf. For instance, the Earth Liberation Front published its *Ozymandius* manual online, a several-hundred-page resource providing tactical and strategic information on the ways to affect job sites and heavy equipment used in construction and logging industries. These manuals have been used in various bombings by ELF actors, such as the burning of a Vale, Colorado ski resort using a device with the same design as one found on an ELF website.[57]

The amount of data available online can also be used by terrorist and extremist groups to acquire information on prospective targets and to develop pre-mission strategies. For example, satellite images from Google Earth and the street view function of Google Maps provide relatively up-to-date, real-world images of the topography and detail of most major cities throughout the world. This information can be used to develop tactical plans for the execution of an attack against various targets. In fact, one of the conspirators in the 2008 terror attacks in Mumbai, India claimed that Google Earth images were used to plan the attacks.[58] Similarly, information on the physical and virtual topography of public utilities, telephone systems, and other critical infrastructure can be obtained from various public and private websites.[59] As a consequence, attackers can readily obtain tactical and strategic information through online sources with ease.

Overall, the Internet offers many information assets for terrorist and criminal activity, including covert messaging among members of decentralized networks, multimedia communications between organizations and its supporters or potential recruits, and surveillance or operational intelligence gathering, to name just a few. As a result, the technology offers extremist groups unparalleled opportunities to promote their agenda and increase membership.

The Intersection of Hacking and Cyberterror

The Internet also provides a platform for potentially lethal attacks against civilian and government targets. There are myriad sensitive systems now connected to the Internet that act as high-value targets for extremist groups due to the amount of economic and/or physical harm that could be produced, as well as extremely high levels of fear among civilian populations. Such attacks require the use of tools and techniques developed by a hacker community that has evolved considerably over the last three decades.

In the 1980s and early 1990s, would-be hackers needed to develop a sophisticated understanding of technology in order to engage in an attack.[60] The hacker community was also regionally bound, with groups forming in cities or suburbs based on friendship circles.[61] Individuals communicated and shared information via Bulletin Board Systems (BBS) and party lines, and often had to demonstrate their skill in order to gain access to these resources. In addition, hackers would often barter for new resources, whether through trading stolen information or credentials, BBS access, or other valuable resources.[62] In turn, the primary targets of attacks were often corporate entities or telecommunications due to a small proportion of the population with networked computers.

The advent of the World Wide Web and its rapid adoption across the globe in the mid-1990s, coupled with a substantive decrease in the cost of computer technology, forced a significant shift in the hacker community and the ways in which individuals engaged in attacks. Computer technology became increasingly easy to use, requiring hackers to spend less time learning how software and hardware functioned in order to engage in attacks.[63] Additionally, hacker tools became more readily accessible through forums and downloadable files that could be obtained from various websites.[64] The global connectivity afforded by the adoption of technology engendered the formation of hacker communities and collectives that were not bound by geography or region. Individuals could develop a reputation based on their ability, which could extend beyond their location and generate status in the international community. In addition, the development of weaponized malicious software—including viruses, worms, and Trojan horses—enabled individuals to engage in damaging attacks with global impact.[65] At the same time, the availability of these tools allowed attackers with minimal knowledge to carry out attacks previously beyond their level of skill.

As hacking became a global phenomenon in the late 1990s and early 2000s, the mechanics of the hacker community changed. Though tools could still be developed and released as a means of garnering status, a burgeoning marketplace for malicious software and hacker tools on a fee-for-service basis emerged.[66] The development of sophisticated attack tools like botnet malware, which combines the functionality of a virus with the capability to remotely control infected machines through a single Internet Relay Chat (IRC) channel, enabled hackers to establish stable networks of infected computers around the world.[67] These tools can be used for multiple attack strategies, such as the distribution of spam, network scanning, or direct attacks against other networks. The small proportion of skilled hackers with the capability to develop these tools have begun to recognize the monetary value of their products, and now lease out their infrastructure to the larger population of semi-skilled hackers for a fee to engage in attacks.[68] In addition, individuals sell custom builds of malicious software directly to interested parties, enabling semi-skilled hackers to access high quality tools that substantially increase their attack capabilities. Thus, the market for malicious software has changed the process of hacking and created significant opportunities to engage in cyber-attacks that were not previously possible.

The global reach of the Internet also allows attackers to monitor and identify useful tools regardless of the region in which they were created. For instance, a recent study found that the distribution patterns of free-to-use malware often starts in Europe, and circulates through the Middle East, South America, and Asia within a six- to eight-month window.[69] The tools can be identified by a local actor via web forums, and reposted with a new language pack reflecting the regional dialect or preferences.[70] This distribution chain not only allows hackers to identify easy-to-use or high quality tools, but also to obfuscate the creation of malware by taking credit for a tool that was created by someone else. Thus, the international dynamics of the hacker community engender access to tools and attack techniques that may be unique to a specific region or group.

The historic changes in the hacker community provide important context for the current methods and tactics for cyberattacks from extremist communities around the world. For example, the Turkish hacker community, which is driven in part by religious and nationalist agendas, regularly posts videos and tutorials on various types of cyberattacks in order to facilitate learning and attacks by less skilled actors.[71] In addition, Turkish hackers use various social media sites like YouTube and Facebook to draw attention to their attacks against government and private industry targets.[72] Various groups in support of Al-Qaeda also operate web forums to distribute hacker tools and coordinate attacks. Most notably, the hacker Younis Tsoulis promoted the use of hacking tools against various targets in support of global jihad. Using the handle Irhabi 007, or Terrorist 007, he published a manual entitled "The Encyclopedia of Hacking the Zionist and Crusader Websites," which detailed various attack methodologies and a list of vulnerable targets online.[73]

In light of the diverse nature of vulnerable systems and points of attack for hackers, it is critical to identify the most common attack vectors for extremist groups online. One of the most common tactics involves the use of Denial of Service attacks in order to keep individuals from using certain services or resources.[74] In fact, Denial of Service tools have been a part of the arsenal of activists and extremists since the mid-1990s. For example, members of a hacktivist group called the Electronic Disturbance Theater developed an attack tool called FloodNet that overloaded web servers and kept others from being able to access their services.[75] Hackers used this tool in attacks against the U.S. Pentagon, Mexican government websites, and various business targets as a means of protest against their activities and policies. Recently, the al-Jinan forum has been noted for its role in distributing a tool called "Electronic Jihad."[76] This stand-alone Denial of Service tool can be used to attack servers without a great deal of skill on the part of the attacker. In turn, this enables anyone to play an active role in the facilitation of cyberattacks on behalf of their beliefs. Similar tools have been used by members of a group called Anonymous in a series of attacks against government and private industry targets in order to protest attempts to reduce the distribution of pirated media.[77] The group believes that intellectual property laws are unfair, and that governments are stifling the activities of consumers, requiring a direct response from the general public to stand up against this supposed tyranny.

Another valuable attack method in support of political or ideological agendas is web defacements, where an actor replaces the normal html code with an image and message of their choosing.[78] Defacements are particularly valuable as they allow an actor to express their opinions or beliefs, and attribute the attack to themselves or their cause. In addition, the defacer can also choose to simply replace the initial page or cause more substantive harm by deleting the original content. Initially, web defacements served as a way to garner attention and status within the hacker community.[79] Over the last decade, however, an increasing proportion of these attacks are used to express a political or patriotic message.[80] For instance, the Turkish hacker community began a widespread campaign of web defacements after the publication of a cartoon featuring an image of the prophet Mohammed with a bomb in his turban.[81] Many Muslims were deeply offended by this image, and Turkish hackers began to deface websites owned by the Danish newspaper that published the cartoon along with any other site that reposted the image. Hackers defaced thousands of websites in support of their faith, believing this to be their duty on behalf of the Islamic community.[82]

Hacker groups have also used e-mail spam campaigns with some success in order to hamper communications by government and industry. In fact, one of the earliest incidents that may be defined as an act of cyberterrorism occurred in 1998 in Sri Lanka. A group called the Internet Black Tigers, tied to the Liberation Tigers of Tamil Eelam (LTTE), engaged in a series of "suicide email bombings" against Sri Lankan embassies.[83] The group sent over 800 e-mails a day for a two-week period in order to disrupt communications and voice dissent against the government and their actions.[84] Similar tactics were observed in the course of attacks between Russian and Estonian hackers in 2007 as a consequence of real-world protests over the removal of a Russian statue from an Estonian cemetery.[85] Thus, e-mail can be used not only as a communications method but as an inexpensive and uncomplicated attack vehicle as well.

Forecasting the Future of Cyberterror

Given the rapid evolution of technology and the unintended changes they force in human behavior, it is difficult to predict the ways that extremist group behaviors will evolve over time.[86] For example, there have been relatively few incidents of cyberterror across the globe and virtually none within the United States despite the explosion in attacks against sensitive government networks and the financial sector over the last decade.[87] In addition, experts argue that the general cyberattack capabilities of extremist groups like Al-Qaeda are relatively limited by comparison to the larger hacker community.[88] In fact, jihadi hackers attempted to engage in a series of attacks against the U.S. stock exchange and financial institutions. The so-called "Electronic Battle of Guantanamo" did not come to fruition due to bank notifications by law enforcement and preparation against the attacks.[89] The failure of that effort, however, should not be construed as a success for government agencies, but rather act as a warning that Al-Qaeda and other extremist groups are becoming cognizant of various vulnerabilities and identifying techniques to exploit these flaws.

With this in mind, it is necessary to consider the various ways that cyberspace may be used for either communications or as an attack mechanism in the immediate future, and the challenges these threats pose for law enforcement and policy makers. One of the key developments lies in the recent release of the malware program Stuxnet. In late 2010, a flurry of media coverage described a new malware program that appeared to target nuclear power plants in Iran.[90] It is not clear what its true functionality and purpose was, though analyses of the program indicate it was clearly designed to affect a specific Siemens brand control system used in the Natanz nuclear enrichment plant in Iran.[91] By degrading the functionality of this system, it is possible that the program could have caused substantive harm to the functions of the facility. In addition, computer control systems are often segmented from publicly connected computer networks in order to reduce the risk of compromise.[92] The Stuxnet malware however, was initially spread via flash drives, indicating that the creators clearly understood how to affect their target.[93] The code also replicated itself in an extremely limited and cautious fashion in order to minimize its likelihood of detection. Finally, the malware utilized several previously unknown exploits in various computer programs to affect system functionality, suggesting the creators were extremely skilled in computer software and hardware exploitation.[94]

The emergence of Stuxnet clearly demonstrates the potential vulnerabilities that can be exploited in critical infrastructure across the globe. Most power grid technologies, water, sewer, and other critical infrastructure are managed via Supervisory Control and Data Acquisition (SCADA) systems that communicate via hardened or defended networks.[95] Though security researchers regularly attempt to identify and secure SCADA systems from attack, the perception of the likelihood of attack has always been largely antecedent to questions about their overall reliability. As a consequence, Stuxnet clearly demonstrates the need to carefully secure these systems from multiple forms of cyberattack. Though the development and release of this sort of program may be beyond the existing skills of extremist groups, widespread access to this code may encourage attackers to develop similar resources that may be made available through the malicious software market.[96] In fact, the U.S. Department of Homeland Security recently reported concerns over this same sort of code being used as the basis for attacks against U.S. power installations.[97] Thus, Stuxnet represents one of the first true examples of a cyberattack that could directly cause physical harm in the real world.

The problem of Stuxnet also highlights a significant issue in any discussion of cyberterror and cybercrime: attribution.[98] Despite investigations by a number of computer security researchers, it is unclear who created this code. The complex nature of Stuxnet suggests that multiple highly skilled programmers developed the code, most likely in the employ of a nation-state or military entity.[99] No nation or entity however, has come forward to claim responsibility for the program. The lack of attribution here is common among other kinds of crime—both physical and online— although terrorists generally seek public attention through their attacks. Skilled offenders can carefully conceal or obfuscate their identity to reduce the likelihood of detection. This problem is compounded in virtual environments due to various tools that can shield an individual's physical location, such as anonymizers and proxy servers.[100] In addition, skilled actors can use compromised computer systems to obfuscate their location and the actual identity of the attacker. For instance, a botnet can be used to route attack traffic through multiple unsuspecting victim machines across the world.[101] As a consequence, malicious traffic may appear to come from individual systems in the United States or other countries. In addition, attackers can acquire tools from hacker communities across the globe in an attempt to confound actor attribution. For instance, using tools common to Chinese hackers may add a layer of complexity to the investigation of the origins of an attack.[102]

It is also difficult to truly discern whether an extremist group engaging in cyberattacks is acting independently from a nation-state or criminal entity. The complexity of an attack may give some insight into the skill and knowledge of the attackers, but does not provide any information on their sources for funding or training, or any connections they may have to other groups.[103] In particular, the hacker community engenders a horizontal organizational structure, where individuals are judged based on skill and ability. As a consequence, when groups form they are generally short-lived, have minimal leadership, and are structured based on skills.[104] This is different from the general cell-based structure of traditional terror groups off-line that work through intermediaries.[105] As a consequence, virtual terror attacks can occur more quickly and with fewer trails to identify funding and tool acquisition sources than traditional terror groups.

In addition, the nature of virtual attacks may reduce the likelihood of attribution in general. Terrorists and extremists may claim responsibility after an attack in order to garner attention and demonstrate their power and capability in physical attacks. For instance, suicide bombers often post videos online or distribute pre-recorded messages to the media in order to ensure that their justification for an attack is clearly known.[106] The need for attribution in the course of a cyberattack may not be pivotal until well after the act is completed since initial actions to survey and access a virtual target must be kept silent in order to minimize the likelihood of detection. The final attack or outcome produced from initial intrusions may, however, lead the group to take responsibility in order to garner attention for their cause. Thus, the variation in group ideologies, coupled with the anonymity afforded by virtual environments, make attribution an exceedingly difficult challenge for policy makers and law enforcement to appropriately respond to cyberattacks.

A final concern related to attribution is the increasing incorporation of civilian participants in various cyberattacks. For instance, recent attacks by the group Anonymous and its offshoot LulzSec were facilitated in part by tools that could be downloaded for free by interested parties to perform denial of service attacks.[107] In addition, the group provided information on prospective targets and asked participants to rate who they most wanted to attack, and utilized the web to coordinate attacks. As a consequence, the ability for an extremist group to rapidly recruit and radicalize sympathetic individuals, or employ their technical skills on a temporary basis without the need for complete indoctrination or membership into their organization, should not be ignored in light of the worldwide spread of the Internet and computer technology.

The continuous and varied threats posed by cyberattacks from cybercriminals, extremist groups, and nation-states require a substantive retooling of U.S. policies toward cyberspace and cybersecurity in general. While the past few presidential administrations established roadmaps to improve the governmental response to cybercrime and prospective attacks,[108] there have been few unclassified policy responses to potential attacks, making it difficult to understand the true posture toward cyberattacks. In July 2011, the Department of Defense released a policy document detailing their view of cyberspace as a protected domain in much the same way as the physical environments of sea, air, and land.[109] The report recognizes that the current defensive measures used to protect critical infrastructure and the defense industrial base against cyberattacks are ineffective and require significant expansion. In addition, the Department of Defense is now placing a specific emphasis on the need for careful responses to theft of data, destructive attacks to degrade network functionality, and denial of service attacks due to the direct threat they pose to the communications capabilities of the nation, and the maintenance of secrecy and intellectual property.[110] In order to reduce the risks posed by malicious actors and attacks, the report calls for improved relationships with private industry in order to develop an improved total government response and an expanded workforce focusing on cybersecurity.[111]

The issue of collaboration between governmental agencies, public and private companies, and law enforcement is critical, but presents one of the greatest challenges to securing cyberspace. Multiple presidential administrations have made similar policy recommendations, though they have generally failed to produce lasting innovations or strategic change due to the difficulty in linking all necessary groups. For instance, a substantive majority of the power plants, telecommunications equipment, and processing facilities that constitute critical infrastructure are owned by private industry using software and hardware from multiple vendors.[112] As a consequence, it is extremely difficult to develop standards that can be readily adopted across industries in order to effectively reduce the risk of cyberattacks. The creation of initiatives like the Department of Homeland Security's Control Systems Security Program helps to identify general vulnerabilities and improve security standards across all vendors and owners, though their true impact is hard to assess in light of the proprietary nature of private industry practices.[113]

In much the same way, there is a need to more clearly integrate state and local law enforcement agencies into the response to cyberterror attacks. There has been a marked increase in funding for training and equipment to prepare local responders to handle physical terror incidents since 9/11. The same attention has not been given to cyberattacks due to the jurisdictional dynamics that arise in inter-state or international offenses.[114] This perception may, however, unnecessarily diminish the response capability of local law enforcement and hinder investigations which may otherwise reduce some forms of online extremism. In particular, domestic terror groups often emerge as a direct result of conditions within a given region or locale, though they may communicate and share information with others through online networks. Thus, there must be an increase in the training and investigative tools available to state and local police agencies to improve their overall ability to investigate cyberterror incidents and generally improve cybersecurity practices.

Policymakers must also give greater consideration to the integration of individual citizens into the defense of cyberspace. The average computer user can pose a substantive threat to the larger security of private industry and government targets because of their potential to mismanage technological resources or be used as a launch point by attackers. Individuals who do not regularly update their computer software or utilize anti-virus and other security tools face an increased risk of compromise from criminal or extremist groups.[115] Those who engage in media or software piracy or view pornography are also susceptible to attacks since malware is often spread through these vectors.[116] Thus, individuals who act without regard for ethical behavior online or utilize minimal standards for computer security present a substantive opportunity for attackers to gain a foothold into larger networks.

As a consequence, hardening end users from all manner of attacks may greatly improve the total security of the nations' computer systems. This is a substantive challenge given the variations in end users' skill with technology and overall recognition of basic security strategies. Multiple strategies must be employed to effectively target individuals regardless of age, technological skill, or access to technology. National programs that promote awareness of computer security issues, such as October's National Cybersecurity Awareness Month, are useful in communicating the problem of cybercrime and harm to a wide audience.[117] Targeted programs are also necessary at all phases of the educational system to ensure that youth are exposed to proper online conduct and computer security principles from an early age.[118] Adult education programs must also be employed in order to ensure that users are frequently reminded of their role in securing their system and various techniques they can employ to reduce their vulnerability to compromise. For instance, Internet Service Providers could communicate these messages to their customers via e-mail and during login periods in order to constantly expose users to computer security issues. In turn, these measures may help to reduce the overall efficacy of attacks by both extremists and criminal entities against individuals and government targets alike.

Finally, it is critical that national policies toward cyberspace develop in tandem with—and to the extent possible, in advance of—prospective strategies employed by cyberattackers. In fact, there is a need for strategic policy initiatives that carefully consider global variations in law enforcement and governmental policies toward cyberattacks. Most developed nations have laws against certain forms of cybercrime,[119] though there are substantive variations in the ways that they may deal with criminal actors. For instance, there is some evidence that Russian and Chinese law enforcement agencies investigate those individuals who target systems within their national borders.[120] Meanwhile, individuals who attack foreign civilian, business, or government entities may be ignored or under-investigated, creating a sort of tacit approval for certain types of cyberattack. As a consequence, there is a need for clearly defined national polices related to threats from cybercriminals, extremists, and nation-states in order to better protect and defend U.S. critical infrastructure.

In addition to policy responses, there is a clear need for research from both the technical and social sciences in order to better understand the tactical and strategic practices of extremist and terror groups online. For instance, social science research utilizing web forums, blogs, and other online data sources can provide a substantive understanding of the activities of terrorist and extremist groups in their own words.[121] Such data sources can be developed with minimal interaction or penetration into these communities, reducing the risk of researcher contamination or harm.[122] Additionally, these data can be used for both qualitative and quantitative analyses to provide significant insights into the changing dynamics of extremist communities on both the left and right.

Online data sources can also be used to identify the ways that extremist groups are adapting tools and tactics from the hacker community in order to engage in attacks against critical infrastructure and other targets. For example, investigations of the market for malicious software and stolen data across the globe can be useful to identify prospective trends in attack tools and vectors that may be used by an extremist group.[123] Evidence suggests that an Al-Qaeda cell used credit card numbers purchased from an online data market to obtain web hosting services, phones, and engage in fraudulent charges.[124] Thus, explorations of the activities of cybercriminals can be used to expand our understanding of how extremists may utilize these resources. Combining this research with technical analyses of cyberattacks in general can help to better understand the dynamics of the current and future cyber threat worldwide.

Finally, there is a need to identify the behavioral and attitudinal factors that affect participation in politically motivated cyberattacks. The increasing incorporation of citizens into attacks against government targets online may reflect a difference in the nature of extremism on and off-line. For instance, radicalization may not be necessary in order to lead individuals to engage in attacks against targets online since they do not face the same risk of detection or loss of life in support of a cause as in real-world attacks. Instead, they may only need to share a certain outlook on a social or political issue, or hold antagonistic views against a target group. Research utilizing demographically diverse samples can help to determine the influence of nationalism, political beliefs, technological skills, and ethnic antagonism on individual willingness to engage in cyberterror attacks. In turn, we may better understand the relationship between extremist behaviors on- and off-line.

Notes

1. Steven Furnell, *Cybercrime: Vandalizing the Information Society* (Boston: Addison-Wesley, 2002); David S. Wall, "Cybercrimes and the Internet," in *Crime and the Internet*, ed. David S. Wall (New York: Routledge, 2001), 1–17.

2. Heather DiMarco, "The Electronic Cloak: Secret Sexual Deviance in Cybersociety," in *Dot.cons: Crime, Deviance, and Identity on the Internet*, ed. Yvonne Jewkes (Portland, OR: Willan Publishing), 53–67.

3. Jake Brodscky and Robert Radvanovsky, "Control Systems Security," in *Corporate Hacking and Technology-Driven Crime: Social Dynamics and Implications*, ed. Thomas J. Holt and Bernadette Schell (Hershey, PA: IGI-Global, 2011), 187–204; Dorothy E. Denning, "Cyber-conflict as an Emergent Social Problem," in *Corporate Hacking and Technology-Driven Crime* (see previous), 170–186; Thomas J. Holt, "Subcultural Evolution? Examining the Influence of On- and Off-line Experiences on Deviant Subcultures," *Deviant Behavior* 28 (2007): 171-198.

4. Susan W. Brenner, *Cyberthreats: The Emerging Fault Lines of the Nation State* (New York: Oxford University Press, 2008); Dorothy E. Denning, "Activism, Hacktivism, and Cyberterrorism: The Internet as a Tool for Influencing Foreign Policy," in *Networks and Netwars: The Future of Terror, Crime, and Militancy*, ed. John Arquilla and David F. Ronfeldt (Santa Monica, CA: RAND, 2001), 239–288; Jerrold M. Post, Keven G. Ruby, and Eric D. Shaw, "From Car Bombs to Logic Bombs: The Growing Threat from Information Terrorism," *Terrorism and Political Violence* 12 (2000): 97–122.

5. Brenner, *Cyberthreats* (see note 4 above); Bruce Hoffman, *Inside Terrorism*, 2nd ed. (New York: Columbia University Press, 2006); Manuel Soriano, "The Road to Media Jihad: The Propaganda Actions of Al Qaeda in the Islamic Maghreb," *Terrorism and Political Violence* 23 (2010): 72–88.

6. Brodscky and Radvanovsky, "Control Systems Security" (see note 3 above); Dorothy Denning, "A View of Cyberterrorism Five Years Later," in *Internet Security: Hacking, Counterhacking, and Society*, ed. Kenneth Himmaed (Sudbury, MA: Jones and Bartlett, 2006), 123–139; Irving Lachow, "Cyber Terrorism: Menace or Myth?," in *Cyberpower and National Security*, ed. Franklin D. Kramer, Stuart H. Starr, and Larry K. Wentz (Washington DC: National Defense University, 2009), 123–139.

7. Peter N. Grabosky, "Virtual Criminality: Old Wine in New Bottles?," *Social and Legal Studies* 10 (2001): 243–249.

8. David S. Wall, "Catching Cybercriminals: Policing the Internet," *Computers & Technology* 12 (1998): 201–218.

9. See Thomas J. Holt, ed., *Crime On-line: Correlates, Causes, and Context* (Raleigh, NC: Carolina Academic Press, 2010).

10. Furnell, *Cybercrime* (see note 1 above); Wall, "Cybercrimes and the Internet" (see note 1 above).

11. Furnell, *Cybercrime* (see note 1 above); Wall, "Cybercrimes and the Internet" (see note 1 above).

12. Holt, "Subcultural Evolution?" (see note 3 above); Bernadette H. Schell and John L. Dodge, *The Hacking of America: Who's Doing it, Why, and How* (Westport, CT: Quorum Books, 2002).

13. Computer Security Institute, *Computer Crime and Security Survey*, 2010, http://www.cybercrime.gov/FBI2010.pdf.

14. Computer Security Institute, *Computer Crime and Security Survey*, 2008, http://www.cybercrime.gov/FBI2008.pdf.

15. Internet Crime Complaint Center, *IC3 2009 Internet Crime Report*, http://www.ic3.gov/media/annualreport/2010_IC3Report.pdf.

16. IDATE, *Taking Advantage of Peer-to-Peer: What Is at Stake for the Content Industry?* (2009), http://www.idate.fr/an/_qdn/an-03/IF282/index_a.htm.

17. Thomas J. Holt and Adam M. Bossler, "Examining the Applicability of Lifestyle-Routine Activities Theory for Cybercrime Victimization," *Deviant Behavior* 30 (2009): 1–25.

18. Wall, "Cybercrimes and the Internet" (see note 1 above).

19. Niv Ahituv, *Old Threats, New Channels: The Internet as a Tool for Terrorists* (Berlin: NATO Workshop, (2008); Hoffman, *Inside Terrorism* (see note 5 above).

20. Brenner, *Cyberthreats* (see note 4 above).

21. Ibid.

22. Marjie T. Britz, "Terrorism and Technology: Operationalizing Cyberterrorism and Identifying Concepts," in *Crime On-Line: Correlates, Causes, and Context*, ed. Thomas J. Holt (Raleigh, NC: Carolina Academic Press, 2010), 193–220; Hoffman, *Inside Terrorism* (see note 5 above); Gus Martin, *Understanding Terrorism: Challenges, Perspectives and Issues*, 2nd ed. (Thousand Oaks, CA: Sage, 2006); Alex P. Schmid and Albert J. Jongman, *Political Terrorism: A New Guide to Actors, Authors, Concepts, Data Bases, Theories, & Literature* (New Brunswick, NJ: Transaction Publishers, 2005).

23. Ibid., Schmid and Jongman, *Political Terrorism*.

24. Ibid.

25. Hoffman, *Inside Terrorism* (see note 5 above).

26. Ibid.

27. Ibid. Denning, "Activism, Hacktivism, and Cyberterror" (see note 4 above).

28. Ibid.

29. Furnell, *Cybercrime* (see note 1 above); Tim Jordan and Paul Taylor, *Hacktivism and Cyberwars: Rebels With a Cause* (New York: Routledge, 2004).

30. Ibid.

31. Alex P. Schmid, "Frameworks for Conceptualising Terrorism," *Terrorism and Political Violence* 16 (2004): 197–221.

32. Stefan H. Leader and Peter Probst, "The Earth Liberation Front and Environmental Terrorism," *Terrorism and Political Violence* 15 (2003): 37–58.

33. Jordan and Taylor, *Hacktivism and Cyberwars* (see note 29 above).

34. Britz, "Terrorism and Technology" (see note 22 above); Dorothy E. Denning, *Cyberterrorism*. Testimony before the Special Oversight Panel on Terrorism Committee on Armed Services, U.S. House of Representatives, May 23, 2000, http://www.cs.georgetown.

edu/~denning/infosec/cyberterror.html; Bryan C. Foltz, "Cyberterrorism, Computer Crime, and Reality" *Information Management & Computer Security* 12 (2004): 154–166; Mark M. Pollitt, "Cyberterrorism—Fact or Fancy?" *Computer Fraud & Security* 2 (1998): 8–10.

35. Ibid.

36. Pollitt, "Cyberterrorism—Fact or Fancy?" (see note 34 above).

37. Denning, "Cyberconflict" (see note 3 above), p. 178; E. Alshech, "Cyberspace as a Combat Zone: The Phenomenon of Electronic Jihad," *MEMRI Inquiry and Analysis Series* 329 (Washington, DC: The Middle East Media Research Institute, 2007).

38. Foltz, "Cyberterrorism, Computer Crime, and Reality" (see note 34 above).

39. Hollis Stambaugh, David S. Beaupre, David J. Icove, Richard Baker, Wayne Cassady, Wayne P. Williams, *Electronic Crime Needs Assessment For State And Local Law Enforcement* (Washington, DC: National Institute of Justice, 2001).

40. Foltz, "Cyberterrorism, Computer Crime, and Reality" (see note 34 above).

41. Marjie T. Britz, *Computer Forensics and Cybercrime,* 2nd ed. (Upper Saddle River, NJ: Prentice-Hall, 2009).

42. Thomas J. Holt and Heith Copes, "Transferring Subcultural Knowledge Online: Practices and Beliefs of Persistent Digital Pirates," *Deviant Behavior* 31 (2010): 625–654.

43. Gary Bunt, *Islam in the Digital Age: E-jihad, Online Fatwas and Cyber Islamic Environments* (London: Pluto Books, 2003); Lachow, "Cyber Terrorism" (see note 6 above).

44. Ibid.; Marc Sageman, *Leaderless Jihad: Terror Networks in the Twenty First Century,* (Philadelphia: University of Pennsylvania Press, 2008).

45. James J. F. Forest, ed., *Influence Warfare: How Terrorists and Governments Struggle to Shape Perceptions in a War of Ideas* (Westport, CT: Praeger, 2009); and James J. F. Forest, "Influence Warfare and Modern Terrorism," *Georgetown Journal of International Affairs* 10, no. 1 (2009): 81–90.

46. Ibid.

47. Tammy Castle, "The Women of Stormfront: An Examination of White Nationalist Discussion Threads on the Internet," *Internet Journal of Criminology* (2011), http://www. internetjournalofcriminology.com/Castle_Chevalier_The_Women_of_Stormfront_An_ Examination_of_White_Nationalist_Discussion_Threads.pdf; Stormfront website. www. stormfront.org; Robert W. Taylor, Eric J. Fritsch, John Liederbach, and Thomas J. Holt, *Digital Crime and Digital Terrorism,* 2nd ed. (Upper Saddle River, NJ: Pearson Prentice Hall, 2010).

48. Taylor et al., *Digital Crime and Digital Terrorism* (see note 47 above).

49. See the website http://www.newsaxon.com for details.

50. Gabriel Weimann and Katharina Von Knop, "Applying the Notion of Noise to Countering Online Terrorism," *Studies in Conflict and Terrorism* 23 (2009): 883–902.

51. Britz, "Terrorism and Technology" (see note 22 above); Lachow, "Cyber Terror" (see note 6 above); Sageman, *Leaderless Jihad* (see note 44 above).

52. Vivian Salma, "Ask a Terrorist," *Newsweek,* 19 December 2007, http://www.news week.com/2007/12/19/as-a-terrorist.html.

53. See http://www.resistancerecords.com for details.

54. Taylor et al., *Digital Crime and Digital Terror* (see note 47 above).

55. For a description of this and several other terrorist-created video games, see Made-line Gruen, "Innovative Recruitment and Indoctrination Tactics by Extremists: Video Games, Hip Hop, and the World Wide Web," in *The Making of a Terrorist,* ed. James J.F. Forest (Westport, CT: Praeger, 2005).

56. Britz, "Terrorism and Technology" (see note 22 above); Lachow, "Cyber Terror" (see note 6 above); Sageman, *Leaderless Jihad* (see note 44 above).

57. Taylor et al., *Digital Crime and Digital Terrorism* (see note 47 above).

58. Britz, "Terrorism and Technology" (see note 22 above); Max Kilger, "Social Dynamics and the Future of Technology-Driven Crime," in *Corporate Hacking and Tech-nology Driven Crime: Social Dynamics and Implications,* ed.Thomas J. Holt and Bernadette Schell (Hershey PA: IGI-Global, 2010), 205–227.

59. Kilger, "Social Dynamics and the Future of Technology-Driven Crime" (see note 58 above).

60. Paul A. Taylor, *Hackers: Crime in the Digital Sublime* (New York: Routledge, 1999).

61. Gordon R. Meyer, *The Social Organization of the Computer Underground* (Master's thesis, Northern Illinois University, 1989).

62. Ibid.

63. Taylor, *Hackers* (see note 60 above).

64. Ibid.

65. Taylor et al., *Digital Crime and Digital Terrorism* (see note 47 above).

66. Bill Chu, Thomas J. Holt, and Gail Joon Ahn, *Examining the Creation, Distribution, and Function of Malware On-Line* (Washington, DC, National Institute of Justice, 2010), http://www.ncjrs.gov./pdffiles1/nij/grants/230112.pdf.

67. Ibid.

68. Ibid.

69. Thomas J. Holt, "Examining the Origins of Malware," Paper presented at the Department of Defense Cyber Crime Conference, Saint Louis, MO, January 2008.

70. Ibid.; Thomas J. Holt, Joshua B. Soles, and Ludmilla Leslie, "Characterizing Malware Writers and Computer Attackers in Their Own Words," Paper presented at the International Conference on Information Warfare and Security, Peter Kiewit Institute, University of Nebraska Omaha, April 2008.

71. Thomas J. Holt, "The Attack Dynamics of Political and Religiously Motivated Hackers," in *Cyber Infrastructure Protection*, ed. Tarek Saadawi and Louis Jordan (New York: Strategic Studies Institute, 2009), 161–182.

72. Ibid.

73. Denning, "Cyberconflict as an Emergent Social Phenomenon" (see note 3 above).

74. Ibid.; Taylor, *Hackers* (see note 60 above).

75. Ibid.

76. Denning, "Cyberconflict as an Emergent Social Phenomenon" (see note 3 above).

77. Sean Paul Correll, "An Interview with Anonymous," PandaLabs Blog, 29 September, 2010, http://pandalabs.pandasecurity.com/an-interview-with-anonymous/.

78. Taylor et al., *Digital Crime and Digital Terrorism* (see note 47 above); Denning, "Cyberconflict as an Emergent Social Phenomenon" (see note 3 above).

79. Ibid.; Kilger, "Social Dynamics and the Future of Technology-Driven Crime" (see note 58 above).

80. Denning, "Cyberconflict as an Emergent Social Phenomenon" (see note 3 above).

81. Holt, "The Attack Dynamics of Political and Religiously Motivated Hackers" (see note 71 above); Michael Ward, "Anti-Cartoon Protests Go Online," *BBC News*, 8 February 8, 2006, http://news.bbc.co.uk/2/hi/technology/4691518.stm.

82. Ibid.

83. Denning, "Cyber Conflict as an Emergent Social Phenomenon" (see note 3 above).

84. Dorothy E. Denning, *Information Warfare and Security* (Reading, MA: Addison-Wesley, 1999).

85. Ryan Naraine and Dancho Danchev, "Zero Day: Coordinated Russia vs Georgia cyber attack in progress," *ZDNet*, 11 August 2008, http://www.zdnet.com/blog/security/coordinated-russia-vs-georgia-cyber-attack-in-progress/1670.

86. Taylor et al., *Digital Crime and Digital Terrorism* (see note 47 above).

87. Britz, "Terrorism and Technology" (see note 22 above); Denning, "Cyber Conflict as an Emergent Social Phenomenon" (see note 3 above); Lachow, "Cyber Terror" (see note 6 above).

88. Ibid.

89. Ibid.

90. See Paul K. Kerr, John Rollins, and Catherine A. Theohary, *The Stuxnet Computer Worm: Harbinger of an Emerging Warfare Capability* (Washington, DC: Congressional Research Service, 2010).

91. Mark Clayton, "Stuxnet Malware is 'Weapon' out to Destroy... Iran's Bushehr Nuclear Plant," *Christian Science Monitor*, 21 September, 2010, http://www.csmonitor.com/USA/2010/0921/Stuxnet-malware-is-weapon-out-to-destroy-Iran-s-Bushehr-nuclear-plant.

92. Brodscky and Radvanovsky, "Control Systems Security" (see note 3 above); Denning, "A View of Cyberterrorism Five Years Later" (see note 6 above).

93. Clayton, "Stuxnet Malware is 'Weapon' out to Destroy... Iran's Bushehr Nuclear Plant" (see note 91 above).

94. Ibid.

95. Brodscky and Radvanovsky, "Control Systems Security" (see note 3 above); Kilger, "Social Dynamics and the Future of Technology-Driven Crime" (see note 58 above).

96. Clayton, "Stuxnet Malware is 'Weapon' out to Destroy... Iran's Bushehr Nuclear Plant" (see note 91 above).

97. Kim Zetter, "DHS Fears a Modified Stuxnet Could Attack US Infrastructure," *Wired Threat Level*, 20 July, 2011, http://www.wired.com/threatlevel/2011/07/dhs-fears-stuxnet-attacks/.

98. Brenner, *Cyberthreats* (see note 4 above).

99. Clayton, "Stuxnet Malware is 'Weapon' out to Destroy... Iran's Bushehr Nuclear Plant" (see note 91 above); Kerr et al., *The Stuxnet Computer Worm* (see note 90 above).

100. Brenner, *Cyberthreats* (see note 4 above); Chu et al., *Examining the Creation, Distribution, and Function of Malware On-line* (see note 66 above); Kilger, "Social Dynamics and the Future of Technology-Driven Crime" (see note 58 above).

101. Chu et al., *Examining the Creation, Distribution, and Function of Malware On-line* (see note 66 above); Taylor et al., *Digital Crime and Digital Terror* (see note 47 above).

102. Holt, "Examining the Origins of Malware" (see note 69 above).

103. Brenner, *Cyberthreats* (see note 4 above); Kilger, "Social Dynamics and the Future of Technology-Driven Crime" (see note 58 above).

104. Holt et al., "Characterizing Malware Writers and Computer Attackers in Their Own Words" (see note 70 above).

105. Britz, "Terrorism and Technology" (see note 22 above).

106. Brenner, *Cyberthreats* (see note 4 above).

107. Correll, "An Interview with Anonymous" (see note 77 above); Kevin Poulsen, "In 'Anonymous' Raids, Feds Work From List of Top 1,000 Protesters," *Wired*, 26 July, 2011, http://www.wired.com/threatlevel/2011/07/op_payback/.

108. Brenner, *Cyberthreats* (see note 4 above); Taylor et al., *Digital Crime and Digital Terror* (see note 47 above).

109. Department of Defense. *Department of Defense Strategy for Operating in Cyberspace*, (Washington DC: Department of Defense, 2011), http://www.defense.gov/news/d20110714cyber.pdf.

110. Ibid.

111. Ibid.

112. Brodscky and Radvanovsky, "Control Systems Security" (see note 3 above); Kilger, "Social Dynamics and the Future of Technology-Driven Crime" (see note 58 above).

113. Ibid.

114. Ibid.

115. Adam M. Bossler and Thomas J. Holt, "On-line Activities, Guardianship, and Malware Infection: An Examination of Routine Activities Theory," *International Journal of Cyber Criminology* 3 (2010): 400–420; Chu et al., *Examining the Creation, Distribution, and Function of Malware On-line* (see note 66 above).

116. Ibid.

117. Taylor et al., *Digital Crime and Digital Terrorism* (see note 47 above).

118. Bossler and Holt, "On-line Activities, Guardianship, and Malware Infection" (see note 115 above).

119. Brenner, *Cyberthreats* (see note 4 above).

120. Chu et al., *Examining the Creation, Distribution, and Function of Malware On-line* (see note 66 above).

121. Joshua Sinai, "Using the Internet to Uncover Terrorism's Root Causes," in *Influence Warfare*, ed. James J. F. Forest (Westport, CT: Praeger, 2009).

122. Thomas J. Holt, "Exploring Strategies for Qualitative Criminological and Criminal Justice Inquiry Using Online Data," *Journal of Criminal Justice Education*, 21 (2010): 300–321.

123. Chu et al., *Examining the Creation, Distribution, and Function of Malware On-line* (see note 66 above); Thomas J. Holt and Eric Lampke, "Exploring Stolen Data Markets On-line: Products and Market Forces," *Criminal Justice Studies* 23 (2010): 33–50.

124. Brian Krebs, "Terror Webmaster Sentenced in Britain," *Washington Post*, 5 July 2007; Kimberly Kiefer Peretti, "Data Breaches: What the Underground World of "Carding" Reveals," *Santa Clara Computer and High Technology Law Journal* 25 (2009): 375–413.

Index

Page numbers in **Bold** represent Illustrations.

Made in the USA
Las Vegas, NV
11 January 2022

41129750R00111